Radical Issues
in
Criminology

Radical Issues
in
Criminology

edited by

PAT CARLEN and MIKE COLLISON

BARNES & NOBLE BOOKS
TOTOWA, NEW JERSEY

First published in 1980 by Martin Robertson, Oxford.

First published in the USA 1980 by
BARNES & NOBLE BOOKS
81 Adams Drive
Totowa, New Jersey, 07512

ISBN 0-389-20083-2

Typeset by Pintail Studios Ltd., Ringwood, Hampshire, England.
Printed and bound in Great Britain by Billing & Sons Ltd., Guildford, London, Oxford, Worcester.

Contents

Contents

Acknowledgements

We should like to thank Doreen Thompson at the University of Keele for typing and re-typing at the editorial stage.

Introduction

Pat Carlen

Criminology, whether old or new (and with the exception of Durkheim), has consistently been premissed on a promise, the promise of future good triumphing over present evil. The old criminology (still very much with us) is imbued with a faith in the scientific control of criminality; the newer criminology is presently imbued with a faith in the eventual advent of a 'socialist legality'. *Radical Issues in Criminology*, by contrast, is concerned not with future idylls but with current issues. Moreover, these issues have not been designated 'radical' in celebration of any radical political space jointly tenanted by the authors of the articles. The issues are radical in terms of the questions and contradictions that they raise, but no generalized 'radical' solutions are offered. For most of the questions raised in this book are posed in awkward recognition of the dysymmetry between the theory and politics of penal practice and the theory and practice of the criminal law. In other words, strategies of intervention into penal politics cannot be read off from global theories of either crime or law – whether those theories be marxist, feminist or whatever. Therefore, instead of promising either the 'good society' or any socialist nirvana, we limit our analyses to the penal politics of specific issues.

The four chapters in Part One discuss law, rights and penal politics. But this first half of the book is also designed to exemplify the different types of knowledge that can be useful to radicals seeking to intervene in penal issues. Thus, in addition to the opening essay, which reviews the radical traditions in criminology, and in great contrast to Paul Hirst's major and lengthy theoretical contribution, we also include in the first part one chapter that is a legalistic account of police powers, and another that is a straight report and commentary on an important case concerning prisoners' rights. This juxtaposition of four very different articles is deliberate. It signifies our disagreement with those who disdain to take seriously both legal procedure and exposé criminology. As I write (September 1979) a criminal trial is in progress with a jury whose members were vetted (without their knowledge) by the police. A national newspaper has been criticized by a judge for revealing the details of the jury vetting. At this same time the publishers of a weekly journal are threatened with prosecution for alleged contempt of court as a result of a post-trial interview with a juror who served at a recent trial. Maybe journalists have a sharper sense of political relevance than do academic crime theorists. But the point is made. The critique of legal reasoning can no more be left to lawyers and judges than can the monitoring of the criminal justice system be left to the Home Office Research Unit – or, for that matter, to any number of government commissions or inquiries.

Chapter 1, in briefly outlining criminology's radical traditions, also introduces two of the book's major and recurring themes: the plea for specific, rather than global, analyses; and the insistence upon the dysymmetrical conditions and effects of the many discourses that, unevenly and discontinuously, constitute penal politics. The second half of this first essay discusses the relationships between criminalization, subjectivity and the 'rule of law' and then the three other chapters in Part One take up different aspects of this 'rule of law' (or not!) debate.

In Chapter 2, Laurie Taylor pursues the question of left intervention into issues of civil liberty. Detailing the progress of the successful appeal of a number of prisoners against the punitive 'awards' made by the Board of Visitors after the riot that took place at Hull prison in 1976, Taylor argues that test cases of this kind can, independently of their long-term legal effects, have the immediate effect of bringing to public scrutiny issues that are usually shrouded in institutional secrecy. However, the reader who agrees with Taylor's arguments that we can entertain a reserved optimism about the effectiveness of at least *some* civil liberties campaigns will not be heartened by Donald Thompson's essay on 'Civil Liberties and Public Order'. Writing as a lawyer, Thompson demonstrates that, whatever rights people may think they have, the actual enshrinement of those rights in law is very precarious indeed. And Thompson is not merely talking about a 'gap' between legal prescription and police practice; he is talking about the apparent reluctance of the judiciary to give clear guidance as to what the 'rule of law' has ever meant in relation to police powers. This will not surprise lawyers (or the police!) but it should at least dampen the ardour of those who still *unequivocally* invoke the 'rule of law' as a condition of civil liberty. It also highlights the need for wider and more precise knowledge about what this elusive 'rule of law' *is*.

In the final chapter in Part One, Paul Hirst argues (in direct opposition to recent anarchistic and libertarian trends) that the legal regulation of conduct is essential. At the same time, he also provides detailed arguments and examples as to why the 'notions of proprietorial subject and "rights" are problematic in any legal system'. In putting forward these arguments Hirst challenges the 'rights' theses of both Pashukanis and Dworkin and rejects as absurd Foucault's *Discipline and Punish* thesis that the 'disciplinary society' is an emanation of 'capitalism'. But Hirst does not merely question the theories that imply that problems of social regulation are peculiar *either* to capitalism *or* to socialism. In the final section of the paper he illustrates, with reference to abortion legislation, his arguments that socialist states can encounter problems of regulation that are 'in no way different to "capitalist" ones'.

In Part Two we turn to contemporary issues that have either been altogether avoided by radical theorists (the glaring example being the continuing public concern with criminal violence) or have been incorporated into generalized-feminist or utopian–marxist rhetorics (the examples here being the legal control of women and social work interventions into juvenile justice). In Chapter 5, Mark Cousins questions recent attempts to establish a 'feminist' criminology and an argument is made for more specific analyses of the heterogeneous effects that law has on the organization of sexual difference. Chapters 6 and 7 discuss criminal violence and juvenile delinquency. In 'Questions of Violence' Frank Burton deconstructs the disparate discourses that, both together and separately, endow 'violence' with its relevance for party political criminology. Then, in 'Questions of Juvenile Justice' Mike Collison elucidates the conditions under which welfarism displaced on to the 'family' the major responsibility for lawbreaking by juveniles. The contradictions that were either preconditional or consequential to this displacement have been managed by the agencies of social work. In the final chapter, therefore, John Clarke, Mary Langan and Phil Lee discuss the political significance of the present contradictions within social work itself.

To summarize, the overall aim of this book is twofold: to examine

Introduction

the discourses within which penal politics are presently constituted, and to stimulate discussion of the possible discourses within which socialist forms of regulation can be constructed.

PART ONE

Law, Rights and Penal Politics

CHAPTER 1

Radical Criminology, Penal Politics and the Rule of Law

Pat Carlen

INTRODUCTION

This opening chapter serves the triple aim of exposition, argument and illustration. The first half presents a brief exposition of criminology's radical traditions. The second half examines a theoretically specified and ideologically effective relation between crime, politics and civil liberties: the ideological instance that contradictorily presents the law–crime couplet as the condition of both individual liberty and social regulation. The critical argument that informs both parts rejects global and empiricist theories which relate crime unproblematically and in symmetrical fashion either to questions of individual psychology, on the one hand, or to the history, practice or form of the criminal law, on the other. Instead, the argument calls for analyses of individualized and theoretically specified instances within criminal and penal politics. As an illustration of that type of analysis, the second half of the chapter theorizes the effects of that dominant discourse wherein the political economy of crime is conflated with the political economy of right. The practical question concerns the grounds upon which it could be argued that struggles to maintain and increase civil rights may be progressive rather than reformist.

THE RADICAL TRADITIONS

Since the early 1960s there have been four strands of radicalism in criminological discourse: (1) a generalized and radical sociological criminology which has engaged in an enthusiastic but theoretically uneven debate with various existential and marxist positions; (2) a more theoretically specific body of work emanating from the Birmingham Centre for Contemporary Cultural Studies and analysing the ideological conditions particular to different forms of criminalization; (3) a historical criminology centring on the works of E. P. Thompson in England and Michel Foucault in France; (4) marxist critiques of law – included for discussion here because the best of them have little to say about *criminal* law and the worst of them often imply that theoretical problems relating to crime can be seen as mere epiphenomena of the problems that arise in conceptualizing law. (But see Hirst, 1979b, for a new approach.)

Sociological Criminology

Sociological criminology became 'radicalized' in the early 1960s when it was renamed the 'sociology of deviance', a name serving to distinguish it from the 'old' positivistic criminology. By the time *The New Criminology* (Taylor, Walton and Young, 1973) appeared in 1973, however, the criminological revolution was complete, the National Deviancy Symposium which had nursed it was fragmenting, and both in Britain and the United States there were two main currents of radical criminology. Symbolic–interactionist and phenomeno-logical–existential perspectives still had a large following in the United States (and a smaller, though influential, following in Britain), but most 'radical' criminologists were by then seeking to develop more politicized perspectives on crime (Taylor and Taylor, 1973), and the search for a 'marxist' theory of crime (or not) had begun (Quinney, 1974).

The 'marxist theory of crime?' debate received its greatest impetus from the writings (and ensuing critiques of them) of Ian Taylor, Paul Walton and Jock Young (1973, 1975), though, as these authors were themselves quick to point out, the utopianism of their *New Criminology* was difficult to reconcile with any coherent marxism and even with their own concern to develop a 'fully social' theory of crime. While Taylor and Young continued to hammer out the elements of a *politicized* theory of crime (Taylor and Young, 1979), both they and other writers (P. Q. Hirst, 1975 notwithstanding!) debated the theoretical prerequisites for a marxist theory of crime. This determination to displace the *New Criminology*'s sociologism within a marxist problematic led to debates with the Conference of Socialist Economists' Law and State Group and to the recently published book, *Capitalism and The Rule of Law* (Fine *et al.*, 1979). (This book completely breaks with sociological criminology and will be referred to in later sections of this article.) Not all radical theorists were as resolute in turning their backs on sociology. Some, like Richard Quinney, attempted to 'marxicologize' criminology. Others wanted to ask questions about 'deviant consciousness', guilt and tolerance, questions that they did not believe it possible to pose from a traditional marxist perspective. The products of these radical labours have recently been presented in two books: *Class, State and Crime* (Quinney, 1977) and *Deviant Interpretations* (Downes and Rock, 1979).

Richard Quinney's book is rhetorical, economistic and moralistic, but it does read as a serious criminology. In an attempt to develop a political economy of criminal justice, Quinney argues for marxist analyses of class and state as prerequisites to a marxist analysis of the meanings of the 'crimes' and types of 'criminal justice' specific to late capitalism. Further, in denying the possibility of a generalized and formal explanation of crime he does himself combine an analysis of the ideological effectivity of different fractions within classes, with a conception of crime as a representation of an ideological relation, an ideological relation which, Quinney suggests, is materially transcripted as the welfare mode of control. This mode is remarkable for its simultaneous conversion of citizens into clients *and* their interpellation as contradictory citizens/clients, always–already both with and without rights. But this is as far as (and most probably further than) Quinney goes. A reserved economism and a reserved idealism are implicit in his arguments. Ultimately he is less concerned with rigorous analyses of the historical forms and functions of lawbreaking and criminalization than with the idealist search for the 'good' life.

A concern with the good life is a dominant theme of *Deviant Interpretations* (Downes and Rock, 1979), though it is to be a good life conceived in intersubjective tolerance, rectitude and liberal common sense rather than in the changing conditions of production. Stanley Cohen's (1979) article on 'Guilt, Justice and Tolerance' is none the less worth commenting on: first, because it is an excellent

example of how common-sense conceptions of crime are so often conflated in discourses that have no clearly defined theoretical object at
all; second, because its appeal is dependent upon the ideological
effects of that same discourse of right that this article is attempting to
deconstruct and elaborate.

Cohen's major argument is that radical criminologists have been
silent about both the grounds on which individuals can be held
responsible for their actions and the grounds upon which the state is
(or could be) justified in punishing them. 'It is punishment', writes
Cohen, 'which is at the core of criminal politics and always has been'
(Cohen, 1979, p. 25). This is the traditional view of criminal politics. It
is the criminal politics of Bentham and of Durkheim (1964), who see
crime contradictorily as being both the condition of social regulation
and the condition of individual liberty; it is, too, the criminal politics of
symbolic interactionists, who see crime as a transaction between law-
breakers and law-enforcers (Becker, 1963); it is indeed the criminal
politics of sociologists of law, who imply that theories of crime can be
read off from theories of criminal law (Kamenka *et al.*, 1978). It is a
common-sense conception of criminal politics. It needs to be taken
seriously because it has ideological effects; for that reason, too, it also
calls for theoretical deconstruction and elaboration. The form and
substance of Cohen's argument is particularly important for the
purposes of this chapter because it exemplifies the ideological site
where left, right and centre politicians and theorists meet under the
auspices of a most tenacious and historically effective conception of
law and crime: the prehistorical and ahistorical conception of the 'rule
of law' as a necessarily effective and unitary condition of humanity
and democracy.

One of the major obstacles to effective and radical intervention in
criminal politics, to attempts to change the common-sense conception
that criminal justice is solely to do with punishing the guilty in
order to establish the 'good society', is that the history of common-
sense criminology has always represented the law–crime (or
rule–deviance) couplet as being *the* condition of individual liberty, of
human personality. And this conception of law as the condition of
human personality (difference and unity balanced in an equivalence
known as freedom) is based upon a chronic méconnaissance of the
sources of value and power (Foucault, 1979, pp. 85–91), upon an
imaginary human nature entrapped in the laws of its own self-
knowledge, terrified to say 'No' to the conditions of its own existence.

While law is seen thus as being the condition of human freedom, questions of crime are dispersed in a variety of discourses and are not inscribed solely in penology. Rooted in a morality both assumed and unspecified, common sense repeatedly demands a general theory of crime wherein law-breakers and the criminalization processes of the state always–already balance in a symmetry of already known relationships designated (variously) as 'capitalist justice', 'socialist legality' (Taylor, Walton, Young, 1973) or 'the good society' (Rawls, 1972; Dworkin, 1977; Cohen, 1979).

Common-sense conceptions of crime, however, whether incorporated into marxist discourse or whether the constituent elements of bourgeois–liberal discourse, none the less inseminate ideologically effective representations of criminal politics. To that extent Stanley Cohen is correct in implying that theoretical work should not result in a refusal to recognize that common-sense conceptions of crime have ideological effects. Where Cohen is wrong is in his assumption that the common-sense categories of 'guilt', 'justice' and 'tolerance' can be used uncritically as constitutive elements of a theoretical discourse (cf. Engels, 1970, pp. 365–6). Theoretical discourse on crime needs both to change common-sense conceptions of crime (a political task) and to calculate theoretically why contemporary discourse on crime takes the form it does (a theoretico-political task). We can refuse Cohen's challenge to attempt theoretical legislation of the modes of subjectivity and representation that will exist under communism and socialism, but we should take seriously (i.e. theoretically and in the fullness of their contradictions) the preconditions and effectivity of modes of representation available to subjects *now*. One such mode concerns the relations between criminal law, human rights and civil liberty. Exactly *why* and *how* are questions of crime and punishment so quickly transformed into questions of human rights and civil liberties?

To attempt both the deconstruction of an ideological representation and the calculation of its effects is to work within a contradiction. But to understand the politics of crime, it is not enough to follow Marx, Althusser (1971), Balbus (1977), Pashukanus (1978) and others and merely to repeat after them that law resides in some place other than the site of its authoritative representation. Such theoretical work is a necessary but insufficient condition for change. Law as an ideological representation has to be confronted in the awkwardness of its dispersions and contradictions. *Because* law is successfully presented as *the* guarantor of human values, radical criminologists have to face the awkward question of civil liberties under the rule of law at the same time as demonstrating that within capitalism the rule of law is not the effective 'rule' at all (Sumner, 1979, pp. 266–77). This confrontation involves both a contradiction and a recognition: a contradiction of law's claims at the level of theory; and a recognition of law's claims and effects at the level of ideology. It is both in recognition of that contradiction and in contradiction of that recognition that it will be argued, in the final section of this chapter, that civil liberties campaigns are not always–already liberal and reformist; that they can have the effect of prising apart the presently conflated relationships between the forms and functions of the criminal law and the forms and functions of the criminal justice system. In the meantime, Cohen's notion that a blueprint for a 'good society' can be constructed on the basis of essential attributes of human nature is rejected. 'Guilt' and 'tolerance' are two of the categories that presently endow subjects with their humanity under the law. It is this very mode of subjectivity and representation of the relationship between 'law' and 'crime' that has to be challenged.

The Birmingham School

Perhaps it is because the work of Birmingham University's Centre for Contemporary Cultural Studies has not been confined to questions concerning crime that it has made at least two distinctive contributions to radical criminology. The Birmingham School has enriched criminology with a *bricolage* of concepts displaced from linguistics, marxism and psychoanalysis; it has also succeeded in writing a politicized criminology, *Policing the Crisis* (Hall *et al.*, 1978). By a politicized criminology is meant:

(1) a criminology that is without a crime and without a criminal;
(2) a criminology that, written within a theorization of a specific conjuncture, displaces a common-sense conception of crime (in *Policing the Crisis*, 'mugging');
(3) a criminology that, in the absence of the common-sense object, produces knowledge of the political and ideological conditions within which 'mugging' as a social phenomenon becomes possible – or not.

But *Policing the Crisis*, although engendering a politicized theory of crime, remains (as the authors themselves point out at the beginning of the book) peculiarly within and without a politics. Writing from a theoretico-political position which enables them to make explicit the ideological and political conditions of current and dominant conceptions of crime, the authors none the less do not address questions concerning the possibilities (or not) for radical intervention into judicial and penal politics.

Historical Criminology

Although it would be inappropriate to characterize E. P. Thompson and Michel Foucault as criminologists, their respective writings on criminal law (Thompson, 1975) and incarceration (Foucault, 1978a) should be central to any serious study of crime. It is Foucault's work, however, that is most relevant to this chapter.

Apart from a few isolated studies (Carson, 1974; Chambliss, 1964; Duster, 1970; Gusfield, 1963; Platt, 1969; Radzinowitz, 1966; Tobias, 1967), sociological criminology of the 1960s tended to ignore history. The peculiar isolationism of 'criminology' meant that sociologists of crime could plead for more historical studies of crime without acknowledging that histories of labour and political movements have repeatedly been histories of lawbreaking and criminalization. Within these histories a constant theme concerned the effectiveness (or not) of lawbreaking as a political strategy (see, for just two examples Hobsbawn, 1964, on machine-breaking and Raeburn, 1973, on militant suffragettes). But, within criminology, Poor Law history and the history of 'welfare' were also overlooked, despite the fact that Marx had commented at length in *Capital*, Vol. I, on the bloody legislation that had, from the fifteenth century onwards, regulated the movement of labour. Compartmentalism in the teaching of sociology meant that undergraduates could be familiar with, say, Stedman-Jones's book on *Outcast London* (1971) without ever thinking it to be relevant to criminology! In the last few years the situation has changed. One can now expect to see the works of Bellamy (1973), Samaha (1974), Hay *et al.*, (1975), Thompson (1975), Cockburn (1977) and Ignatieff (1978) on criminology book lists where, together with others, they may constitute a section on 'Historical Studies on Crime and Law'. The works of Michel Foucault, however, could be more difficult to 'place'.

Foucault's books have all been concerned with analyses of the discursive formations within which specific events were recognized as constituting particular phenomena. His books are systematic descriptions of discursive objects whose histories are always fragmented, whose engendering relationships appear and disappear (dysymmetrically) as conditions and effects of quite disparate events. Whereas Kuhn (1970) argued that scientific paradigms are supplanted in revolutionary fashion, Foucault has insisted that paradigms are forever in a flux of discursive submergence and re-emergence, of discursive dispersion and realignment. A recurring theme in his books has concerned the articulation of archival knowledges as power relations. The two dimensions of his work that are most relevant to this chapter are, first, the insistence that phenomena should be individualized in their actual modes of existence, rather than 'explained' by reference to either an originary source (reductionism) or a noumenal condition (idealism); and second, and more substantively, his own regional analyses of how the political economy of right has been repeatedly conflated with the political economy of punishment.

Discipline and Punish (1978a), an analysis of why nineteenth-century penology took the form it did, is in many ways reminiscent of Rusche's and Kirchheimer's *Punishment and Social Structure* (1939). Both books insist that questions of crime should be released from the analytic symmetries into which they have been traditionally compressed. Rusche and Kirchheimer, for instance, wrote that 'the bond, transparent or not, that is supposed to exist between crime and punishment prevents any insight into the independent significance of the history of penal systems. It must be broken. Punishment is neither a simple consequence of crime, nor the reverse side of crime' (1939, p. 5). However, whereas Rusche and Kirchheimer presented an analysis of the structural relationships between punishment and the European labour market from the late Middle Ages to the 1930s, Foucault's emphasis in *Discipline and Punish* is upon the discursive modalities wherein the power to punish was (and still is) represented as a right. This theme is taken up again and stated more explicitly in *The History of Sexuality*, Vol. I (1979):

> The juridical is increasingly incapable of coding power ... [but] One remains attached to a certain image of power-law, of power-sovereignty, which was traced out by the theoreticians of right and monarchic institution. It is this image that we must break free of, that is, of the theoretical privilege of law and sovereignty, if we wish to analyse power within the concrete and historical framework of its

operation. We must construct an analytics of power that no longer takes law as a model and a code. [pp. 89–90]

The only English book that has so far succeeded in breaking this imaginary bond between crime and punishment is *Policing the Crisis* (Hall *et al.*, 1978). The last pages of *Whigs and Hunters* suggests that E. P. Thompson, Britain's major historian of crime, lawmaking and criminalization, is incapable of making any such break (Thompson, 1975).

Marxism and Law

It has sometimes been implied (Carson, 1974; Taylor, Walton and Young, 1975) that the development of a marxist theory of law will one day displace criminology's traditional concern with crime and punishment. Maybe it will. At present, however, there is no developed marxist theory of the *criminal* law. Writers who have rediscovered Pashukanis's general and formal theory of law have either remained silent about the criminal law (Edelman, 1979) or have argued that 'coercion is at best only a secondary element in bourgeois legal relations' (Kinsey, 1978, p. 204) and that 'the law must be understood in terms of the facilitation and organisation of commodity circulation rather than as a technique of repression or coercion' (Kinsey, 1978, p. 205). This latter point expresses the classic marxist position: Mr Moneybags always did go to market as a *legal* subject (Marx, 1967); *ideally*, market relations and factory discipline demand an internalized self-control rather than the penal technology of a coercive social control (Marx, 1967; Foucault, 1978a; Ignatieff, 1978; Scull, 1979). But ideal market relations have never existed, and one history of nineteenth-century policing and incarceration is a history of attempts to school industrial and rural labourers in regular working habits and the keeping of restrictive contracts (Playfair, 1971; Burchill and Ross, 1977; Ignatieff, 1978; Collison, 1981). Although one would have to be a fool to imply that penal coercion is peculiar to capitalism (one could, of course, argue that the particular form of its representation *is*), one has to be neither an economistic nor a conspiracy theorist to know what the conspiracy laws have in fact been used for (Pritt, 1971; Arnison, 1974; Spicer, 1976). In short, a general and formal theory of crime cannot be 'read off' from either a general or specific theory of law because the theorized relationships between the criminal law, juridical relations, criminalization processes and lawbreaking are embedded in asymmetrical practices and discourses. These discourses are neither mirror images of each other nor reducible one to the other. 'Today,' as Foucault points out, 'criminal justice functions and justifies itself only by . . . perpetual reference to something other than itself, by its unceasing reinscription in non-judicial systems' (Foucault, 1978a, p. 22). Thus, for example, although it can be accepted that a politicized theory of crime must be underpinned by a theory of law, state and the possible forms of their representation during a transition to socialism, it can, at the same time, be argued that the politics of criminalization are today more specifically related to changes in the composition of capital and the resultant new fractions within the working class than they are to the *general* juridical relations within which capitalist social relations are represented as natural relations (Engels, 1970, p. 365). The foregoing, however, is an example of the simplest level at which it can be argued that criminal law, juridical relationships and criminalization processes are asymmetrical to each other. Once they are inscribed within and around notions like morality, freedom, guilt and retribution, *then* they fragment into ironic icons of juridical relations whose effectivity is dispersed *not* in criminological but in economic, religious or political discourses.

PENAL POLITICS AND THE RULE OF LAW

Contemporary work on the relationships between crime and politics has been engaged in three slightly differing theoretical projects. Stuart Hall and his associates have concentrated on the political economy of crime. Matthiesen and Taylor and Young have concentrated on questions relating more to a politics of criminology. Most recently, the National Deviancy Symposium in conjunction with the CSE Law and State Group have published their *Capitalism and The Rule of Law* (Fine *et al.*, 1979), a book that, more than any other, insists on specificity of analysis. It has already been suggested that *Policing the Crisis* (Hall *et al.*, 1978) is an excellent example of a politicized theory of crime. It differs from books like Quinney's (1977) in so far as marxist concepts not only *inform* the analyses, they also put under erasure their common-sense object. In place of common sense is a theorization of the precise political conjuncture that made 'mugging' possible. The authors, however, limit their project to theoretical production. They recognize that practical remedies involve struggle with contradictions and they claim only that their book might be a theoretical contribution to that struggle.

Thomas Matthiesen, Ian Taylor and Jock Young have been less cautious than the authors of *Policing the Crisis*. Not only have they attempted theorization of the relationships between changes in penal policy and changes in the composition of capital; they have also examined the possibilities for radical intervention into penal politics. With regard to the latter, one concern has been with the tendency for radical critique to be incorporated into reformist measures. A second concern has been with the possibility of alliances between radical criminologists and the criminalized working class.

Capitalism and The Rule of Law (Fine *et al.*, 1979) is concerned with just that — the relationships between law and capitalist production. Criminalization is (correctly) theorized as being but one among several modes of social control. In the main, though, the articles tend more towards theoretical exposition and elaboration of the relationships between 'state' and 'law' than to calculation of the conditions for specific and progressive interventions into penal politics.

This chapter is concerned neither with the problem of radical co-optation by the state nor with the possibilities of alliances between criminologists and the criminalized working class, though the importance of the issue of co-optation is recognized. The aim here is limited to theorization of the political implications of the prevalent and dominant conception that criminalization and the criminal law are necessarily preconditional to social cohesion and individual autonomy united under the sign of democracy. It is argued that a dominant effect of the popular conflation of the political economy of punishment with a political economy of right is that questions of crime are repeatedly transformed (at the level of rhetoric) into questions of civil liberty. The theoretico-political implication is clear: a radical criminology which attempts to change contemporary conceptions of the relationships between criminal law, crime and social regulation will, if it is to be effective, also have to address the question of civil liberty under the law. The strategy adopted here is, first, to follow Pashukanis and to deny the necessity of causally relating criminalization processes to a 'rule of law' which conflates notions of equivalence with notions of individual responsibility; second, to argue that, even though the 'rule of law' must be denied its ideological effects, at the same time those ideological effects do have an effectivity that could facilitate denial of the 'rule of law' through recognition of the concept of 'legality'. The logics of the two final sections, therefore, are incommensurate with, and irreducible to, each other. This dysymmetry is provoked by the theoretically awkward recognition that, at the limits of theory, the present conflation of the relations between criminal justice, rule-of-law and civil liberty cannot be dismissed as being merely the site of an imaginary subjectivity; it can also be a site of ideological struggle.

Crime Without a Knowing Subject

> Fundamental to our law and civilisation is the principle of the abstract equality, equivalence and imputed moral freedom and responsibility of the parties. [Tay, 1978, p. 9]

> The imperative of right is: 'Be a person and respect others as persons. [Hegel; quoted in Pashukanis, 1978, p. 111]

Eugeny Pashukanis quotes Hegel at the commencement of his disquisition on the relation between the commodity form and the legal subject. He argues that within Marx's *Capital* the analysis of the commodity form predicates an analysis of the legal subject. According to Pashukanis, the juridical element in human conduct inheres in the exchange that recognizes opposed interests, but the *legal* element emerges only with the commodity form. The law that facilitates commodity exchange represents legal personality as being both subject to things and as having free will over things. Thus 'the social bond appears simultaneously in two incoherent forms: as the abstract equivalence of commodity values, and as a person's capacity to be the abstract subject of rights' (Arthur, 1978, p. 14). But, writes Pashukanis (1978, p. 167), 'criminal law is the sphere in which legal intercourse is most severely tested', for it is in the arena of criminal justice that the rule of law is necessarily called into question.

Pashukanis's writing on criminal law and lawbreaking again concentrates on the problematic subjectivity of the legal subject. The notion of juridical equivalence is now manifest as retributive justice. But 'criminal law starts out not at all from the damage suffered by the injured party, but from the violation of the norm established by the state' (Pashukanis, 1978, p. 177). The extent of the penalty is determined as much by the *guilt* of the individual as it is by the *damage* suffered by the injured party. There is no space for a notion of collective or community responsibility for crime. Law-breakers are not only located within the juridical relations of civil society; they are interpellated (and isolated) by the state as guilty individuals. Such interpellation endows them with guilty (i.e., knowing) subjectivity as a condition of existence of legal personality. This subject-in-subjection to law, though presently over-determined by capitalist social relations, also is subject to the signifying practices that are constitutive of value in general. These are the elements that, according to Pashukanis, 'give the juridical abstractions of crime and punishment their reality, and ensure them their practical significance in the framework of bourgeois society, *despite all the efforts of the theoretical critique*' (1978, p. 184; my emphases). So, Pashukanis calculates that 'since social relations are not confined to abstract relations between abstract commodity owners, so too the criminal court is not only an embodiment of the abstract legal form ... it is also a weapon in the immediate class struggle' (1978, p. 176). Here, at the limits of theory but within ideology and politics, the displaced consequences of Pashukanis's theory of law and the legal subject cohere as a contradiction: class struggle calls into question an existent and unitary subjectivity which is both preserved (as a condition of representation of value) and denied (as a condition of present exploitation). In citing Van Hammel, who had declared that 'the main obstacles to modern criminology [are] the three concepts of guilt, crime and punishment', Pashukanis again emphasizes that 'the forms of bourgeois consciousness cannot be eliminated by a critique in terms of ideas alone'. Guilt exists and has effects. Its relationship to criminalization, however, is not a causal relationship: it is an element in the interpellatory form within which right is not thought independently of criminalization. This is not to argue that subjects are interpellated only as legal subjects. (Under the sign of welfare capitalism, for instance, many subjects are also hailed as clients.) Nor is it to argue that law is the only ideological form within which subjectivity is constituted. It *is* to argue that this specific interpellation effectively obstructs radical arguments that *today* actual law enforcement and criminalization are more closely related to the social relations of a capitalist mode of production than to any ideal and subjectively desirable rule of law.

Subjectivity, Legality and the Rule of Law

TOM: Why do our governors put many of us poor folks into prisons against our will? What are jails for? Down with jails, I say. All men should be free.

JACK: Harkee, Tom, a few rogues in prison keep the rest in order
          and then honest men go about their business afraid of
          nobody; that's the way to be free.
          [Hannah More, 1792, p. 5; quoted in Ignatieff, 1978,
          pp. 12–13]

The rule of law itself, the imposing of effective inhibitions upon power
and the defence of the citizen from power's all-intrusive claims, seems
to me to be an unqualified human good. [Thompson, 1975, p. 226]

It is doubtful whether the 'rule of law' has ever existed in the form
lauded by E. P. Thompson, and it is even more doubtful whether we
learn much about the 'rule of law' by embracing its shadow as an
'unqualified human good'. The conditions of its existence (and effects)
within and without subjectivity, however, require elaboration.

In examining the ideologically effective relationship between crime
and the 'rule of law', I have been tacitly addressing two questions
which students of crime often pose when it is suggested to them that,
even though criminalization processes are only tangentially related to
the 'rule of law', the Left should intervene more frequently in judicial
and penal politics. From those concerned with democracy comes the
question: 'But doesn't the "rule of law", however unsatisfactory its
operation, at least guarantee against a totalitarian state?' From the
theoreticist Left comes the question (usually posed as a statement of
fact): 'Doesn't the struggle for justice or civil liberties merely result in
a reformism which strengthens the existing system?'

In order to answer the first question it is necessary to distinguish
very carefully between the notion of the 'rule of law' and the actual
administration of criminal justice. Following Pashukanis, I have
already argued that the 'rule of law' is subjectively desirable because it
is recognized as a condition of existence of legal personality.[1] The
actual administration of criminal justice, however, bears very little
resemblance to its imaginary conception in law.

One has neither to romanticize law-breakers nor to put forward a
crude theory of the criminal law as having effect *only* as a mechanism
of class oppression to adduce evidence for Pashukanis's claim that:

> The machinery of the state represents a very powerful weapon. On this
> battlefield, relations do not appear in the least to be in the spirit of
> Kant's definition of law as a minimal limitation of the freedom of the
> personality indispensable to human co-existence. ... The norm is
> determined, not by the possibility of co-existence, but by the domina-
> tion of some by others. [Pashukanis, 1978, p. 150]

Today, as previously, it is recognized both in popular discourse and in academic and official reports (e.g. President's Commission, 1967, p. 4) that the burden of criminalization is borne disproportionately by working-class offenders. But working-class people do not only suffer a disproportionate amount of criminalization; they also suffer disproportionately from visible criminal activity. Given, too, that the visibility of working-class law violation is amplified by the mass media, it is small wonder that the perennial demand for 'law and order' is enthusiastically supported by people from all classes. Moreover, as social security recipients struggle for their supposed rights (see Piven and Cloward, 1972) as clients of a state increasingly having to intervene in support of a mode of production unable to legitimate itself on its own logic, new forms of crime are created which function to displace the causes and effects of structural contradictions on to the backs of 'scroungers', 'immigrants' or 'vandals'. Further, the hapless working-class criminal is not only vulnerable to popular stereotyping; (s)he is also likely to receive, from sectors of the marxist Left, the more esoteric characterization as a reactionary element – as being *more* 'lumpen' and *less* 'proletarian'. (For a good discussion of this see Taylor and Young, 1979.) Add to this generalized abhorrence of the working-class criminal (and the alternative is *not* romanticization of law-breakers) the nihilistic (and economistic) belief that, until there is a transition to socialism, *all* struggles for justice must necessarily be reformist, and it then becomes easier to understand why questions of criminal justice and penal politics are an embarrassment to many on the Left. For even E. P. Thompson, who has recently rebuked the Left for abandoning issues of civil liberty, and who has himself done an immense amount of work in this area (1978a, 1978b, 1979) has tended to overlook the necessarily asymmetrical relationship that exists between his beloved 'rule of law' and the actual administration of criminal justice. Which leads to a consideration of the ways in which civil liberties questions have been variously theorized by radical legal theorists.

Isaac Balbus (1977, p. 580) rejects all forms of legalism:

> The legal form is a specifically bourgeois form; those who would simultaneously uphold this form and condemn the capitalist mode of production which 'perverts' it simply fail to grasp that the part they uphold is inextricably tied to the very system they condemn.

Balbus's distrust of legalism is echoed by Clarke, Langan and Lee at the end of this present book when they raise doubts about the likelihood of progressive effects being engendered by a 'Back to Justice' movement (see Von Hirsch, 1976). But whereas Clarke *et al.* merely (and correctly) remind us that on its own the classical formula can never work, Balbus's position celebrates an essentialist conception of law, one that forecloses any possibility of short-term intervention in penal politics.

It has already been argued that the ideological effectivity of classical criminal jurisprudence is not determined solely by the capitalist mode of production. This is partly because criminal law as a discourse is dependent upon signifying practices which are constitutive of value in general; partly, and relatedly, it is because any specific discursive formation has the metonymic power to produce entirely new (or, conversely, very antiquated) representations of value. For these reasons, what is presently known as 'criminal justice' will not be 'transcended' by socialism; its deconstructed elements may well have metonymised effects in entirely new representations of value. The form and substance of those representations, moreover, will result neither from a political faith in 'transcendence' nor from a morality whose reward is the 'good society'. Future representations of value will depend upon the outcomes of present political struggles. What are the implications of such arguments?

Pashukanis, who, like Balbus, put emphasis on the form rather than the content of law, also recognized that at certain times the specific contradictions between the rhetorical claims of law and its actual administration could open up a space in which the 'rule of law' could be denied its primacy of jurisdiction over certain social issues and in which, at the same time, class antagonisms would be revealed. This advocacy of irony as a strategy of ideological intervention is nowadays fashionably derided as 'exposé criminology', the justification for such derision being that the force of irony depends upon an acceptance of the very forms that irony denies. I am well aware of the theoretical rectitude (rationalism) of this argument. I am less convinced that it makes sense politically. The secrecy and elitism of the criminal justice and penal systems (see Carlen, 1976a; Cohen and Taylor, 1978) alone seem to offer good reason to expect a radical criminology *continuously* to expose the fraudulent claims (to distributive justice) of a law whose administration is over-determined by exploitative social relations. However (and unlike Pashukanis), I am not trying to erase these contradictions through invocation of any ideal law, whether it be characterized as 'bourgeois', 'socialist' or neutral. The impossibility of law's claims does not negate the reality of law as a set of institutionalized practices which can be recognized as being coherent in their contradictions. On those grounds I would go further than Pashukanis and expect that sometimes 'exposure' could be followed by struggle over a practice and that such struggle could result in legislative and administrative reforms with progressive effects.

But Pashukanis did realize (and more acutely than any other theorist) that, however much the criminal law could be exposed as being the adversary, rather than the instrument, of justice, the process of criminalization could in itself be argued for by right-wing theorists as being not only the sanction against law-breakers, but also the condition of civil liberty.

> The more wary of the bourgeois criminologists are not at all ignorant
> of this connection between criminal law and the legal form in general.
> ... That is why their very reasonable response to the demands ... that
> they should lay the concept of crime and guilt to rest ... is the ques-
> tion: in that case, what about the principles of civil liberty?
> [Pashukanis, 1978, p. 188]

And it would be in answer to Pashukanis's 'bourgeois' criminologists that I would argue for a criminology (whether 'theoretical' or 'exposé') that continually questions any assertion that the present operation of the criminal law strengthens juridical relations in civil society. Such a criminology is already practised by organizations like NACRO (with the distribution of their monthly *Nacro Information*) and by the NCCL (both in their legal work and in a series of fact sheets and other publications).

So what, then, *is* the point of theory, particularly of theory the effects of which cannot be guaranteed; of theory that may in certain situations have a lesser effect than ironic description or other non-theoretical (but always calculated) forms of intervention? The task of theory remains what it always should have been: the constant questioning (and maybe erasure) of the most taken-for-granted concepts, whether they be presently favoured by either Right *or* Left. (For an example of this type of theoretical work see Mark Cousins's 'Men's Rea' – Chapter 5.)

CONCLUSION

Recently there has been qualified support for E. P. Thompson's plea that the Left should resume the fight for the maintenance and extension of civil liberties. The reasons for that support vary. Thompson's own argument is that the struggle for civil liberties is a struggle for democracy, a struggle against statism. In his enthusiasm for *this* struggle, Thompson has rather unreservedly given his support to what is popularly, loosely and erroneously called the 'rule of law'. However, as a result of analyses that recognize either the asymmetrical relationship between criminal law and criminalization processes (e.g. Young, 1979) or the contradiction between state forms and the economy (e.g. Picciotto, 1979), several contributors to the book *Capitalism and The Rule of Law* (Fine *et al.* 1979) have given qualified support to struggles for justice, though always emphasizing that at the same time there must be continual struggle for the 'transcendence' of bourgeois forms of social organization by socialism.

This essay has not been concerned with 'transcendence'. Its concern has been with calculation of the conditions in which radical explanations of crime will more immediately and effectively undermine popular conceptions of the relationship between crime, rule of law and individual (egotistical) existence. It is argued that, because the discourse of right has been conflated with the discourses of crime and individual autonomy, subjects at present have few modes of self-representation outside law. As a result, attempts to deny the rule of law its rhetorical claims are also seen as threats to personal autonomy. Until, therefore a non-capitalist mode of production is constitutive of, and demands, new representations of value, people who already know the language of totalitarianism will not easily have their fears assuaged by the unknown language of 'socialist legality'. In the short term, therefore, and at a time when many people still equate socialism with stalinism, the law must be both denied and preserved as a condition of value. One result of such a contradictory strategy might be the assuagement of prevailing fears that the transition from capitalism to socialism must necessarily encompass the Gulag in order (mistakenly) to promise Utopia.

CHAPTER 2

Bringing Power to Particular Account:
Peter Rajah and the Hull Board of Visitors

Laurie Taylor

My title comes from E. P. Thompson's 'Introduction' to *Review of Security and State* (1978b) and appears at the end of a particularly incisive analysis of the pessimism about the struggle for civil rights that is induced by certain 'marxist' emphases upon the mystifying character of the law and the reactionary character of the police. Thompson writes:

> This rhetoric can be seen to unbend the springs of action and to discount the importance of any struggle for civil rights ... if *all* law and *all* police are utterly abhorrent, then it cannot matter much what *kind* of law or what *place* the police are held within; and yet the most immediate and consequent struggles to maintain liberty are, exactly, about kinds and places, cases and precedents, and the bringing of power to particular account. [Thompson, 1978b]

The allusion to Thompson may be somewhat presumptuous in that this chapter deals solely with a test case in which the challenge to power was something less than direct, and in which the actual gain to civil liberties was a matter for debate rather than assertion. But perhaps this is necessarily the case with any issues of civil liberty in the present political climate. The possibilities for the legal and political establishment to recover the situation through a variety of secret and semi-secret administrative manoeuvres means that what seems like a clear gain the day after the verdict has been delivered, perhaps the firm establishment or re-establishment of a principle of civil liberty, can, in the absence of active public defence of that gain, be quickly transformed into a mere technical qualification of existing anti-libertarian practise. However, it is this very tendency that I believe justifies the present exercise.

For although Thompson refers approvingly in the same paper to the 'long and dogged record of the National Council for Civil Liberties', it is often the case that legal victories gained by the NCCL and other libertarian organizations become imperilled or fail to make sufficient impact upon other potential litigants, because the resources of those organizations limit the publicity that can be given to their achievements. *The Guardian*, *The Times* and the *Criminal Law Review* may note their significance in inside columns, but frequently such news items appear only at the moment when the final judicial decision has been made. They are not seen as the successful culmination of a long debate in which the principle of civil liberty at stake has been comprehensively rehearsed.

The difference between the United States and this country in this respect is quite dramatic. Of course, there are important constitutional differences between the countries which may enhance the effect, but in sheer terms of relative concern about issues of civil liberty it is interesting to contrast the coverage given, say, to the Bakke positive discrimination case in the United States and the case (described in this chapter) in which Hull prisoners went to the Appeal Court and confronted a fundamental tenet of British penal policy – namely that legality stops at the prison gates.

This contrast between the two countries is undoubtedly enhanced by the general lack of concern with civil liberty issues among British lawyers. The small legal staff at NCCL (at present two full-time solicitors) does not have a large outside reference group that can be counted on for support when important issues arise. Perhaps this is a fatalistic response engendered by past defeats; certainly one can observe some renewed signs of activity by radical lawyers now that the European Court of Human Rights provides another site where remedies may be sought. But, in general, the remarks made by the Legal Director of the American Civil Liberties Union in 1971, still carry weight:

> Because it is law on which we rely to protect our liberties, the legal profession and the courts are their special stewards. But the British lawyers and courts seem more often to ignore that stewardship in favour of the more lucrative work of defending property rights. In addition, I find them an uncreative lot. Though American lawyers may have more room for maneuvre because of the power of the courts to declare legislation unconstitutional, there is nevertheless room within the British Law to influence the interpretation of statutes and the development of case law – but I find hardly any evidence of the legal profession applying its ingenuity to the development of law affecting personal freedom. [quoted in Grant, 1971]

The NCCL's lack of resources to publicize their achievements (and indeed their failures – for a proper record of these may be just as important as any success story in alerting others to the present attacks upon civil liberties) is unfortunately not greatly alleviated by the left-wing tendency to fight shy of detailed legal issues. While the dramatic Hull riot and the equally dramatic subsequent trial and conviction of Hull prison officers on charges of assault received full coverage, there were very few column inches devoted to the prisoners' successful Appeal Court action against the sentence that they themselves received from the local Board of Visitors. It is difficult not to find affinities between this imbalance and E. P. Thompson's remarks on the Left's 'pitiful absence of concern displayed towards the recent modification in jury procedure' – a lack of concern, which, as we have already indicated, he adduces to their general belief in the inappropriateness of the courtroom as a site for political action or, as Jock Young puts it in his critical characterization of 'left idealism', the belief that 'the law itself represents a universalistic patina thinly covering the interests of the powerful whereas the police and the prisons represent the direct coercion on which the State is based' (Young, 1979). But that will do. This is not intended as a vindication of the NCCL at the expense of the Left. That would be to compound the problem rather than resolve it. For there is certainly some truth in the claim that an immersion in legalism can easily become an excuse for political inaction. And a present regret about the Left's relative aversion to issues of civil liberty should not be allowed to obscure the considerable political bravery that has been recently demonstrated in an increasingly difficult climate by individual socialist groups over such issues as race, employment and trade union activity.

THE RAJAH CASE

Elsewhere, Stan Cohen and I have documented the Home Office's determined and successful attempt to construct an apparatus of secrecy that will ensure that neither prisoners themselves, nor those on the outside (lawyers, journalists, teachers, researchers, relations) will know what is really happening to them (Cohen and Taylor, 1978).

When lawyers have intermittently threatened this state of affairs (as in the Golder case) the Home Office has shown that it is quite prepared to engage in the deliberate and secret subversion of a verdict issued by the European Court in order to thwart their claims (Cohen and Taylor, 1978). On the whole, by fair means or foul, the Home Office (aided by pusillanimous judges) has managed to maintain the state of affairs characterized by Graham Zellick: 'In Britain ... the law for most purposes tends to stop at the prison gates, leaving the prisoner to the almost exclusive control of the prison authorities' (Zellick, 1974).

It is this that gives such significance to the Rajah case. For the first time we find the courts declaring that the prison is not a closed world; that notions of 'natural justice' extend to within its walls; that prisoners like other human beings have a right to expect some degree of 'fairness' from the officers and governors who guard them. What follows is a record of the tortuous path that finally led the Appeal Court to this conclusion.

Following the riot that took place at Hull prison from 31 August to 2 September 1976, a large number of charges were brought against inmates who were thought to have been involved. In all, proceedings were taken against 185 out of the 310 prisoners in the jail and the total number of individual charges was over 500. As many of the prisoners were transferred immediately after the riot, a large number of the hearings took place at different prisons with the Board moving around from one to another to hear the cases. Such a situation did, of course, seriously interfere with the prisoners' opportunity to call their own witnesses – a matter that figured strongly in their subsequent objections to the proceedings.

The nature of the offences and the summary manner in which justice was dispensed cannot be better illustrated than by reproducing the transcripts of the proceedings for the three charges that Rajah faced.[1] Before this, however, it is relevant to mention a few general features of the prison adjudication system. The adjudication is conducted by the Board of Visitors, which in the Hull case was composed of two Justices of the Peace and one other person. Although token references are made in Home Office reports to the Board's independence, it is clear from other statements that this independence is rather narrowly defined. In the *Annual Report of the Prison Department* (1972), for example, we find the following:

> If the Boards are to be effective there must always be good communication between them and the Prison Department at every level. The main points of contact will always be the governor who will keep his Board in touch with current developments both in general policy and in relation to his particular establishment.

In adjudications the importance of this link is emphasized by the presence of the governor or a senior officer representing him. The *Home Office Working Party on Adjudication Procedures in Prisons* suggests disingenuously that the sense of the independence of the Board may be preserved in such circumstances by moving some of the furniture around: 'the seating arrangements should be such as to avoid the impression that the governor is one of those conducting the adjudication'.

There are a number of 'awards' that may be made by the Board including stoppage of earnings, cellular confinement and loss of remission. It is the last that is the most serious, in that it may effectively increase the actual sentence that a prisoner has to serve by up to two years. It was this setting and these punitive consequences that Peter Rajah faced on the 16 December 1976. He was first of all charged under:

Rule 47, Para. 6: 'Absents himself without permission from any place where he is required to be whether within or outside prison'. The proceedings were as follows (nothing has been omitted).

Gov./CLERK: Do you plead guilty or not guilty?
RAJAH: Not guilty.
SENIOR OFFICER DUDDING: At 20.00 h on 31/8/76 in C Wing I was S.O. i/c. I checked Rajah's cell at 20.00 h and found him to be missing.
CHAIRMAN: Were you in your cell at 20.00 h?
RAJAH: No – I was in the showers – I was in my cell at 10 past 8.
CHAIRMAN: Was a body check taken?
S.O. DUDDING: Yes – all the doors were locked – either occupied or empty. If he wasn't in his cell at 20.00 h he couldn't have been in his cell 10 minutes later.

RAJAH: He didn't look in the showers.

S.O. DUDDING: Rajah was one of a group on the centre at 7 o'clock.

CHAIRMAN: All the cells, showers and recesses were checked – you weren't there and were not on the list of those who were there.

RAJAH: I was in the shower at 5 to 8.

CHAIRMAN: Case proven.

Altogether, Rajah faced four charges. The entire hearing of these lasted 15 minutes and the deliberation of findings (as timed by Rajah) took 1 minute 40 seconds. He was 'awarded' 390 days' loss of remission, 154 days' loss of privileges, 154 days' loss of earnings and 154 days' exclusion from associated labour. Lord Justice Lane commented in the Divisional Court: 'Whatever other criticism may have been levelled at the Board, no one could fail to admire their industry and application and no one could fail to applaud the way in which the proceedings were recorded and documented.'

The other criticism levelled at the Board was basically the case made by Peter Rajah and five fellow prisoners in their attempt to obtain an order of *certiorari* against the Board of Visitors of Hull Prison. In Rajah's case it was specifically claimed that:

Applicant was not informed of the charges laid against him as soon as possible.

Applicant was not given adequate time to prepare his defence.

Applicant was prevented from cross-examining sufficiently or at all.

Applicant was prevented from calling evidence.

Applicant was prevented from addressing Board of Visitors.

Chairman gave hearsay evidence.

Governor gave hearsay evidence.

In other words, it was argued that there was a general denial of the usual conditions of natural justice which typically accompany any adjudication that carries with it a determination of guilt and a sentence. Peter Rajah said that he was kept in solitary confinement prior to the hearing, and that 'no information was provided to me about the case other than the list of charges'. The Chairman referred to statements that Rajah was not given the opportunity of reading, made by officers who were not present to be questioned. He also felt that some doubt might have been thrown on the proceedings by the fact that the chief witness against him in one of the cases (see above) was Senior Officer Dudding, who had been subsequently convicted of conspiracy to assault and beat prisoners detained in Her Majesty's

Prison, Hull. In court Dudding had pleaded not guilty, given evidence on oath, and received a nine months' suspended sentence.

The initial request for an order of *certiorari*, however, is an attempt not to establish whether such infringements of natural justice occurred in any particular adjudication, but rather to show that the occasion was such that the basic elements of natural justice – right to cross-examination, to call witnesses, to speak on one's own behalf – should apply. It is, in other words, preliminary to the actual examination by the Court of the specific content of the proceedings.

Some brief historical remarks about the order of *certiorari* are relevant to our account of the Divisional and Appeal Court's deliberations. The order is legally classified alongside *habeas corpus*, prohibition and *mandamus*, as a prerogative writ. Essentially, *certiorari* started its legal life as a royal demand for information about the operation of inferior tribunals.

> The theory is that the Sovereign has been appealed to by some one of his subjects who complains of an injustice done to him by an inferior court; whereupon the Sovereign, saying that he wishes to be certified – *certiorari* – of the matter, orders that the record, etc. be transmitted into a court in which he is sitting. [de Smith, 1973]

Although the remedial jurisdiction passed from sovereign to courts in the course of history, the essential authoritarian function of the order, particularly in the late seventeenth and early eighteenth centuries, was to prevent other judicial or quasi-judicial bodies from usurping the functions of superior courts or persons. But, of course, the pursuit of this authoritarian aim also provided an opportunity for ordinary citizens to appeal against convictions and orders made by a variety of authorities who had taken it upon themselves to maintain discipline by acting in a semi-judicial manner. Thus it was that the procedures of the Hull Board of Visitors could at least in principle be regarded as the proper object for an order of *certiorari*. After all, the Board set itself up as a judicial body; it inquired about guilt or lack of it, and pronounced sentence.

THE DIVISIONAL COURT

At first it seemed that the case for natural justice operating in Board of Visitors' adjudications was so overwhelming that none of the three

judges in the Divisional Court could resist it. Lord Chief Justice
Widgery observed:

> One looks at the circumstances and visualised the Board of Visitors'
> setting very much like a bench of magistrates ... [*two were in fact*
> *magistrates* L.T.] with the applicant prisoner standing before them.
> With that mental picture, one can say it looks as though this is a case
> for *certiorari*. Instinctively one would think that this would be within
> the category to which the Order applies. That is reinforced by the view,
> which I hold at any rate, that the Act which the Board of Visitors
> perform under this jurisdiction is a judicial act.

Neither could the judges readily find any escape clause in precedent. *Certiorari* had never been specifically limited to certain sorts of
judicial settings. Lord Parker had declared in 1967:

> The position as I see it is that the exact limits of the ancient remedy by
> way of *certiorari* have never been and ought not to be specifically
> defined. They have varied from time to time being extended to meet
> changing conditions. . . . The only constant limits throughout were that
> it was performing a public duty.

There seemed only one other way of escaping the inevitable conclusion: this was to argue that the Board of Visitors was administering a
piece of private discipline, rather like a schoolteacher or an army
officer (or, indeed, a prison governor), and was therefore technically
not involved in an adjudication. But this avenue was also blocked.
Lord Goddard had ruled in rejecting the case of a fireman who applied
for *certiorari* after being disciplined for refusing to clean the bucket of
his superior officer (*sic*) that '*certiorari* goes to courts or to something
which can fairly be said a court'. Surely that had to include the Board
of Visitors.

And then at the very last minute, when it seemed that the scales had
tipped so far towards the applicants that they threatened to over-
balance, there appeared upon the legal scene, stepping crudely over
historical precedents and careful logic, the figure of crass expediency.
Widgery invoked a statement made by Denning in 1972 in *Becker* v.
Home Office, which although not concerned with *certiorari* was
nevertheless very definitely concerned with the power of the Home
Office and its immunity from legal intervention.

> If the courts were to entertain actions by disgruntled prisoners, the
> governor's life would be made intolerable. The discipline of the prison
> would be undermined. The Prison Rules are regulatory directions only.

Even if they are not observed, they do not give rise to a cause of action.

Natural justice be damned: the governor's life and prison discipline were suddenly the real issues. Lord Chief Justice Widgery concluded his judgement with Denning's remarks and the statement, 'I respectfully agree with that'.

The other two judges quickly fell into line behind their expedient mentor. Lord Justice Cumming Bruce had no doubt about the judicial character of the proceedings and had even noted the word 'adjudication' appeared in the Prison Rules themselves. But what use were legal arguments when you were dealing with a case like this? Consequences, not principles, were the decisive factor:

> It gradually became clearer and clearer to me that as a matter of commonsense there would be very grave public disadvantages in allowing the writ to go to . . . a Board of Visitors.

THE APPEAL COURT

The sight of three eminent judges wriggling so uncomfortably on the hook of precedent before swimming off into the murky waters of common sense and expediency was quite enough to prompt further action by solicitors representing the prisoners. Five of the seven (including Peter Rajah) who had initially applied to the Divisional Court for orders of *certiorari* now proceeded to appeal against the refusal of the application. The case was eventually heard in the Court of Appeal on 3 October 1978.

Once again three judges applied themselves to the question of whether or not a Board of Visitors' adjudication might reasonably be said to be a judicial proceeding. Further indications of the appropriateness of *certiorari* appeared. Lord Justice Megaw was confronted with the details of Form 1145 which is handed to prisoners when they are to appear before an adjudication: the form made it quite clear that the Home Office saw the proceedings as analogous to a criminal trial. As Megaw observed:

> It [Form 1145] shows that the prisoner will be asked whether he pleads guilty or not guilty to the charge; that there will be evidence of witnesses in support of the charge; that he may question such witnesses; that after the evidence against him he may make his defence to the charge, or if he has pleaded guilty, offer an explanation.

The transcript of one of the other hearings involving Peter Rajah demonstrates the lack of congruence between the statements on Form 1145 and the actual conduct of the adjudication: once again the entire proceedings are given.

Rule 47, Para. 11: 'Wilfully damages or disfigures any part of the prison or any property not his own'

GOV./CLERK: Do you plead Guilty or Not Guilty?
RAJAH: Not Guilty.
HOSPITAL OFFICER HENDERSON: At approx. 09.15 h on 1/9/76 I was in the admin. block when I saw a number of inmates hurling bricks and roof slates from the Seg. Unit roof in the direction of the main prison wall. Rajah was one of these inmates.
CHAIRMAN: How far away were you?
H.O. HENDERSON: 20–30 yds.
CHAIRMAN: Do you know Rajah?
H.O. HENDERSON: Yes.
RAJAH: I've never seen him before.
H.O. HENDERSON: He's been on sick parade.
CHAIRMAN: Therefore you've spoken to him and he's lying.
H.O. HENDERSON: Yes.
MR BRADY: Have you been sick?
RAJAH: Yes.
CHAIRMAN: Any questions?
RAJAH: He said he saw me twice.
CHAIRMAN: That's the next charge.
RAJAH: I'll leave it till then.
CHAIRMAN: Case proven.

It is important to re-emphasize at this point that the arguments advanced on behalf of the Board of Visitors in these proceedings were only partly a justification of the conduct of such adjudications. In the face of clear evidence that they hardly conformed even to the requirements set out in the Home Office's own Form 1145, the defence concentrated on arguing that the Board of Visitors was a domestic tribunal which was a master of its own procedure and that therefore the rules of natural justice could have no relevance to its proceedings – in other words, that an order of *certiorari* was inappropriate. But at this point Home Office duplicity caught up with itself. The very claim that the Board of Visitors by virtue of being a domestic tribunal did not need to offer a full and fair hearing of a case such as would occur in other judicial settings was precisely the *opposite* of that which Home Office lawyers had advanced to the European Commission of Human Rights in *Kiss* v. *United Kingdom*. In this case a prisoner,

Laslo Kiss, had cited Article 6(1) of the European Convention of Human Rights with regard to his own inability to have access to outside legal advice in connection with a Board of Visitors' adjudication. Article 6(1) states: 'In the determination of his civil rights and obligations, or of any criminal charge against him, everyone is entitled to a fair and public hearing within a reasonable time by an independent and impartial tribunal established by law.'

The lawyers forcibly argued on behalf of the Home Office:

> The Government conclude that the proceedings against the applicant were of a purely disciplinary nature to which the provisions of Article 6 need not have applied. In any event the Government submit that the *applicant had a full and fair hearing of his case before the Board of Visitors which is an important and independent authority.* [my italics]

This example of the Home Office being hoisted by its own petard is an interesting indication of the additional room for legal manoeuvre which is provided by the existence of the European Convention of Human Rights. This is hardly a libertarian charter – but then, so grossly illiberal are many of the present Home Office practices that the Convention's provisions have proved quite strong enough to embarrass the defenders of the British penal system. The Rajah case provided civil liberties' lawyers with the chance to contrast the Home Office's European and domestic defences of its illiberality – and thereby demonstrate not just their inconsistency but their calculated hypocrisy.

The Appeal Court having then found further arguments for making an order of *certiorari*, and having dismissed new reservations entered by the defence, moved towards a judgement. Would they, like the lower court, turn at the last minute to the road marked 'common sense' and 'expediency'?

Lord Justice Shaw provided the answer in a series of extremely important statements about the rights of prisoners. First of all, he dismissed the argument that prisoners should be denied natural justice on the grounds of their special status:

> Prisoners are subject to a special regimen and have a special status. Nevertheless they are not entirely devoid of all the fundamental rights and liberties which are inherent in our constitution ... despite the deprivation of his general liberty, a prisoner remains invested with residuary rights appertaining to the nature and conduct of his incarceration.

And then turning directly to face the Division Court judgement, he forcefully declared: 'To deny jurisdiction on the grounds of expediency seems to me, with all respect to the views expressed in the judgement of Lord Widgery ... to be tantamount to abdicating a primary function of the judiciary'.

It would be difficult to find a clearer example of the way in which an essentially authoritarian statement about the central importance of the judiciary simultaneously affirmed a fundamental principle of civil liberty – namely the necessity of keeping political, expedient and 'common-sense' arguments well away from considerations of natural justice.

And once back on this path of legal principle, Lord Justice Shaw was also quite prepared to dispatch that whole range of arguments that seek to impair basic liberties by reference to practical difficulties – in this case the threat of large numbers of prisoners trying to claim similar rights.

> It may be inexpedient or perhaps stultifying in relation to prison discipline that recourse to the courts should be available to a prisoner who advances some capricious complaint as to the manner in which he has been disciplined. There are no finite limits to the extent of the jurisdiction of the High Court in this regard. The practical limits are to be sought in the exercise of the power to grant relief which is always a matter of discretion.

Neither did the personal characteristics of the complainant constitute any grounds for refusing him access to the courts. Lord Denning's 'disgruntled' prisoners had the same rights as any other inmates. After all, '"disgruntled prisoners" may have serious grounds for complaint of some award which is not only peremptory but arbitrary'.

Although the other judges accepted this point of view, and the appeal was allowed, we should not, as suggested at the beginning of this chapter, regard the Appeal Court's decision as exactly flinging open the prison gates to legality. Lord Justice Lane's summary indicated that, even if judicial minds could not quite tolerate the behaviour of the Hull Board of Visitors, their sentiments were still firmly on the side of the authorities:

> We confess it is with some reluctance that we came to this conclusion, because there is inevitably a feeling that the Board may have reached the right result ultimately in spite of the irregularities. These men were prisoners. Some of them were dangerous. Most of them were difficult. All of them were no doubt to some extent untrustworthy.

With the order of *certiorari* granted, the matter then went back to the Divisional Court for a detailed assessment of the extent to which principles of natural justice were actually violated in specific cases. As a result of these proceedings a total of sixteen findings of guilt against six prisoners were quashed and privileges and remission duly restored.

CONCLUSION

The significance of this case for civil liberties in general and for prisoners' rights in particular does not depend wholly upon the fact of its successful outcome. If adequate publicity had surrounded the proceedings, and the judicial recourse to expediency and the actual nature of the Board of Visitors' proceedings thereby become public knowledge, there might have been some significant gains in the general appreciation of prisoners' lack of rights, an appreciation that might in future cases even have done something to point judges more firmly towards the judicial standards that they claim to embody. After all, the ability to opt for expediency in cases where principles are supposedly at stake is, as every successful politician well knows, very much related to the degree of public visibility that the issue enjoys.

The necessity of such publicity when test cases are being heard is made even more urgent by the relative scarcity of such cases. There are not many second chances in this area. In the Rajah case, for example, there were several formidable obstacles that nearly kept the matter entirely out of the courts. First there was time. An order of *certiorari* must be sought in the six-month period following the questionable adjudication (this has recently been reduced to three months). Peter Rajah, as we have seen, appeared before the Board of Visitors in December 1976 and immediately petitioned the Secretary of State to complain about the adjudication. Home Office officials are old hands when it comes to bureaucratic delay and they managed not to reply until 1 April 1977. Their actual letter gave no indication that the time had been taken up by careful official reflection on the rights and wrongs of Rajah's case: 'The Secretary of State has considered your petition but is not prepared to take any action in respect of the adjudication by the Hull Board of Visitors on 16th December 1976.'

Rajah then proceeded to contact the NCCL in May of that year and it was only the success of his solicitor in arguing that there were special reasons for the delay that eventually allowed the case to be heard 'out of time'.

The NCCL faced one other principal difficulty in their attempt to pursue the Rajah case: the difficulty of obtaining the necessary legal aid to finance the appeal stage of the proceedings. On the face of it this looks like a technical problem, but rather as in the case of Home Office time-wasting over dealing with petitions, it soon begins to take on a subtle political colouring.

Application for legal aid is made to an area committee composed of lawyers which listens to opinions on the case from Counsel and from a solicitor. In the present case every one of the conventional considerations for the granting of legal aid seemed to be satisfied. Counsel advised that there were strong grounds for appeal; there was every sign from the transcript that the matter had been taken most seriously by the Divisional Court, and of course an extremely important legal point was at stake. Indeed, before the Divisional Court decision, lawyers were confidently expecting the Home Office to appeal if the decision went against them. In such circumstances it was extremely surprising that the local legal aid committee should refuse the request, and more particularly that they should justify their refusal by a mere statement of their agreement with the Divisional Court: 'The Committee, having considered all the information and documents submitted including Counsel's advice on appeal, agree with the reasoning of the Divisional Court and they consider that your proposed Appeal is unlikely to succeed.'

There is no right of appeal against such a decision. An aura of secrecy surrounds the committee and its proceedings, such that even the names of the members are secret and there is no publicized way of actually becoming a member. It is known, however, that those who eventually 'emerge' are relatively senior lawyers who may well not be as sympathetic to certain kinds of cases as their younger colleagues. Fortunately, the NCCL were able on this occasion to exploit a little known anomaly in the legal aid procedures. They gave up their local committee and applied to other areas, finally obtaining legal aid from the Newcastle committee. It seems disturbing that a case that eventually produced such a significant legal decision should have depended for its continued existence upon such fortuitous circumstances.

This paper is not intended as a celebration of a famous victory. It is rather an attempt to provide a more detailed analysis than has hitherto been available of an important case concerning prisoners' rights. Neither is it intended as a vindication of legalism. The irony of the use of *certiorari* in the service of civil liberties has been emphasized, as has the non-libertarian legal impulse that prompted the final decision.

Prisons have not changed as a result of the Rajah verdict. Boards of Visitors are still dispensing 'kadi-justice', and the vigorous criticisms made years ago by the Jellicoe Committee about their inability to act as both independent witnesses to 'the state of the prison . . . and the treatment of prisoners', and 'as an adjudicating body', remains unheeded.[2]

But some specific personal injustices have been righted, some judicial remarks made that can be cited on future occasions, and once again the Home Office's attempt to keep legality from its prison doors has been temporarily thwarted. For a variety of reasons, some democratic and libertarian, some authoritarian and legalistic, power has been brought to particular account.[3]

CHAPTER 3

Civil Liberties and Public Order

Donald Thompson

The relationship between issues of civil liberties and issues of public order is subject to much confusion, largely because attitudes to police powers are themselves confused or, at best, ambivalent. The presence or absence of constitutional guarantees protecting civil liberties will not itself determine the extent to which police powers are permitted to reduce individual rights and liberties, but some authoritative pronouncement can be invoked as the underlying statement of values. In England the theoretical and even philosophical basis of the interaction between police power and individual rights is nowhere authoritatively stated in any legal provision. Both statute and case law applicable in this complicated area combine the piecemeal with the *ad hoc* to a degree that assures a generous dose of the worst of both worlds, the authoritarian and the libertarian.

Public order issues arise mainly from public meetings, demonstrations, marches or disorderly gangs on the rampage. This is the more visible and more widely chronicled aspect of public order, but there is another no less important side concerning police powers more generally: those who are concerned with organized public protest as part of a wider aim to change or to preserve the society we live in can arouse police interest in far more than their marching and demonstrating. If, like the Angry Brigade, they resort to bombing they will obviously attract the attention of special police squads designed to deal with bombing or terrorism. If they pour out subversive literature they may be visited. For this reason the public order question is not confined to streets and public meetings; it concerns the use of police powers in a wider sense if the police begin to investigate the activities of organizations that show prominently in public protest or dissent.

The use of police powers in entering and searching premises and questioning suspects is thus important in a discussion of civil liberties generally and in the public order context. It is important also as an indication of the ethos according to which the police may operate with a view to securing convictions.

Many practical questions arising from the exercise of police powers are unanswered in English law. The legality of the exercise of police powers is usually tested in a civil action brought by an individual or in a prosecution for assaulting or obstructing a policeman in the execution of his duty. The legality of police methods is not as such an issue in a criminal prosecution and a convicted defendant is not likely to seek damages in a separate civil action for any wrong such as trespass, unlawful arrest or wrongful seizure of documents.

Thus, while the need for the rule of law in a variety of senses is constantly urged, and we become painfully aware of the incidence of crime of the kind that violates individual safety and security, the need to examine and re-examine the framework of rules within which the police are required to operate is itself crucial. Police powers relating to the investigation of crime, with this inevitable detraction from the rights and freedoms of the individual, involve the acceptability of encroachment not only on the rights of the innocent but also on those of the guilty. The powers and authority conferred on the police are designed as much to enable pursuit of the guilty as they are to protect the innocent. They also authorize the mistaken but bona fide pursuit of the innocent and protect the guilty. It would be wrong to concern oneself only with the righteous indignation of the innocent, who have been the unfortunate victims of police activities; the acceptability of how one investigates and proves guilt is also a matter of concern in the case of those who are genuinely guilty of the offence charged.

This point is important for a number of reasons, perhaps the most important of which is that it conditions the law's response to one of the central problems of law enforcement, viz. whether the primary concern is to uphold the rights of the individual, as is inherent in the due process approach, or to get the actual decision right, at the expense if necessary of concern over whether it was properly arrived at (Packer, 1968). In English law, in sharp theoretical contrast to the position in the United States, the main concern in permitting the police to adduce relevant evidence without worrying (subject to exceptions) over how it was obtained indicates that the courts are concerned mainly with the relevance of the evidence submitted;[1] in the United States the rule that excludes from the courtroom evidence obtained in violation of the constitution guarantees against unreasonable searches and seizures,[2] or of the privilege against self-incrimination,[3] displays a concern with respect for the rights of the individual (as well as for police observance of legality) even when the evidence may be perfectly reliable, as it is in the case of an illegal search and seizure.

Similarly, in the area of public order, although the United States is a society of a greater diversity of culture than this country and of greater public excitability, the courts there have chosen to rank the constitutional guarantee of freedom of speech and assembly ahead of police power to prevent public disorder by prohibition on either.[4] Despite our cramped opportunities to find a public venue to process or assemble there is the clear statement of priorities in *Hague* v. *CIO*:

> Wherever the title of streets and parks may rest, they have immemorially been held in trust for the use of the public and, time out of mind, have been used for purposes of assembly, communicating thoughts between citizens, and discussing public questions.[5]

In England the position under combined law and in practice may not be significantly different from that in the United States; but the absence of firm legal underpinning leaves much to the discretion (or inability to cope) of the police. Judicial decisions are often distressingly brief and formalistic.[6] Moreover, the way in which, even under the rules applicable, the police can break rules with little danger for the successful outcome of a prosecution can scarcely encourage respect for rules, or even for the rule of law.

A convenient starting point for a general appraisal of police powers in relation to civil liberties in England is the recognition that the voluntary (wittingly or unwittingly) waiver of one's right not to co-operate or comply with police requests is an indispensable help to the police as they seek to investigate crime. The process of fingerprinting an entire neighbourhood or asking all drivers of a particular model of car to account for their movements on a particular occasion usually elicits a generous public-spirited response if some shocking crime has outraged the local community. Less publicized is the need for the police to secure individual co-operation where they have no authority to compel. Many members of the public, guilty or innocent of an offence, volunteer information or make confessions, 'assist the police with their inquiries', move on when told to do so, allow the police to search them or their premises, and generally co-operate in doing things on which the police are not empowered to insist. One of the first and most important legal questions concerns the effect that such acquiescence by the individual has on the eventual outcome of the prosecution; whether police action was in the circumstances lawful is a matter which, however important otherwise, does not of itself affect the outcome of the prosecution.

COMPLIANCE WITH POLICE REQUESTS AND DEMANDS

To an individual who does not know whether a policeman is lawfully entitled to arrest him (search him, enter his premises, etc., tell him to accompany him or to move on, or to empty his pockets, etc., or to hand over correspondence or give his fingerprints), the distinction between a request and a command will not always spring to mind and the police need not in most instances worry unduly whether the distinction is appreciated. The reason for this is that the conduct in question either is not, or, by virtue of consent, ceases to be, a legal wrong.

Thus, the entry of police on to private premises with the permission of the occupier is not legally wrongful, and it does not become legally wrongful as a trespass simply because the occupier failed to realize that he need not have allowed the police to enter. It is not usual for the police to have lawful authority to search premises without a warrant, but many premises are entered without permission. What is understood to be permission or consent can sometimes surprise the lay observer of such matters, but it seems clear from the cases that a clearly and firmly worded refusal is desirable if the police are not to succeed in claiming that their entry was permitted by the occupier. Standing by without protest as police enter and search is tantamount to permitting the entry and search, even when the absence of protest is based on ignorance of the legal position. In any event there is no rule in English law that excludes as admissible evidence (solely because of the illegality) anything obtained through an illegal search.

There is, however, one case where an assertion by the police that they have an authority which in reality they have not can ground legal liability, and that is the case of an arrest. If an individual submits to an assertion of authority by a policeman requiring him to go to the police station this amounts to an arrest if in the circumstances the reasonable inference is that he is being ordered to do so (Leigh, 1975, pp. 37–9). This 'show of authority' rule is important as far as the knowledgeable citizen is concerned, since he can refuse to go or at any rate make it quite clear that he is submitting to an arrest. Where in the circumstances there is no power of arrest such an exercise of authority is construed as an arrest and the policeman may be sued for the arrest if it is unlawful. In one bizarre case where it was necessary for the police to establish that they had arrested the accused (more usually they wish to show that he had voluntarily accompanied them) the rule operated the other way, with the result that the common formula, 'I must ask you to accompany me', was held not to amount to an arrest.[7]

PROBLEMS OF SEARCH AND SEIZURE

It is usual to require a warrant authorizing the entry and search of private premises, although it is important to note the power to enter private premises without a warrant to search for anyone reasonably thought to be on the premises who is reasonably suspected of having committed an arrestable offence.[8] Search warrants must specify what is to be searched and what is to be searched for, and there is an understandable long-standing concern that searches beyond what is authorized by the warrant should not be permitted. It can be said at once that, although the issue of the lawfulness of the search does not determine whether what is discovered and taken away may be used in evidence,[9] it does determine civil liability at the instance of the aggrieved party.

It is not unlikely that a search for one thing might uncover something else, either similar but not covered by the warrant or something quite different. Thus a search for suspected stolen goods has uncovered other suspected stolen goods,[10] or drugs;[11] a search for explosives has uncovered documents indicating involvement in sedition.[12] A search without a warrant for a suspected offender could well uncover stolen goods or other material relevant to proof of a crime. In all these cases the objects not covered by the warrant (or by any warrant where the search was one for which no warrant was required) were discovered in the course of a search (one of which was itself unlawful) and the legality of their seizure becomes an important practical issue. Provided action were taken in time, the recovery of such objects could be sought before they have been used in evidence, and the effect of the absence of a rule excluding illegally seized objects from evidence would be negatived. However, the cases show a readiness by the courts to treat as lawful the seizure of objects found in the course of a lawful search where neither search nor seizure of those objects was specifically authorized. Even if the search was unlawful, it is only in exceptional cases that they will be excluded from evidence.[13]

It is important to consider whether the power to search must be delimited by the nature of the quest. A warrant to search for drugs clearly authorizes the most penetrating scrutiny of miniscule and remote corners of premises and of cupboards, desks or filing cabinets; the power to search for a suspected offender would not. A finding that a search is lawful must, it is submitted, take into account what is being looked for and where. In so far as the legality of the seizure of objects not specified in the warrant depends on the lawfulness of the search being conducted, it is important to examine where and how in the circumstances the search for the objects specified could be carried out. It is submitted that search warrants do not authorize the ransacking of parts of premises where the objects sought could not conceivably be.

A further important question arises in relation to the decisions that permit the seizure of objects discovered in the course of a lawful search. Since the objects seized were not covered by the warrant, it can be argued that the decisive criterion is not the lawfulness of the search, since no search for the objects seized was authorized, but simply the lawfulness of the circumstances in which the objects were discovered. It is obvious that to admit a policeman into your home or office when he calls and asks to see you is not a licence for him to conduct a search of the premises. But if his eye should catch sight of something openly visible, which indicates that an offence has been committed, and should he wish to seize it, it is not obvious under case law why he cannot lawfully do so.

It has been argued that the power to seize these additional objects may be limited to entry carried out under a search or an arrest warrant (Leigh, 1975), and the suggestion has the attraction that it would set relatively narrow limits to the extended power. On the other hand, since the search is not being conducted for that object and its seizure is not covered by the warrant, the fact that a search is being conducted for something else would serve merely to indicate that the object in question was discovered lawfully. If the object were one for which a search warrant could not be issued anyway, the relevance of searching under a warrant is not clear. It may well be that the lawfulness of the circumstances is the appropriate test, and that carrying out a search under a warrant is merely one instance of such lawful circumstances. It would be useful to know. What is clear, as Dr Leigh observes, is that there have been major departures from old established rules in recent cases.[14] The problem of compliance with a police request or demand again arises. Many people do what a policeman tells them to do, such as (reluctantly) handing over a passport, as in *Ghani* v. *Jones*. A statement that 'I shall have to take that' may well lead to acquiescence, i.e. consent. In such cases the 'seizure' is done with consent, and unless the 'show of authority' rule applicable to arrests were similarly applicable no legal wrong would be committed. It is, however, important to bear in mind that an action for the return of such objects can always be brought if second thoughts or legal advice should belatedly stiffen resolve,[15] but this course is clearly less satisfactory from the point of view of the individual for at least two reasons: first, it can be more troublesome and expensive than simply to refuse to part with the objects in the first place; second, in so far as correspondence and other documents are involved the damage may be done simply by perusal, especially with the possibility of photographic reproduction.

A relatively recent innovation recognizes a power to search premises, as distinct from the person, as ancillary to the power of arrest.[16] In such cases the link between the person arrested and the premises on which he is arrested must clearly be something more than physical presence: any notion that when the police arrest a burglar they may add to the householder's chagrin by searching his premises is surely derisory. On the other hand, it is clear that the relationship need not be proprietary. Some vague notion that the person arrested must be in some degree of authority over the use of the premises, or his part of them, was indicated in *Elias* v. *Pasmore*, where a warrant of arrest was executed on premises which were then searched. The search must relate to matters connected with the crime for which the person is arrested. There is no inherent reason why a similar rule to that laid down in *Elias* v. *Pasmore* should not apply to an arrest effected without warrant, assuming that the entry to effect the arrest was lawful, as it quite easily could be. Again, the criterion of lawfulness seems more appropriate than whether or not the action was due under a warrant, and therefore the extended power is as appropriate to a lawful arrest without a warrant as to a lawful arrest with a warrant, at any rate as long as presence on the premises was lawful.

It is clear from this cursory examination of some of the problems concerning police powers that there is much doubt and uncertainty in this area. Must you do what the policeman says? Must you let him in? Must you let him take what he says is to be kept as evidence? Where lines should be drawn is a question on which attitudes vary, but many whose views might differ as to where lines should be drawn – are we for due process or are we for law enforcement? – would agree that the lines are not drawn with sufficient clarity. This creates problems for both the police and the individual.

The police recognize that they depend for the effective discharge of their duty in investigating crime on the co-operation of individuals. They may enjoy this co-operation from the knowledgeable, who are prepared to do voluntarily what they know they are not compelled to do, or from the less knowledgeable, who either would agree anyway or who do so reluctantly in ignorance of their rights, or from those who in one way or another are bluffed or persuaded into reluctantly agreeing to do what the policeman wants. Some recent decisions have allowed the police significantly wider powers, but perhaps of even greater importance is the large area of uncertainty introduced by the judgements in the Court of Appeal in *Ghani* v. *Jones*. The effect of an important part of this decision is that criteria laid down for some cases where the police have lawful authority to seize and retain are that the crime involved should be 'serious' and that giving up the object should be in the circumstances 'reasonable'.

A qualitative term such as 'serious' or 'reasonable' is clearly a desirable limitation if there is not to be a general power for the police simply to exercise and act on their judgement as they think fit. But both terms are sufficiently imprecise to ensure that there will be significant differences of opinion over whether a particular offence is serious or whether in the circumstances it is reasonable that something to be used as evidence should be handed over to and retained by the police. Is the individual to be told that the (unspecified) offence is serious and take his chance as to what it is? Or must he be told what the offence is, to enable him to decide whether to comply with the policeman's demand? Must he be told sufficient to enable him to exercise his judgement on whether something would or would not be reasonable? It seems clear that if the offence is serious, and if it would in the circumstances be unreasonable to refuse to allow the police to take the item of evidence, refusal to comply with a policeman's demand would amount to obstructing the police in the execution of their duty. If this is so the question arises how far must knowledge by the accused of the circumstances that give rise to the duty be proven. It appears that an intention to obstruct has to be shown.[17]

There may well be determined individuals who will insist on knowing what the circumstances are and also who reserve the right to form their own view of 'seriousness' and 'reasonableness'. They may well discover in the criminal courts whether or not they were correct, but for those who do not relish this particular kind of empiricism the prudent course is to do what the policeman says. Unless the criteria laid down by Lord Denning in *Ghani* v. *Jones* are hedged around with the safeguards embodied in the principle that knowledge of the circumstances that make conduct criminal must normally be established, the rule rapidly becomes that a policeman's statement that he is investigating a serious offence, and that he has reason to believe that the object is evidence relating to that offence, creates an obligation, backed by the sanction of criminal proceedings, to give him what he demands. Perhaps this is desirable, but it would be a remarkable and disturbingly vague formulation of an important new rule. It also discourages insistence on what one conceives to be one's rights by virtue of their precarious uncertainty. Obstructing a policeman is in some cases easily translatable into assaulting a police officer in the execution of his duty, and for that offence it is no excuse to establish that one honestly and reasonably believed on the facts that the policeman was exceeding his lawful authority.[18]

Another point of disquieting uncertainty facing one who is reluctant to yield to authority wrongly asserted by the police is the notion that not every trivial wrong committed by a policeman results in his actions being no longer in the execution of his duty.[19] The broad and simple view which had until recently held sway was that when a policeman exceeded his powers an assault on him was not an assault on him in the execution of his duty. If we all knew what was trivial for this purpose there would be little practical difficulty, but in one important case the curious view was taken that a policeman who was trespassing on private property was still acting in the execution of his duty when he prevented the householder on whose land he was trespassing from entering her own home.[20]

SUSPECTS AND POLICE POWERS

A few years ago debate raged furiously over whether the silence of the accused could be taken into consideration by a jury together with all the other circumstances to determine whether the accused was guilty. The vehement opposition aroused by the proposal that it should seems to have resulted in the burial of the proposals made on that and other matters by the Criminal Law Revision Committee in its *Eleventh Report* (HMSO, 1972). The report of the Royal Commission on Criminal Procedure may deal with a range of wider and related issues in a more rounded context. But in recent years the rules relating to police powers in relation to suspects have continued to occupy attention.

When the police question suspects there are rules of law and rules of practice that regulate the admissibility of confessions. In addition there are administrative directions given to the police by the Home Office. The legal effect of these various categories of what to the police amount to instructions is significantly different. Legal rules can create legal rights and duties, and the overriding legal rule governing the questioning of suspects is that a statement made by an accused person shall not be admitted in evidence unless it was made voluntarily.[21] Unless a judge is satisfied that the statement was made voluntarily he must reject a statement attributed to the accused. In addition there are the Judges' Rules – rules drawn up by the judges for the guidance of the police when taking statements; these cover the cautioning of suspects and other matters. The Judges' Rules do not have the force of law, and breach of these rules simply means that a trial judge in the exercise of his discretion may (but need not) decline to admit a statement by the accused.[22] As far as administrative directions are concerned they can, it would seem, similarly result in a judicial refusal to admit a statement in evidence.

Apart from the Judges' Rules themselves there is in the introduction to the Rules a statement, not part of the Rules and also not part of a legal rule, that, subject to important limitations, a suspect in custody has the right to consult privately with a solicitor.[23] There is no such right, although one judge did, unusually, refuse, in the exercise of his discretion, to admit a statement solely on the ground that the accused had not been allowed to consult a solicitor.[24] This is another example – for quite different legal reasons – where breach of rules does not prevent the prosecution from using evidence obtained through such a breach. It has already been pointed out that evidence obtained through an illegal search is admissible; now we see that what look like further legal rules (but strictly are not) can also be broken without the evidence, in this case confessions, being excluded. These statements by the judges are directed to the police: they do not create legal rights. The pity is that the formulation in terms of imperatives is in the language of the legal rules.

Thus there is further ground for disquiet, not because the content of the Judges' Rules is as such good, bad or indifferent, but because in numerous cases rules that are supposed to be applied by the police are not applied, and such failure, often deliberate, is countenanced by those who drew up the rules and have to apply them. The lawyer can make a formal apologia by pointing out that the Judges' Rules are not legal rules. Unfortunately, however, the rarity with which breach of the Rules is visited with the sanction that a statement is excluded appears to add to the catalogue of situations where illegal action by the police is treated as a matter separate from the admissibility in evidence of material obtained by such action.

Similarly, the frequency with which one continues to read that someone at a police station is spending several days 'assisting the police with their inquiries' makes ironic the statement that 'police officers, otherwise than by arrest, cannot compel any person against his will to come to or remain in any police station'. Once a person has been arrested problems of bail and appearance before a magistrate arise well before the suspect has finished 'assisting the police with their inquiries', and, of course, the chances of obtaining such assistance are very considerably diminished once the suspect is arrested and charged. These patent legal irregularities do not affect the prosecution process, and convictions, doubtless of the guilty, seem to close the book on such cases.[25] What damages would the convicted person obtain for the illegal detention?

PUBLIC ORDER

There are many offences concerned with public order in the sense of demonstrating, marches, processions, public meetings and so on; and obviously no attempt will be made to provide a complete list of such offences. Current concern is to see that the very considerable powers that may be invoked in the public order field are used in respect of genuine public order problems and not to stifle dissent.

Foremost among the law's weapons in the range of measures to protect public order is the Public Order Act 1936. Although the genesis of the Act is in the tumultuous 1930s, with Fascist marches in uniform through sectors of London with a large Jewish population, the Act is by no means limited to displays of political aggression.[26] Under s.5 it is an offence to use 'in any public place or at any public meeting threatening, abusive or insulting words or behaviour, or distributing or displays any writing, sign or visible representation which is threatening, abusive or insulting with intent to provoke a breach of the peace or whereby a breach of the peace is likely to be occasioned'.

It is fair to say, as far as reported decisions show, that the emphasis is on the immediate threat to public order rather than longer-term threats by outspoken radical critics. Causing offence is not the same as insulting, which, presumably like the other words used in the Act, is a word with an ordinary meaning capable of being understood and used without further legal gloss.[27] The important point – that words might be provocative to a particular audience but not necessarily to another – was dealt with in *Jordan* v. *Burgoyne*,[28] where it was held that a speaker must take his audience as he finds it and that the likelihood of a breach of the peace in the circumstances was the test to apply. In that case a British Nazi was addressing an audience that included Jews and people of left-wing views who were incensed by his offensive observations about Jews and went to the meeting fully expecting to hear them.

The offence of unlawful assembly, previously long dormant, once again became prominent with the disturbances of the late 1960s. This offence is laden with problems of definition and understanding. Part of the definition includes a common *lawful* purpose carried out in a manner such as to endanger the public peace or to give firm and courageous persons in the neighbourhood of the assembly reasonable grounds to apprehend a breach of the peace in consequence of it. The resurgence of prosecution for unlawful assembly has done little to clarify the law, with all the attendant difficulties of definition and the citing of cases on their facts as if each embodied a proposition of law. A lawyer may pick his way through cases that go apparently different ways by treating them, no doubt accurately, as decisions on whether there was on the recorded facts evidence capable of justifying this, that, or the other conclusion, and can reconcile in legal terms that which to the non-lawyer may look frighteningly unpredictable in terms of prosecution and conviction. Perhaps more to the point, apart from spectacular cases of serious damage or injury caused by the disturbance, is the likelihood of violent clashes between the police and assemblers once the police have formed the view that an assembly is unlawful.

Writing in 1967, David Williams quoted the Home Secretary (Henry Mathews) in the House of Commons in June 1890 on the uncertainty inherent in the definition of unlawful assembly:

> ... it is not always very easy to determine at what point an assembly previously lawful becomes an unlawful assembly. There are moments of excitement which, in some circumstances, may be overlooked, but the borderline of danger to the peace is not always easy to discover, even by a calm and impartial onlooker. [Williams, 1967, p. 237].

Little has occurred since 1890 to simplify that task of discovering the borderline. For those who believe, perhaps naively, that as long as they do not incite violence or act violently they commit no offence, the law relating to unlawful assembly can provide a salutary awakening. So too can other important legal provisions, of which perhaps the most important under the general law is that contained in the Police Act 1964, s.51 (superseding earlier provisions), which provides that it is an offence if any person 'resists or wilfully obstructs a constable in the execution of his duty'.

Many decisions on police powers generally concern this provision or its predecessors, since a conviction will depend *inter alia* on whether the constable was exercising lawful authority when resisted or obstructed. Conduct not unlawful becomes unlawful if a policeman gives a specific instruction, such as to move on or to disperse a meeting, or to take a particular route. Every constable has the duty to preserve the Queen's peace and is empowered to take whatever steps are reasonably necessary in order to do so. English legal science being more empirical than theoretical, it is perhaps not surprising but is nevertheless disturbing that a notion as central to public order and police powers is not properly defined. Indeed, the late Sir Carleton Allen delivered a series of Hamlyn Lectures in 1953 entitled 'The Queen's Peace' and made no attempt to define it.[29] Suffice it to say for present purposes that it includes at least the notion of security from violent disorder. A policeman's response to such disorder or the threat of such disorder is likely, given discretion, to vary according to the circumstances. The law gives him such discretionary authority and reinforces his authority by linking the offence of obstructing a constable with the steps that he takes to preserve the Queen's peace.

The famous case of *Duncan* v. *Jones*[30] (Williams, 1967) effected that link. Mrs Duncan was about to speak at a meeting outside a training centre for the unemployed when she was told by a police inspector not to hold the meeting there. She was told that she could hold it elsewhere. The Chief Constable and Inspector Jones took the view that, in view of a disturbance inside the centre on a previous occasion, there were grounds for apprehending a breach of the peace. Mrs Duncan began to address the meeting and was then arrested for obstructing Inspector Jones in the execution of his duty. The Divisional Court of the Queen's Bench Division upheld her conviction for that offence, on grounds that are not altogether clear. One problem arises between the facts stated (as found by the Deputy Chairman of Quarter Sessions) included a finding that Mrs Duncan must have known that a probable consequence of holding the meeting would include a disturbance and possibly a breach of the peace, and one judgment (that of Lord Hewart) seems to treat that finding as relevant. For Humphreys J it was enough that the policeman reasonably apprehended a breach of the peace, and he did not refer to what Mrs Duncan foresaw. Since the police appear not to have told her of their apprehension, the finding that she must have foreseen a disturbance may be relevant to her awareness of the policeman's duty. In any event, it is clear that Mrs Duncan did not herself commit, incite or provoke any breach of the peace.

Thus, when the police reasonably apprehend a breach of the peace they in effect have power to disperse a meeting or at any rate to move it on. Nothing in the brief judgments in *Duncan* v. *Jones* suggests that the offer of an alternative venue was a necessary condition of the exercise of the police power. Public utterances that are neither threatening nor insulting nor abusive are not unlawful, but if a policeman gives an instruction not to repeat them because he apprehends that there will be a breach of the peace, from then on any further utterance risks prosecution for obstructing a constable in the execution of his duty.

One major issue here is of public order versus freedom of expression, and it is by no means clear that an offender must be shown to have known that he was likely to cause a breach of the peace. Another was pointed out in a reluctant concurring judgment in the Irish case of *Humphries* v. *Connor*, in which a policeman had removed (lawfully the

Court held) an orange lily by force from a woman in a district where it was likely to provoke violence: 'we are making, not the law of the land, but the law of the mob supreme'.[31] Such clashes are not on occasions that lend themselves readily to debate on the spot between the policeman and the speaker or demonstrator, and it seems clear that as long as it is brought home that the policeman apprehends a breach of the peace anyone who disregards the policeman's instructions risks arrest and conviction. He would not be convicted if the court took the view that the apprehension was unreasonable or that the steps taken were not reasonably necessary, but his meeting would be broken up by the police if they decided to act on their view in that particular way. On 'reasonableness' Lord Parker had this to say in 1961:

> I think that a police officer charged with the duty of preserving the Queen's peace must be left to take such steps as, on the evidence before him, he thinks are proper.[32]

Obviously, the police lack the resources and indeed the wish to break up any meeting simply because they think that there might be a disturbance. There are powers to deal with those who disrupt meetings without resorting to the extreme step of ordering the meeting to disperse. The chronicling of cases of intervention and evaluation of neutrality and fairness are not easy tasks. In any event, the holding of a meeting in certain places requires permission, and the use of the highway for the purpose of holding a meeting can always be stopped under laws applicable to the highway. The fact of an obstruction is politically neutral, and in theory those who come to cheer and applaud are as capable of causing an obstruction of the highway as those who come to protest. One would also have thought that, whatever the strict legal position, if an area has been used repeatedly to hoid a meeting without police intervention, it is invidious to intervene in the case of a particular meeting, at any rate unless this is the first step in putting an end to the previous irregularity. In *Arrowsmith* v. *Jenkins*,[33] Miss Arrowsmith contended that her obstruction of the highway by means of a meeting was not wilful because the area had frequently been used for meetings, but this and associated arguments were rejected by the Divisional Court. The streets of this country are not held as trust for the use of the public for purposes of assembly.

Of the various assemblies that may gather, the category of a procession is of special importance. The legal category 'procession' includes various forms of activity that can otherwise be described as a march or a demonstration. The power to regulate processions includes the power to prohibit them, a power not available to other forms of assembly generally. Professor Brownlie's work, *The Law Relating to Public Order*, gives a full account of powers specifically relating to the use of streets. Particularly important are the provisions of the Metropolitan Police Act 1839, s.52 which authorizes the Metropolitan Police Commissioners to make regulations prescribing routes to be taken 'by all carts, carriages, horses and persons and for preventing obstruction of the streets . . . in all times of public processions, rejoicings, or illuminations . . . and also to give directions to the constables for keeping order and for preventing any obstruction of the thoroughfares . . . and in any case when the streets or thoroughfares may be thronged or may be liable to be obstructed'. Similar provisions are applicable outside the metropolitan area under s.21 of Town Police Clauses Act 1947, as amended.

The powers so conferred can keep antagonistic groups apart or away from particular places, but there is no power to ban a procession altogether. Such a power is conferred by the Public Order Act 1936, s.3, which also contains provisions authorizing the police to direct the route to be taken by any public procession on the grounds that 'serious public disorder' may occur. This is a narrower power in some respects (preventing obstruction or mere disorder is covered in the other legislation) and wider in others, in that the chief officer of police may give instructions dealing with matters other than the route to be taken.

> s.3(1) If the chief officer of police, having regard to the time or place at which and the circumstances in which any public procession is taking place or is intended to take place and to the route proposed to be taken by the procession, has reasonable ground for apprehending that the procession may occasion serious public disorder, he may give directions imposing upon the persons organising or taking part in the procession such conditions as appear to him necessary for the preservation of public order, including conditions prescribing the route to be taken by the procession and conditions prohibiting the procession from entering any public place specified in the directions; Provided that no conditions restricting the display of flags, banners, or emblems shall be imposed under this subsection except such as are reasonably necessary to prevent risk of a breach of the peace.

The power to seek a ban on processions is contained in s.3(2) generally and in s.3(3) for the Metropolitan and City of London police areas.

s.3(2) If at any time the chief officer of police is of opinion that by reason of particular circumstances existing in any borough or urban district or in any part thereof the powers conferred on him by the last foregoing subsection will not be sufficient to enable him to prevent serious public disorder being occasioned by the holding of public processions in that borough, district or part, he shall apply to the council of the borough or district for an order prohibiting for such period not exceeding three months as may be specified in the application the holding of all public processions or of any class of public procession so specified either in the borough or urban district or in that part thereof, as the case may be; and upon receipt of the application the council may, with the consent of a Secretary of State, make an order either in terms of the application or with such modifications as may be approved by the Secretary of State.

This subsection shall not apply within the City of London as defined for the purposes of the Acts relating to the City police or within the Metropolitan police district.

s.3(3) If at any time the Commissioner of the City of London police or the Commissioner of police of the Metropolis is of opinion that, by reason of particular circumstances existing in his police area or in any part thereof, the powers conferred on him by subsection (1) of this section will not be sufficient to enable him to prevent serious public disorder being occasioned by the holding of public processions in that area or part, he may, with the consent of the Secretary of State, make an order prohibiting for such period not exceeding three months as may be specified in the order the holding of all public processions or of any class of public procession so specified either in the police area or in that part thereof, as the case may be.

Several important points need emphasis. Under s.3(2) a local council is empowered to act solely on the initiative of the chief officer of police; the ban sought must be over all public processions or any class of public procession and not just for a specific occasion; the power of the Home Secretary to modify the terms applied for does not include modification so as to impose a ban on a specific procession. Under s.3(3) the local authority concerned with the area, the Greater London Council or the City of London, has no power to deal with the application in any way – the matter is dealt with by the chief officer of police, and the Home Secretary; just as the council may make no order under subsection (2) unless a chief officer of police applies for the order, so under subsection (3) the Home Secretary is powerless to act except to approve an order made by the chief officer of police. Such an order will clearly strike at more than one procession and can clearly cause great inconvenience to those whose processions in no way threaten serious public disorder if they fall within the class on which the ban is imposed, *a fortiori* if the ban is on all processions.

At any rate directions and bans equip the police, if they so wish, to take action to keep violent disturbances out of vulnerable or sensitive neighbourhoods or, with the approval of local and or central government as the case may be, to stop them temporarily altogether. The balance between the autonomy of professional judgement and action by constitutionally responsible organs of government is a curious one. It would clearly not be satisfactory that a ban could be imposed by the police alone; it is debatable whether it is satisfactory that no ban can be imposed unless the police seek one.

Summary

Breaches of law or rules of practice by the police (a distinction without much meaning to a layman at the receiving end) are not effectively sanctioned by the rules of criminal procedure, so that the products of successful but illegal searches are useable and the denial of the supposed rights of a suspect is ignored at a trial where discretion to exclude statements by the accused is very sparingly exercised. Recent cases have further accentuated the difficulty of knowing when a policeman can lawfully search and/or seize objects for use in evidence.

The main legal difficulty concerning police powers is that of uncertainty. This means that even an informed individual may in cases where the extent of police power is uncertain feel obliged to submit to the exercise of authority because the penalty for being wrong is one that he does not wish to risk. For those who are not so well informed, yielding to an assertion of authority, often bluff, is the usual practice. Even where a police officer has acted wrongfully, recent cases create a grey area where supposedly trivial wrongs do not take him outside the course of his duty, with consequent criminal liability for those who obstruct, resist or use force against him.

CHAPTER 4

Law, Socialism and Rights

Paul Hirst

This chapter will be concerned with the role of law in socialist states. It will be concerned with three major problems:

(1) the question of 'civil liberties' under socialism – in practice, the conditions for securing forms of regulation, inspection and interdiction of the action of state agencies;
(2) whether the elimination of a certain legally sanctioned class of agents – 'private' owners of the means of production – problematizes the existence of the institution of 'law' itself;
(3) whether 'laws', whatever the political and economic system, must necessarily constitute subjects as possessive bearers of 'rights'.

The last problem links the two preceding: in marxist theory the proprietal subject enjoying certain 'rights' is considered an irredeemably bourgeois notion, arising from the realities of individual private possession. While it is possible to argue that the notions of proprietal subject and possessive rights are in no sense specific to the organization of production in terms of commodity exchange, this point will be secondary in our argument. It will be argued that the notions of a given proprietal subject and of 'rights' are problematic categories in *any* legal system; that they create severe problems in securing the objectives towards which legislation is directed; and that attempting to solve questions of divergent interests in terms of 'rights' can only lead to impossible contradictions. This is because questions of 'rights' and of the priority of the 'rights' of one class of agents over another tend to generate ontological doctrines which seek to necessitate the agent's possession of or priority to 'rights' by reference to its nature. These problems are in no sense specific to socialist states; we will illustrate them by reference to a salient example, the problems of abortion legislation in contemporary Britain.

The arguments advanced here challenge the theses of two leading legal theorists: in the marxist camp E. B. Pashukanis, and in the liberal camp Ronald Dworkin. Both, by completely different methods and to different ends, argue that the subject endowed with rights is the vital element in law. Certainly it is a prominent component of legal ideologies, but I would argue one whose role must be minimized in the legal framework of any socialist state that seeks to avoid the abuses so evident in the USSR and minimized, whatever the dominant form of property law, in the resolution of certain complex dilemmas of social policy by means of law.

We will begin with the second of the three major problems outlined above and, therefore, with the work of Pashukanis.

LAW AND SOCIAL AGENTS

Pashukanis attempted to establish a general theory of law based on marxist method, a materialistic counter to bourgeois jurisprudence. In this theory law is explained as specific to, and as a necessary form of expression of, the relationships of commodity–capitalist society. In explaining law thus it is assigned a necessary content: law consists in the recognition in the form of 'rights' of the realities of the possession of alienable things by individuals. Law is, in consequence, assigned a set of limits it cannot transgress, just as much as in theories that conceive the laws as embodying certain principles that are definitive of their nature (justice, equity, etc.). Pashukanis ends up adopting positions that have striking similarities to certain of the bourgeois theories whose method he repudiates. Law is for him, however, confined to the commodity form and will disappear along with that form.

I have criticized Pashukanis's work in *On Law and Ideology* (Hirst, 1976), but I must return to it because it is a direct and vigorous challenge to the enterprise of this paper. The notion of a legal framework of a socialist state as something to be constructed and elaborated is for Pashukanis a nonsense; the work of socialists in respect of the law can only be its progressive deconstruction, the facilitation of its 'withering away'.

Pashukanis sets out in his theory to avoid the reduction of law to class interests. In doing so he posed two questions:

(1) What is the *form* of law, i.e. what is specific to and definitive of legal institutions?

(2) Why is the *legal*, rather than some other, form of regulation of social relationships necessary?

The answers he gives are less satisfactory than the questions. The form of law is defined by the categories of 'subject' and 'right': law consists in the recognition of the rights of subjects concerning possession, and serves as a medium of resolution of disputes concerning possession between subjects. Law arises because it is necessary to the system of production that individual subjects be guaranteed full recompense on alienation of the fruits of their labours. Law is the means of regulating the social process of production, the connection of specialized individual private labours through the exchange of their products as commodities. Economic subjects are independent, linked only by mutual alienation of things, and interdependent – they require that alienation in order to exist. Law resolves the antagonisms of this realm of differentiated individuals: law, the recognition by a supra-individual instance of their 'rights' to possession, is a condition of those individuals' relationships with one another. In these answers law is equated with and confined to a certain conception of property rights and with commodity–capitalist social relations.

Pashukanis, therefore, conceives law as *recognizing* prior realities and *regulating* an already given realm of relations between agents. Recognition and regulation are necessary because of the specific problems of the relationships of autonomous and potentially antagonistic bourgeois individuals. This conception may be challenged in each of its elements, and yet it retains something of value. I have argued that it is by no means the case that the subjects 'recognized' and the activities regulated are given in their form prior to law, pointing to significant instances of the *construction* in legislation and application of categories of subject. Further, legal regulation is not confined to *antagonistic* relations between agents (questions of restitution, equity, etc.), or to agents of a particular form – human individuals as bearers of commodities. Regulation is definitive of agents and imposes requirements of action on them: regulation also establishes a relation between agents and the 'public power', not merely a relation between agents with the public power as adjudicator.

The value of Pashukanis's explanation of the form of law is that it sensitizes us to the problems posed by a realm of differentiated agents. Pashukanis supposes these agencies are human individuals (conceived as given social subjects) and that the form of their relationship is an exchange of commodities ('things'). But a realm of differentiated agencies of decision is in no sense limited to these forms. In order for such a realm to exist the scope and limits of these agencies' actions must be defined and limited: this is a condition of their having a determinate capacity for decision. This is not merely a matter of *ordered* relations between these agencies (the classical 'problem of order' posits just such a realm of agencies with capacities for decision and asks how their actions can be made compatible; the 'problem' arises simply because the agents are made prior to their regulation), but of the existence of the agents in a determinate form. Agents are never *given*, be they tribal elders or the Factory Inspectorate. It is not merely a matter of making agents' actions *compatible* (such cannot be done by regulation); rather, it concerns the form of *definition* of the agents as agents. This necessarily arises whenever a realm of differentiated agencies of decision must be constituted, whether or not these agents are directly concerned with production, and *whether or not the relations between those agents take a commodity form*.

For Pashukanis neither pre-capitalist nor socialist societies entail such realms of differentiated agencies of decision. Commodity production alone creates the necessity of regulating 'autonomous' individuals. In pre-capitalist societies relations of personal dependence and hierarchy – subordination to the tribal community or the feudal lord – prevail, while in socialist societies centralized planned production expresses the conscious will of the associated producers. On the contrary, 'feudal' societies do involve differentiated agencies of decision, complexes of distinct organizations and public powers – monastic orders, urban corporations and guilds, barons and landlords, etc. – and, certainly in England, elements of contractual relationships between landlord and tenant. The socialization of economic relations, as we shall see, cannot operate without differentiated agencies of decision. Laws and courts are a vital means of definition of the powers of feudal agencies, a power themselves and a means of regulation of disputes between agencies. Forms of legal regulation cannot be dispensed with under socialist forms of property.

Accepting for the time being this somewhat abstract notion of differentiated agencies of decision, we will attempt to define the form of law in a way that does not limit law to one particular set of property rights or to the legal system of the 'bourgeois' states. Law is an instance of regulation: an institutionally specific complex of organizations and agents, discourses and practices, which operates to define (whether in codified rules or not) the form and limits of other organizations, agents and practices. Law, therefore, consists in the elements necessary to this instance:

(1) an apparatus of legislation: 'laws' issue from definite organizations advancing claims as to their scope and capacity (these *claims* differentiate laws as 'laws' from other classes of rule);
(2) rules produced by this apparatus defining the status and capacities of agents:
    (a) the definition of these agents' *form of existence*, that is, the forms of organization and activity constructed as following from a legal personality (legal 'personalities' are differentiated; who or what is recognized as a person in one statute may not be recognized or may be recognized in a different form in another; legal persons such as limited companies, doctors, married women, etc., are complexes of statuses, powers and requirements imposed by various statutes);
    (b) *norms of conduct* and requirements of regulation: these relate differentially to agents' statuses and to the realms of activity regulated (e.g., companies are required to file accounts, households to admit health visitors, etc.);
(3) an apparatus of adjudication in infractions and disputes, norms of conduct for its operations, and an apparatus to compel acceptance of the process of adjudication and its results.

Two qualifications need to be entered here. First, (1) and (2) are differentiated here but, given autonomy of decision in adjudication, the rules cannot remain unaffected by the process of their application; this applies no less where there is no 'common law' and a lesser role for precedent than in Anglo-Saxon courts. Second, there is no reason why the apparatus of enforcement should be institutionally separate from the legal agencies proper, as in the case of modern armies and police forces, before the development of these organizations, officers of the courts, bailiffs, etc., served to enforce judgment.

Pashukanis supposes a 'prior' realm of activity (production and exchange), given independently of its definition and regulation, which is homogeneous and inclusive and concerns a single category of agent (the proprietal subject). Each of the elements of this statement is challenged in the notion of a realm of differentiated agencies of decision subject to definition and regulation given above. First, it has been stressed that law does not necessarily consist in the recognition and expression of entities already existing outside it, 'organic' products of social life. Legislation and application are processes of the construction of agents and the organization of their existence through the form of a legal personality: I have argued this in respect of the limited company in *On Law and Ideology* (Hirst, 1979b), and Jacques Donzelot demonstrates the construction of the mother as 'responsible agent of socialization' (a site of medicalized social superintendence distinct from the obligations of the 'wife') from the late nineteenth century onwards by legal rules and administrative practices concerned with social health legislation in *La Police des Familles* (Donzelot, 1977). Law (as an institutionally differentiated instance) cannot be the sole means of construction of agents. Various forms of administrative rules, practices and policies (state and semi-state; viz. the importance of 'private' charities in welfare provision and supervision in countries like Italy or Ireland) also serve in this direction, e.g. Board of Trade rules in respect of companies, DHSS rules in the case of mothers. These agencies are not, however, 'outside' the law: they are in turn differentiated agencies of decision constituted in a particular way in public law. Second, there is no homogeneous and inclusive realm of social life for law to express: Pashukanis conceives the essence of social relations as a *totality* of production and exchange; 'society' is a singular entity unified by its material life process. Social relations are conceived here not as a totality governed by a determinative principle, but as complexes of institutions, agents and activities which have no necessary unity, which permit of differentiation, divergence and non-intersection. Third, and following from this, all agents are not at par with one another, nor are they engaged in a single intersecting realm of activity: thus limited companies and mothers are both specific legal persons, but there is no identity of status or requirements of regulation and no necessary realm of contact between them.

Nothing differentiates 'laws' as such in the definitions given above from other classes of rule. Customs overseen by tribal elders and the rules of administrative bodies may equally well define agents and set norms of conduct. Village meetings and administrative tribunals may decide cases according to procedural rules just as courts do. Nothing differentiates laws, *as categories of rule*, from other forms of regulation of agents and their activities. What differentiates 'laws' are the claims in that regard made by the institutionally specific instances of regulation issuing and enforcing them.

Pashukanis's search for the 'form' of law, for the definitive features of its rules, which would provide its *raison d'être*, was a chase after a chimera. It is legal *institutions* that differentiate the rules they make as 'laws'. Pashukanis's privileging of 'private law' was a profound error: law became an expression of social relationships, which required it and yet which determined how it met those requirements. Legislation and the form of legal institutions became a non-problem, a medium necessary to private law but one governed by its form. Challenging this organicist conception means taking the construction and application of particular laws by specific institutions within a framework of public law seriously. 'Laws' depend on the instance of regulation issuing them taking a definite public form, as bodies within the legal framework of a state.

Laws are effective *as laws* precisely because they are the products of certain institutions presented as a sovereign public power and because specific state agencies and practices pursue their enforcement. The regulatory instance has a specific form as a complex of institutions and has political conditions of existence of its operation and effectivity. These institutional and political conditions of legislation and application have specific effects on the rules that can be passed and enforced; these conditions are not some neutral medium for the 'expression' of prior and determining social needs. Public law is thus central to 'law' in two senses. First, it is the condition for the differentiation of 'law' from other categories of definitive/regulatory rules – the creation of an institutionally specific instance of regulation as a public power. Second, in order that public power of regulation is itself regulated, definite limits of scope and action are placed on legal institutions.

We have argued that rules of definition and regulation are conditions of existence for a realm of differentiated agencies of decision; this requires a regulatory instance. Further, we have argued that a condition of existence of 'law' is an institutionally specific instance of regulation, which is itself presented in the form of public law. We will now attempt to systematically link these two propositions.

A realm of differentiated agencies of decision is an abstraction which implies:

(1) that a definite sphere of activity (production, distribution, war, cultural propagation, etc.) requires to be organized in the form of a number of distinct agencies (whether this be due to limits of information, control techniques, division of labour, geographical division is not pertinent here); these agencies may perform the activity in series or in combination;

(2) that the agent is a unit of organization of the activity which acts on calculation; the agent's actions, however much circumscribed by conditioning factors, are determined in their form by calculation and not given to them by some other agent. The classic examples of such agents are capitalist firms, but others are just as pertinent, like monastic orders deciding whether and where to establish a new house, or feudal landlords deciding to establish a local market or to use fines more systematically, or the leadership of an autonomous expeditionary corps determining what strategy to pursue;

(3) that it operates in a sphere of activity in parallel with, opposed to or in combination with other organizing agents; thus feudal landlords may hold manors in the same village, or socialist enterprises may recruit labour in the same locality or perform services for one another, etc.

The assignation of status and the imposition of norms of conduct is a condition of the agent's action in that it sets it definite forms and limits. This makes definite forms of calculation and organization possible, even if those involve breaching the limits; a feudal landlord bent on increasing the scope of fines has a set of instances of their use and a calculation of the possible. Definitory and regulatory rules are a form of construction of agents or organizational design. These rules are not merely 'legal'; viz., the rules of a monastic order for the regulation of houses serve as a plan for new establishments as well as for the conduct of existing ones. But 'laws' (rules issued by institutions making certain claims) serve an analogous function: laws construct the *form of existence* of subjects and organizations as agents in definite arenas (feudal tenant, on the one hand, juryman and keeper of the peace, on the other; mother as agent of socialization, wife as bearer of certain property rights, etc.). Laws and administrative rules co-ordinate the action of agencies, producing means of co-operation, reconciliation and control. Co-ordination of the interaction of agencies depends in the first instance on the delimitation of their permitted form and the field of their action. Legislation is constitutive of agents in setting limits and prescribing norms of conduct, and in that way 'regulative' in a more basic sense than any policing or settling of disputes.

In order to define and regulate a realm of agents the instance of regulation in question must be presented as external to each of the agents and 'superior' to them. It cannot without difficulty be an agent at par with them and perform this regulatory function. If that were the case then one agent would define the form of existence and terms of conduct of the other agents in an activity in which it was involved. This would tend either to decompose the differentiated nature of the realm by compromising the autonomy of the other agents, or, to the extent that the definitary agent operated on the principle of *primus inter pares*, it would subject its own operations to its own rules, and thereby tend to differentiate itself into a regulatory and an operational instance. Regulation requires a specific agency which is not at par with those to be regulated.

There is no reason why for any given activity this instance should take the form of a state, a single dominant public power. For the regulation of definite spheres of activity other forms are possible: governing councils, trade associations, agreed arbitrators, etc. Nor does the invocation of the 'state' resolve all difficulties. For, however much it may be *presented* as a single public power, the 'state' is itself a complex of differentiated agencies of decision: ministries, local councils, specialist bodies, etc. *As an assemblage of organizations it stands as much in need of definition and regulation as any other realm of agents.* Public law serves this regulatory function by defining the component parts of the 'state' as agencies of decision with definite powers and spheres of activity; as a specific instance it reviews and regulates the actions of those state agencies.

As such, law is at once definitive *of* the state and at the same time a complex of institutions *within* it; as a regulatory instance it is a mere portion of the state's agencies and activity. The state cannot be explained by the legal forms in which it is presented, or by the requirement to define and regulate spheres of activity. Further, as we have seen, the legal characterization of the state as a single public power is at variance with its being a realm of distinct agencies of decision, and this realm raises all the problems of control and regulation any other would. Our discussion will not lead us down the slippery slope to 'state derivationism' or to conceiving state apparatuses as exhausted in their character and action by the forms of their presentation in public law.

For all the qualifications and limits to a legal analysis of state apparatuses, public law is a vital component of the state, it establishes the formal limits and scope of state power, the conditions of access to and the means of its exercise. The role of public law may be schematized as follows:

(1) the definition of the component elements of the state and their 'powers' — a *constitution* (organizational design — legal form of existence);
(2) through the legislative, applicatory and adjudicative elements thus defined, the definition of the status and capacities of non-state entities.

Public law involves the 'fiction' that the state exists in the form of law and that law is not merely one definite sphere of state activity but is definitive of the whole. Public law as outlined above is no peculiarity of 'capitalist' states; feudal states, the Roman Republic, the USSR all had or have constitutions and participate in this 'fiction'.

The very notion of 'law', as an institutionally distinct and superior category of rules, is implicated in this 'fiction'; that is, the legal instance is not a member of the classes of agents it regulates (it is not an agent at par with others), and yet it is subject to itself; it is not outside or above the rules of law. Law is always the product of specific agencies of decision and yet is supposed to be subordinate to itself. This 'fiction' is a condition of its action: it *is* a fiction (1) because laws and regulatory instances are not a homogeneous sphere of legality (Law) — there is no 'Law' in general, only specific bodies of rules and definite apparatuses regulating particular spheres of activity (there is no necessity for these bodies' categories and practice to form a coherent system); (2) because the rules of procedure that legal agencies follow are specific constructions of other agencies of decisions, legislatures and higher courts. The notion of a 'rule of Law' embodies this fiction — that legislations and higher courts are themselves bound by procedural rules. It is a doctrine that unifies the complex of rules and agencies into a single entity, 'Law'; this unification serves as the ground of certain claims, for example, that *all* laws are equally valid and should be obeyed.[1] Laws *always* have an 'outside': laws and procedural rules are subject to transformation by definite agencies (legislatures, Supreme Court, etc.).

In public law this 'fiction' – whereby the 'outside' is placed within the law – is presented in the doctrine of 'sovereignty'. The sovereign is the source of law and procedural rules: state and legal agencies represent (are delegated protions of) the sovereign power. The doctrine of sovereignty transcends different forms of state and constitution; it is in no sense alien to feudal constitutions, retained and reinforced by the doctrines of the liberal era, and, as we shall see, its analogues affect profoundly marxist conceptions of the socialist state.

We have contended that state apparatuses and practices are not reducible in their practices and effects to law or in their action to the limits of their own legal form. Public law constructs administration and state activity as a realm of differential agencies of decision, agencies that it purports to define and regulate. But it cannot subsume them, precisely because they must be assigned a definite autonomy of action in order that the state's activities be organized. The very legal definition of state agencies necessarily poses the problem of 'control' of administrative agencies: legal agencies define capacities that they do not exercise. The very notion of a limit imposed by regulation implies an agency capable of exceeding it and not subsumed as part of the regulatory instance. The very notions of 'constitutionality' and 'rule of law' are symptoms of this problem: legislative and adjudicative agencies are merely one portion of the complex of agencies and practices that exist within the constitutional confines of the public domain; they are a necessary part but in no sense necessarily primary, as constitutional doctrines assert.

The state as a realm of differentiated agencies of decision is a problematic notion. The limits of and conditions of access to the public domain are set by laws, but the realm of agencies thus established is 'policed' by definite agencies with limited capacities of supervision and control. Access to and operation of 'public' agencies is necessarily problematic: the doctrines of 'constitutionality' and 'rule of law' attempt to cover this paradox, and serve as claims to intervention and review by particular state agencies (select committees, higher courts, etc.). The paradox is doubled in that the agencies closest to being definitive of the constitution (the limits of public power, whether formalized and codified or not) have the greatest capacity (in the formal claims of the public law) to transform it. Constitutional doctrines and the form of legislative agencies therefore can be matters of political consequence; the 'fiction' is not an illusion despite its paradoxical and problematic nature. The notorious Article 48 of the Weimar Constitution is an example. Public law and legal agencies are not above politics (even if such claims are advanced for the impartiality of higher courts' functions of review), but they can be an independent factor in it, depending on the complex of political conditions. Constitutional courts can set limits and serve as a vital factor in politics (a factor with conditions in other political agencies' support of these institutions' practice), as the example of Chile shows: Allende's government could be formed as a parliamentary and elected administration only on conditions set by the Electoral College and the Courts.

The state is given coherence and limits in the legal form of a constitution; as a doctrine of delegated powers this defines away the problem of the state as a complex organization of differentiated and interacting agencies of decision. 'Sovereignty' defines the state as a homogeneous space of realization of the will of the sovereign subject (monarch, people-in-representation). 'Sovereignty' as a constitutional category serves a dual function:

(1) It resolves in doctrine the paradox involved in the notion of 'law' (an institutionally specific instance of regulation advancing claims); that is how 'law' (legal agencies) can at once be 'above' the activities it regulates, and yet subject itself: law is the will of the sovereign appropriately expressed, the sovereign because sovereign is competent to make law and set its procedures.

(2) It therefore serves ideologically to prioritize certain agencies and activities within the apparatuses of state; these are held to express the 'will' of the sovereign, as for example with Parliament.

Doctrines of 'sovereignty' construct the state in the form of a hierarchy of expression of the sovereign will. The state can thus be thought of and held to be a unity, as a single, homogenized and hierarchized medium of a will that emanates from its centre. This notion of a 'sovereign', a centre as a subject with a will, is a 'fiction' no less than the notion of law as subject to itself. As a consequence of this 'fiction' certain agencies are presented as empowered vis-à-vis others.

Law and public law cannot be separated; this is because what differentiates 'law' from other classes of rule are the claims advanced by institutionally specific instances of regulation. We have dwelt here

on the 'fictions' involved in making those claims; law and doctrines of
the nature of the public power cannot easily be separated. Definition
and regulation – establishing the form of existence, scope and limits of
action of 'its' agencies – are necessary to *any* form of state. The question we will consider later is whether the doctrines of 'rule of law' and
'sovereignty' can serve any constructive purpose in resolving problems
of the organization of socialist states, in particular the problem of
securing the effects of 'civil liberties'. The difficulty as we can see
already is that problems of 'policing' state apparatuses are *not*
removed by a framework of public law, by doctrines of 'rule of law',
'sovereignty' or 'rights of the citizen'. All states, as complexes of
agencies of decision, *must* take a public law form. The USSR is no
exception. It will be argued that both the notions of a 'withering away
of law' and of 'socialist legality' are equally problematic. The invocation of 'legality' and the call for its abolition are *parallel* responses and
are not the answer to the problem.

LAW AND SOCIALISM

Pashukanis is consistent and rigorous in supposing law to be confined
to commodity–capitalist relations. His conception of law is consistent
with the central tenet of marxist political theory, that socialism is a
transitional phase in which the state 'withers away'. The objectives of
socialist construction are twofold: the formation of a planned
economy, and the deconstruction of state power arising from class
antagonism. Law arises from the necessities of commodity production: private law will disappear with private production. The legitimation of the repressive apparatus of the state in the form of law (derived
from analogies with private law) will disappear with the abolition of
class exploitation and class struggle.

   The condition for this 'withering away of law' is the elimination of
commodity production and with it the *necessity of differentiated
agencies of decision* ('private' property = individuals separated from
one another acting as agents of production and exchange). This
elimination of differentiated agencies of decision is consistent with the
marxist conception of socialism:

(1) Planned production replaces the circulation of commodities;
    distinct units of production become mere technical necessities

rather than economic agents – *the plan is the centralization of economic decisions*;

(2) The plan is the economic expression of popular democracy: the specialized administrative agencies and institutions of the 'bourgeois' state (a public power 'separated' from the people) will disappear and are replaced by popular democratic, legislative–executive bodies which are the direct expression of the popular will (soviets, commune state).

Retained in marxist political theory are analogues of the categories of 'sovereignty' and 'general will': popular democracy is the means of action of the people-as-sovereign. The representative bodies of bourgeois democracy are rejected in favour of a doctrine of direct representation of the masses (the notion of 'people' remains central *despite classes*; the organized working class are conceived as the representatives/leaders of the whole people, the 'vanguard' which represents the objective interests of the masses as a whole). Popular democracy depends on a concept of representation of the 'general will' through the politically active working class and on a notion that power resides in the people, that they alone by their own self-action can organize their own emancipation. The transitional state has its own doctrine of legitimation which counters and parallels bourgeois conceptions of 'sovereignty'. Marxist political theory rejects the administrative centralization of the 'bourgeois' state, the concentration of capacities in distinct agencies to which access is limited. It stresses, however, the centralization of decisions: planning can work only by concentrating resources and decisions in a single centre; this is possible because the people (acting through a complex of bodies – soviets, communes) are capable of formulating a general set of interests which reflects their fundamental unity. The plan can be centralized and democratic because, ultimately – in spite of clashes and contradictions – the people are one agency of decision, a unity with a single interest.

This notion of the elimination of distinct agencies of decision haunts marxist political theory: Lenin and Mao stumbled and staggered away from it in their attempts to cope with the organizational problems of socialist states, but they never broke with – indeed, they further valorized[2] – the notion of people as a unitary agency of decision. This unity rested on common objective interests which the masses, given the means and the time to overcome obstacles, could not but express.

Leninist socialism has been criticized from the 'Left' and the 'Right' in an attempt to account for and seek means to overcome what is considered to be the particular problem of the phenomenon of 'stalinism'.

Trotskyists have predominated in formulating the main lines of 'left' criticism: this has sought to find the sources of stalinism in the two elements of political organization absent from Marx's *Civil War in France*: political parties and the retention of the centralized state administration. Thus the critique of 'substitutionalism' stresses the danger of the vanguard party; that the party isolates itself from the self-action of the working class and the leadership of the party is in consequence able to bureaucratize and subordinate the party apparatus. Parallel to this is the failure to 'smash' the state, the retention of bourgeois institutions and bureaucratic personnel separated from the people. Often these criticisms are traced to the backwardness of the economic and political development of Russia; the weakness of the working class and the absence of a developed centralized economy made bureaucratic organization necessary. These criticisms further valorize the notion of popular sovereignty: a developed economy and working class will make a non-repressive centralized system possible; it will homogenize the 'people' (drawing them into industrial production and wage labour) and make them capable of united autonomous action. Planned production without repression will be possible because the objective basis of contradictory interests has been eliminated and the means for democratic mass decision will be created.

The problem with these critiques is that in them parties and states are thought as at best regrettable necessities imposed by the conditions of fighting the 'old society'. They are deformations of the 'self-emancipation of the working class'. The whole political content of socialism is here predicated on the notion of a unitary 'working class' (as representative of the people) capable of realizing its 'interests' in mass action if not held back or sold out by its own leadership. This predication is nothing but a disaster: classes cannot be political actors, and 'interests' — political objectives — are not given. Political struggle *always* takes the form of definite organizations with formulated programmes operating in particular institutional/political conditions. These organizations may make claims to *represent* classes, but they are not classes: the specific form of their organization is not derived from classes, but is a matter of available institutional forms and means of construction. The SPD was a mass electoral party conditioned by the voting system and conditions of struggle; it succeeded *because* it organized and competed in national elections, *not* because of its doctrines or claims of representativeness (other German groups also claiming to be socialist and to embody the 'interests' of the working class failed to do this). Again, the soviets were definite institutions, with definite personnel and limited organizational capacities, *not* the 'people' in action. Kautsky saw this clearly when he defended the specificity of political organization against the economistic doctrines in the early 1900s, and again in *The Dictatorship of the Proletariat* (Kautsky, 1964), when he argued – *against* Lenin (who had adopted Kautsky's earlier position) – that while classes may 'rule' (whatever that means)[3] they cannot 'govern'. Socialism must mean the organization of politics by parties, and of government (specific capacities of control and decision) by state and other agencies.

The critique of stalinism from the 'right' accepts that questions of the form of organization of the socialist state cannot be resolved by the supposition of a popular 'will' prior to and independent of them which they must express. The 'rightist' critique has followed two lines:

(1) *Of the problems of planning.* It is impossible to centralize all decisions concerning the utilization of productive resources and their distribution in a single agency. This involves decentralized decision-making by enterprises and other organizations (welfare agencies, etc.). This critique stressing the problems of information and span of control has been primarily formulated by 'market socialists' (Bruz, Sik, etc.), but the critical point being made here with great force is not confined to meeting the difficulties of control through market allocation and monetary calculation. The necessity of differentiated agencies of decision (enterprises, etc.) remains even if their relationships do not take the form of monetary exchange.

(2) *Of the problems of authoritarianism.* This confronts the problem of organizing state activities in such a way that elementary 'civil liberties' – freedom of correspondence, association, right of criticism – are not violated. This is seen in terms of limiting the prerogatives of the central party apparatus, the political police and so on. Two main lines of response predominate: calling for the restoration of 'socialist legality', the implementation of the violated formal rules of institutions like the party, respecting the provisions of the Soviet constitution, etc., or reintroducing 'pluralism', as in the various Eurocommunist strategies. These

criticisms have serious defects but they do pose definite problems of organization as specific issues to be resolved at their own level. First, the forms of institutional organization of the economy (how enterprises relate to one another and to state agencies): it is recognized here that the apparatuses of control and decision-making are not given as some necessary 'expression' of the basic production relations. Second, how the imposition of a definite scope and set of limits on state agencies' actions can be assured: this too demands specific organizational means.

Classical marxism has resolutely refused to think through such questions of organization because it has refused them autonomy. Socialism's structure is a matter of the effects of the basic relations of production and the conditions of class struggle. The resolution of political problems is located in the, ultimate, unity of action and interests of the working class. The discussion of the specific forms of institutions, organizational practices and legislation cannot anticipate this dialectic. To do so is to fall into the illusions of rationalism. Socialism is a transitional phase of social relations, the period of the 'transition to communism'. It is governed by the necessities of the class struggle and of transforming social relations. The one necessity makes all questions of organization conjunctural; institutions, laws, etc., can have no fixed form but depend on the needs of the struggle and the creativity of the leadership and masses in responding to them. The other necessity makes limits to mass and state action unthinkable; nothing that preserves the capacities of the bourgeois class or impedes the transformation of social relations can be permitted. Under communism questions of organization will cease to be *political*. Organization is a matter of the 'administration of things', of socially neutral and consensual technique. Relations of production cease to be constraints because they are nothing but the conscious and rational direction of society to the fulfilment of its material needs. These needs and interests are unproblematic because they are the expression of a single popular will. This rejection of the 'rationalism' of attempting to determine the organizational problems and requirements of 'socialist' states is made in the interests of a 'realism'. But this realism is a curious hybrid. On the one hand, it is a scientism: socialist social relations are an effect of the basic determinants of material production and class struggle. This 'realism' depends on a certain causal doctrine which treats socialism as a totality governed by its determinative principle.

On the other hand, in order that the categories of this scientism be sustained, it involves notions of a popular 'general will' and of communist society as governed by the teleology of a communal rationality. These notions are *valorizations* necessary to the 'realism', the conditions of socialism's objective evolution into a desirable form of society. They are, moreover, undemonstrable by this scientism, if as is claimed the construction of socialism is an objective process whose form and course cannot be predicted. But it is only an 'objective process', compatible with the objectives of marxist political theory, on condition that it gives rise to a *subject* capable of making the process 'its' conscious collective action. The supposition of this subject is no more 'realistic' than the notion that specific processes of organizational construction are both possible and necessary.

This latter supposition rests on the conception of social relations as something other than a totality governed by a determinative principle. It accepts the specificity and potential discontinuity of social relations. It does not involve the acceptance of the notion that social relations can be merely legislated for, that there are no constraints; rather, it involves the analysis of organizational construction as a means of overcoming constraints. This conception of social relations is no novelty (although its capacity for self-defence against orthodox Marxism is). G. D. H. Cole in his *Social Theory* (1921) conceived social relations as a specific complex of 'associations' with no given form and with no necessary interrelationships. Cole, at the time a non-Marxist socialist, took the question of the specific forms of organization of socialist social relations seriously. *Guild Socialism Re-Stated* (Cole, 1920) is a blueprint or institutional design. Cole based his theory on a critique of the concept of 'representation' (a challenge to the Webbs' schemes for a Socialist Commonwealth with a plurality of representative institutions). Representative bodies can never 'represent' their electorate – the diverse wills and personalities of their individual electors – and representation is merely a mechanism of providing the personnel of certain bodies. This critique of representative democracy as a principle of organization is not made in the service of a doctrine of popular democracy. There is no concept of the 'people' as a unity or 'sovereignty' in Cole's political theory. These categories involve the problematic notions of a 'general will', or of will-in-delegation, that are no less problematic than the conception of the representation of individual wills through elective mechanisms. Cole styled his political theory 'functional democracy'. 'Associations' are definite bodies established to adminster or pursue a particular activity (sport, sociability, production, co-operative consumption); they are freely entered into by members. Suffrage was to be based on *activity*; an individual had as many votes as associations and as much say as his involvement. Members of associations would be assigned to collaborative bodies to pursue the business of their mutual co-operation.

The classic criticism of Cole's guild socialism is that it ignores the general problem of co-ordination of these associations and, therefore, the need for a central instance of co-ordination, the state.[4] To the extent that it recognizes this problem, its solution restores the state in all but name. This criticism is correct as far as it goes, but it supposes that the answer to a plurality of associations lies in the *centralization* of force and economic decision-making. This very centralization generates a plurality of differentiated agencies of decision, which pose problems no less acute than a plurality of associations freely entered into. The critics are correct that Cole's merely *ad hoc* and consultative conception of the co-ordination of the activities of a complex of interacting associations is inadequate. But why? First, there are requirements of information and division of labour that necessitate continual co-ordination, not a constant process of ad hoc adjustment. But these are no better handled by the notion of a single centre rather than a centreless plurality. There can be no *general* solution to the questions of information collection and relay, of techniques of control, etc. Second, what all questions of organization involving a plurality of associations or agencies generate are the problems of the definition of their form and the regulation of their action in the form of limits. Associations *cannot* be co-ordinated if no limits are placed on their competencies and actions: the absence of such limits generates a plurality of agencies of decision limited only by their own objectives, dependent on each other's compliance and goodwill as to the areas in which the respective decisions of each pertain. The absence of imposed limits inhibits organizations' calculation and the performance of definite tasks: competition for resources in the absence of imposed conditions of interaction and multiple performance of functions would be the result.

Cole proposes a realm of differentiated agencies of decision. Such a realm, as we have seen, requires a regulatory instance which imposes limits in the sense of requirements placed on agents by the definition of their *forms of existence* (status, scope and capacities of action) and *norms of conduct*. The regulatory instance serves as a mechanism of organizational design and supervision. It does not and cannot solve all the problems of the co-ordination and control of a realm of differentiated agencies of decision; it does make such a realm possible and, therefore, the appearance of *definite* rather than *generalized* problems of control of, co-ordination of and interaction between the agencies. This differentiation/limitation of agencies must have a general support, a regulatory instance, that is, a locus of decision not at par with the agencies but 'above' them. This locus – to be capable of effects – must be independent of any of the agencies to be regulated and must have a capacity to enforce limits upon them. This general support can only have the form of a 'public power': a specific instance of regulation advancing claims in this regard. Cole's associationalism indicates why. *All* agencies that interact must be assigned limits and brought into definite relations; the regulatory instance must have a scope adequate to the realms of agencies in question. The regulatory instance must itself take a definite form, assign limits to its action, and resolve (in definition) the problem of itself as a realm of differentiated agencies.

Posed in this problem of 'co-ordination' set by Cole's plurality of autonomous but interacting associations is the necessity of some form of 'constitution', in the sense of an organizational design and certain conditions of its regulatory maintenance. An instance of regulation, itself definite and limited, is nothing less than a framework of public law. Law, as we have seen, is *not* the entirety of the state; it is the regulatory instance that defines the public domain and agents in general. Which agencies and activities are part of the state as a legal unity cannot be specified in general. A framework of public law is *not* solution to all the problems of co-ordination and control of state or other agencies, nor does it have a general definite content or effectivity. It can be made to have definite effectivities as part of the overall design and setting of the conditions of action of state and other agencies.

To recapitulate, a constitution is the definition of the entities in the 'public' domain, their capacities and limits of action vis-à-vis one another and other agents. The 'state' always entails a set of differentiated agencies, with capacities to dispose of resources and make decisions in respect of spheres of activity: it therefore entails a regulatory instance. *Socialist states, by increasing the scope and variety of state agencies and functions, accentuate rather than reduce the need for an effective framework of public law to regulate the 'public' domain and its relations with other agents.*

Existing socialist societies are not without a framework of public law. The definition of state property, the form of enterprises, state agencies and so on necessitates this. The USSR and the People's Republic of China both now boast constitutions; the former has a developed apparatus of administrative law and courts. The weakness of these constitutions is not their absence; constitutional documents and legal institutions are just as present in the USSR as they are in the USA. Law is neither inoperative nor systematically 'violated', but limited in its role. It is not a question of 'arbitrariness', of power without legal definition. Kirchheimer (1961) explains the failure of legal regulation of the actions of state agencies and the non-institutionalization of 'civil liberties' or political rights in the Eastern Block in his book *Political Justice*. He does so without falling into the crudities of the conventional concept of 'totalitarianism', of an unlimited and arbitrary state. What he stresses is that the legislative and adjudicative instances exist and function; they define state property, make rules, try criminal cases, etc.; but that they lack, as institutions, autonomy as political agencies in decision-making. Thus the Soviet or DDR constitution and state organization is not constructed *in order to* attempt to limit, inspect, supervise and control the actions of certain crucial state agencies. In his examination of the DDR he takes full account of the fact that there are competent legal specialists, that 'due process' is followed and so on. The crucial point is that the courts are part of an administrative hierarchy and are directly subject in their adjudicative decisions to orders from, interventions by and more subtle pressures emanating from the Ministry of Justice. A similar point can be made about legislation: the Supreme Soviet in the USSR does not function as an autonomous political body setting norms for and reviewing the conduct of the state administration and Party. This is not merely because the Party manipulates the election of candidates, or because opposition is subject to police measures. There is no conception of or room in official Soviet ideology for the differentiation of political functions in such a way that the higher levels of state and party decision-making be subject to limit and review. Without this differentiation, without political autonomy of the legislative and adjudicative agencies, the 'rule of law' or 'socialist legality' means very little. In fact, the repression of the opposition in the contemporary USSR is generally by legally defined and sanctioned institutions and means: dissidents are tried under rules and sentenced by the courts; the police, frontier guards and prisons are institutions established in public law; and even the incarceration of dissidents in mental hospitals works through the decisions of legally specified agents (doctors and psychiatrists) with the power of assessing grounds for committal.

The current Soviet state is hardly the ideal of most sections of the Left, a few hardened 'marxist–leninist' ultras apart. But the Left, in the interests of attaining a radical and complete transformation of social relations, is if anything even less committed to constructing legal and organizational limits to state and mass actions. Without such limits, which if effective must create bases for opposition and obstacles to change, all references to 'rights' of opposition, criticism, etc., are pious cant. The 1936 Constitution included an impressive collection of 'rights' of the citizen, but no specification of the mechanisms of enforcement that would make these 'rights' practical capacities. The 1977 document is little better in this respect. It is not a matter of individuals being endowed with 'rights' in the abstract, but of agencies being capable of limiting the practices of others.[5] The problem is the absence of institutions to defend certain agents' capacities for action and to limit those of others. In large part these institutions must be legislative and adjudicative agencies; to be effective these agencies require differentiated capacities for enforcement (their own police powers, review bodies and inspectorates) and an ideological commitment of political leaders and the mass of citizens to such forms of regulation. There is virtually no place for such commitment in the classical forms of marxist political theory. Courts, specialist review bodies, supervision by legislative, administrative police, etc., are hardly institutions to commend themselves to marxists. Yet these and others like them are none the less necessary if public discussion of, criticism of and opposition to the policies of socialist state agencies is to be possible. Such freedom of criticism and opposition, like the legal regulation necessary to support it, is not something alien to socialism, a concession to liberal 'pluralism'; it is a constituent part of any conception of a viable socialist state.

'Socialization' – the conversion of activities and resources to a public or communal property form, the administration and distribution of activities and resources in non-commodity forms – extends the 'public' sphere, the scope and capacities of state and co-operative agencies. To the extent that it does so it increases the complexity of the public domain and the need for regulation. 'Socialization' is not an automatic process, nor are its forms of organization and objectives given by basic property and economic relations. 'Socialization' must create, for this very reason, accentuated problems of differences of policy line and objectives, and clashes between specific 'interests' within the institutions of state and among organized bodies of citizens. Unless these differences can be openly expressed and discussed the prospects for effective, lasting and practical resolutions of such questions of organization and policy are dismal. Freedom of criticism is not a 'concession' to avoid certain unpleasant consequences; it is before all else a condition of efficiency in administration. Free discussion itself cannot resolve severe clashes of organized interests; it is absurd to suppose a dialectic of reason or a spontaneous process of compromise. Policy decisions must take place according to procedures, which include means for resolving 'hard cases' and subjecting decisions to review. These procedures must inevitably mean assigning legislative and adjudicative bodies a central place in policy inspection and review: it is only by developing and extending means to permit serious examination of alternatives according to rules of procedure that socialist states can make any claims to advances in political organizations over 'capitalist democracies' like the USA or Sweden.

We will now consider in more detail how and why the alternative marxist conception of the solution to the problems of policy-making and regulation of state agencies – 'popular democracy' – cannot function, *on its own*, as an effective means of legislation, inspection and control.

Legislative bodies are necessary to any instance of regulation; they are a condition for defining agents and limiting their action in the form of rules. These rules are not a formality, but must be adjusted to serve certain objectives and conditions of practicality. In consequence these bodies must be composed of personnel with competence and information to make rules relevant and workable. This requires cognizance of different forms of agents and their conditions of action. These bodies require an ideological commitment to the process of regulation on the part of members and other agents, a style of deliberation that is not limited by other agencies and bodies.

These remarks are not made in order to impose a model of parliamentary or representative democracy on socialist social relations. The effectiveness of legislative bodies cannot be assessed in terms of their 'representativeness', in the sense of purporting to represent the wills or interests of a constituency from which is derived the mandate or membership of the body. Ironically, doctrines of parliamentary and popular democracy both involve this concept of 'representation': it serves to legitimate the claim of legislative bodies to be 'sovereign', unlimited in their right to make rules because they are authentic expressions of majority will. Democracy is often identified with 'representativeness'. But 'democracy', in the sense of electing the membership of legislative bodies (whether directly as with Parliament or indirectly in the case of half of the delegates to the Supreme Soviet) is *a mechanism for the provision of a personnel*. This objective is served and is no more or less 'representative; if 20 per cent of the electorate vote in order to do this (as in some UK local government elections) or over 90 per cent (as in elections in the Soviet Union). Voting does not mean endorsement of the policies (if any) advocated by parties and candidates (this is blatantly obvious in the USSR, but occurs elsewhere; voting studies – however problematic – have shown that preference bears no necessary relation to support of party policies). Measuring the effectiveness of democratic mechanisms as 'representation' depends on a conception of what the 'interests' to be represented are, and of necessity the only way of measuring this effectiveness is to use *some other mechanism of representation of interests* (opinion polls, local committees, referenda or whatever). The circle of 'representation' can never be closed, however much it is doubled by other representative mechanisms and measures. Democracy – forms of election – must be assessed as a way of providing personnel for bodies and the work those personnel do, and not in terms of some doctrine of the 'representation' by those personnel of the interests of some constituency.

The personnel of a legislative body need not be at par with one another in status or arrive by the same mechanism – a point that will be elaborated later. We are conditioned by doctrines of parliamentary and popular democracy to suppose that the membership of legislative bodies should be homogeneous and equal in status, all alike in being representatives of their constituents. This derives from the notion that there is a sovereign subject to be represented, the 'people', and each component member of this subject is equal to any other. Each representative of the members must therefore be equal to any other. But legislatures have included and do include members of different status and routes of arrival; the House of Lords or the Business and Universities votes before 1947 are examples in this country; the USSR has its Soviet of Nationalities; while feudal parliaments were characteristically divided into 'estates'. This may appear an absurd pendantry, but membership must be dictated by considerations of effectiveness in producing workable rules. This may demand a diverse personnel with different roles, as sources of information, rapporteurs to other decision-making agencies, etc. Personnel are homogenized by the notion of a sovereign and unitary constituency whose interests must be represented. There is no such given constituency.

The personnel to be provided and the mechanism of their provision are to be determined by the objectives of the legislative body. In this case they are twofold and the conditions of their attainment are twofold also. The first objective is to supervise a complex of agencies of decision (enterprises, ministries, parties, etc.) in order to make forms of their co-ordination and interaction possible. The second is to supervise certain of these agencies (police, political parties, etc.) in order to inhibit certain consequences – suppression of opposition and criticism in particular. The first condition is that the supervisory body must have a definite autonomy from the agencies it must inhibit (ministries, parties, police). This cannot be received merely by enunciating a doctrine of the 'separation of powers'; legislative bodies may indeed need to inquire more closely into administrative activities than the conventions of such doctrines would envisage. The second condition is that those bodies have the capacity to deal with complex administrative and organizational problems by means of rules in a way that is both practical and directed toward the political objective of securing against abuses. Regulation cannot therefore consist either simply in general 'norms' applicable to all citizens ('rights and duties' in the 1936 sense are a thin icing on an unpalatable cake) or in presenting the state as a unitary hierarchy of the realization of the sovereign will (that is as good as employing a watchdog with cataracts). *It is precisely because doctrines of right and sovereignty ignore the problem of the conversion of rights into capacities and the state as a realm of differentiated agencies of decision that they cannot serve to resolve the problems of socialist states.* These central categories of traditional legislation and public law are not much use. Regulation must involve mechanisms whereby administrations and administrators watch and check others (in forms that are limited): legislative and judicial specialists must have competence in problems of economic, welfare, military, etc., administration. Administrators must take part in practices of regulation, be conditioned to accept them and be interpellated by ideologies that sustain those practices. This raises the necessity of the presence on legislative bodies of the members of certain of the main agencies of decision as a condition for informed rules and their conditioning in an ideology of the necessity of preserving freedom, of administering within limits, etc. Thus enterprises, hospitals, unions, groups of specialists and so on require a presence on legislative bodies. This is not to try to resurrect Cole's ad hoc co-ordination of associations in a new form; the regulatory and control bodies in question must be specific apparatuses with capacities and a role specific to them, reaching decisions independently of the bodies they supervise and from which some of their members come. Merely to list the bodies from which personnel should be drawn as spokesmen/rapporteurs or experts (not 'representatives') would demonstrate that there could be no unitary constituency or set of 'interests'. The same mechanism of provision could not be used for these very different 'constituencies'.[6]

This role of control and supervision in so far as it is considered at all has been assigned in marxist political theory to popular democracy. The state, while it continues to exist as a complex of specialist administrative agencies, can be checked only by a real basis of popular power. This basis is threefold: soviets/communes, factory councils, and a militia. The first point to notice here is that the category of the 'people' or 'working class' is transformed into definite organizations. The 'people' *as such* cannot act. Indeed, what the 'people' as a political entity *is* must be defined by specific organiza- tions and by laws: its composition is the result of political decisions as to *nationality*. (Marxism provides no means of determining the scope of a state territory and grounds for inclusion; socialist states are therefore forced to use criteria identical with those of bourgeois states: birth within a definite territory as with the USSR, or cultural and ethnic characteristics of persons as citizens – any ethnic Chinese can on certain conditions claim citizenship of the People's Republic, for example), age, sex and competence (madmen or former capitalists and 'bourgeois' elements may be denied political rights). The second point to notice is that, while the particular organizations of 'popular' power have *limited* administrative, supervisory and policy formation capacities, the 'people', as the creative force in socialist construction, are assigned an *unlimited* sovereignty.

It is necessary to examine what these capacities are, to see what can be attained by direct democratic organization. The objective is not to deny popular democracy and self-administration any role – far from it – but to point out that it cannot perform certain tasks of administration or serve as a means of supervision of the state agencies made necessary by these very limits in its capacity.

'Direct' democracy – rule-making and administrative bodies in which every member involved in a certain activity is or can be involved – *can* be an effective means of organization under certain conditions. Units such as village communes, small factories, schools, housing estates and so on can be run in this way. It is necessary to design the scale and scope of tasks of such bodies to permit direct democracy; it is both an economical form of control and provides masses of ordinary people with an education in basic organizational skills.[8]

The limits of direct democracy arise above commune or plant level. There are three main problems. The first is the co-ordination of the activities and use of resources of a multiplicity of units engaged in similar activities – plants producing products needed by others, or drawing on common pools of labour, raw materials, energy, etc. Co-ordination of activities and distribution of resources require agencies of decision above plant/commune level. As organizations these agencies are irreducible to plant level: they are forced to make decisions affecting plants involving clashes of line, allocations between competing resources, etc. This is true even if they are composed of personnel drawn from plants through some mechanism to which a doctrine of 'representation' is attached. This level uses distinct means of administration and criteria of decision. The second problem arises from the fact that units of administration of distinct activities are not at par with one another; plants, hospitals and battalions are not of the same type. Production, medical welfare and war are distinct activities requiring different conceptions of administration and different limits of action. This means it is difficult to put the 'basic units' of any set of social relations together as the foundations of a political system:

(1) Plants or communes – capable of being administered by direct democracy – cannot organize residence, welfare, etc., beyond the most basic level. The greater the 'enterprization' of non-productive activities, the more restricted is the ability to change the form and size of the enterprise (such changes dislocate residence, welfare funds, etc.). The provision of residence and welfare outside enterprises, e.g. a number of enterprises sharing common facilities

in the form of a 'town', makes more sophisticated welfare provision and flexibility in production organization possible: otherwise the expansion, contraction and differentiation of plants poses severe problems. 'Enterprization' also introduces severe rigidities into the labour force (plant = 'home'). It follows from this that 'towns' are aggregations too complex to be administered by direct democracy, that division of labour and specialization of activity create different interests and claims on resources. 'Factory councils' or 'communes' cannot be the exclusive basis of local organization: hospitals, schools and office councils would parallel them, while 'town councils' and means of controlling planning and allocative bodies involve elections or systems of appointment. 'Factory councils' are easily identifiable with the notion of 'workers' power' and a basic identity of interests. Social workers, nurses and doctors, economists and other specialists organized in the councils of their equally necessary agencies, and, perhaps, far outnumbering production workers, are less easily fitted to a doctrine of an homogeneous 'workers' ' power.

(2) War is not a continuous activity and military units do not have autonomy to make decisions in this regard – battalion direct democracy is confined to matters of discipline and housekeeping; in other relevant matters units act on orders from higher authority.

The third problem is that direct democracy is not an 'essence' or 'spirit' that informs the higher levels of organization made necessary by its limits. The People's Republic of China illustrates this point well: extensive direct democratic institutions and practices in communes, factories, battalions, etc., are well documented, but this parallels an absence of developed institutions of control of centralized political and economic decision-making bodies, of means of discussion and criticism at regional and national level not dominated by party and state officials. Direct democracy does not achieve 'popular' control over the higher levels; merely sending delegates 'upwards' to other bodies is not the answer. It assumes that recall to the base can police a series of layers of administration each of which sends delegates to the next. But no specific *means* of supervision and control of these higher bodies are proposed. Libertarians may wish for a world without nation states, extended division of labour, complex problems of economic control and allocation, the problems of urban areas,

political differences and wars: let them wait for it. Under such conditions direct democracy cannot suffice as the primary means of
administration and control. Marxist/leninists stress the democratic
'dictatorship of the proletariat' over the borgeoisie, and popular
democracy is the keystone of that dictatorship. But against a single
disciplined party machine and state agencies whose actions are
unfettered by special purpose bodies competent to do so, local committees can have little impact. The absence of defined and enforced
limits on the masses' action in conceptions of the commune state is
mirrored by the actual absence of limits on the party and state
apparatuses in states espousing 'marxist–leninist' ideologies. This conception of state stems from giving priority to the interests of transformation of social relations. In the USSR the result of this conception of
state and an unfettered state machine has been the exact reverse: a
block on political development. To say 'unfettered' is not to resurrect
the chimera of 'absolute' power. *Any* agency is limited by the means of
exercise of its activity at its disposal and the capacities of other
agencies. At issue here are *limits constructed in pursuit of policy*.

It is not a matter, as we have seen, of counterposing parliamentary
democracy to popular democracy. Parliamentary 'representative'
democracies can also place precious few effective limits on the action
of state agencies. However, the election of 'representatives' to legislative bodies by the (competent) population as a whole does have certain
political advantages and can serve control functions: but its role must
be assessed in terms other than its 'representativeness' (i.e of certain
prior 'interests'). There are two main advantages in such a system of
voting:

(1) Certain minimum political requirements are placed on *all*
    (competent) agents; a legal capacity and requirements to vote
    interpellates all persons as political subjects. Elections serve as a
    means of *political education* and induction on a wider scale, just
    as direct democratic organization provides an introduction to
    administrative competence on a limited scale. The dangers of
    Cole's suffrage based on *activity* are that it ignores the problems
    of induction to and mobilization for political activity (it treats
    association as a 'natural' human attribute). Elections, the
    interpellation of persons as political subjects, also serve to stress
    the importance of the legislative and regulatory agencies. Elec-
    tions can serve as an ideological focus reinforcing a generalized

and mass commitment to enforcing limits on and ordered forms of the action of state and mass agencies.

(2) Elections in the USSR have served primarily as means of mobilizing expressions of 'support' for the regime. Mobilization through elections must involve such a role of reinforcement of party and certain state agencies' capacities for unregulated action if the agents, organizations and issues entering into elections are set by these very agencies. 'Pluralism' is a precondition for elections serving the functions of provision of personnel for agencies of control and development of mass political involvement and competence. Only if the means of agitation, opposition and the conduct of campaigns are widely available can different policy lines be openly debated, state and other agencies' conduct publicly reviewed, and mass commitment to enforcing regulated and ordered forms of political decision-making generated. (Conventional liberal ideologies cannot be an adequate support for this particular 'pluralism', precisely because they stress the primacy of 'representation'. A doctrine of representative democracy is not the sole answer to the problems of regulation, organization and control raised by this notion of 'pluralism'. Democratic elitist notions of 'polyarchy' are no more satisfactory; *any* state is polyarchal in the sense of involving a number of centres of decision, constituencies of support and bases for divergence of interest. The problem raised here is not of the *existence* of a plurality of differential agencies of decision, but the forms of their definition and regulation.)

I have tried to stress the central role of autonomous legislative and regulatory institutions in the control of the agencies of socialist states. The prescription of limits and practices of inspection and review cannot merely be diffused throughout social relations, as popular democratic ideologies suppose. Specific institutions claiming a *general* definitive and regulatory competence are necessary; institutions of *last resort* in questions of adjudication, that is, legislature and higher courts. I have also stressed the uselessness of the notion of 'sovereignty'. First, the legislature need have no single source of its members; its claims derive from no 'sovereign' whose will it represents but from the necessity of its functions. Second, what necessitates a complex of legislative and regulatory agencies is that the state does not take the form of a single 'sovereign' power acting according to the 'rule of law' but is a complex of agencies of decision. The delimitation of state agencies' functions and capacities cannot be based on the assumption of the state as a homogeneous public power. It is a heterogeneous domain united by definition and regulation. A legislature recruited partly by nomination, partly by indirect election from certain categories of organizations, and partly by universal suffrage, conforms to no single doctrine of 'democracy'. Social organizations and administration conducted partly by direct democracy, partly by competent specialist agencies, and partly by bodies of elected and appointed 'representatives' has no unity of principle. It conforms to no doctrine of democracy, whether popular or representative. 'Democracy', of whatever form, is *not an absolute value*, but a means of providing personnel to bodies that serve definite functions. Those means need have no unity.

I have contended that socialist states need a firm framework of public law and legislative regulation, precisely because socialization means that functions and capacities of state agencies increase and differentiate. It is not the *presence* of this framework that is at issue but the forms of its effectivity in defining and regulating agents' capacities. This, as we have seen, cannot be attained by merely promulgating rules; it is a matter of constructing organizations with the appropriate capacities, of practices of inspection and review, and of mass commitment to the decisions following from those practices. This cannot be attained merely by creating a legal instance; it is a question of the whole form of the socialist state and of the organized competence of its members. Equally, without certain specific definitive and regulatory institutions this whole form cannot be designed and fixed. It is not a matter of 'legality' but of the work courts and legislative bodies do. 'Legality' can always be achieved – the USSR or Hitler's Germany make the point all too well – and it is an established prejudice of the Left to set the least possible store by it. The reason for this is that courts enforcing rules of procedure and limits to action, public discussion, opposition and organization not limited to certain favoured objectives or 'interests', and so on, are capable of serving as effective blocks to change. That these 'blocks' are a precondition for avoiding 'stalinism', that the centralization of decision-making according to the dictates of a single popular will is a chimera, cannot be admitted except at the price of radically rethinking the character and objectives of socialist states. The orthodox marxist Left wants to avoid 'stalinism', but without forfeiting the political doctrines and conceptions of organizational practice that make it an ever-present danger.

PASHUKANIS AND SOCIALIST SOCIAL POLICY

Pashukanis was committed to the doctrine of the 'withering away of law', but not in the interests of libertarianism. It is the *form* of law that is to be replaced, but this does not mean the elimination of the control of behaviour and the regulation of conduct. Law works through general norms, applicable universally to individuals, and entails categories of subjectivity in its definition of fault (responsibility, intention, guilt, etc.). This corresponds in a hypostasized form to the realities of individuation in relations of commodity exchange, to individuals who make economic decisions independently of one another. Individuals can be regarded as autonomous agents whose actions depend on their will and who can be held responsible for the consequences of those actions. Linkages between individuals are primarily matters of exchange and alienation of things; regulation therefore concerns the acts of specific individuals in relation to others. The *form* of law is inappropriate to the regulation of conduct in a system of collective property and planned, co-operative production. Individuals are not as such autonomous economic agents and must act in concert. The securing and restitution of property, the central element in both private and criminal law, is an irrelevance to the regulation of the process of production. In the transitional period of construction of a communist society men must learn to co-operate. Traditional forms of individualism characteristic of commodity society must be eliminated in favour of socialist patterns of conduct. The notion of certain generally applicable and prescribed standards of conduct, and therefore the possibility of deviation from them, is retained. The management of this deviation for Pashukanis takes the form of 'social defence'. Law and adjudication are replaced by administrative action and political struggle (for Pashukanis's conception of 'social defence' see Sharlet, 1974). Conduct is reviewed by state agencies and one's comrades. Institutions of 'social defence' examine individuals' behaviours not in terms of fixed general rules concerning specific categories of acts, but in terms of their overall contribution to and fitness for socialist construction. Categories of intention and responsibility are not at issue; the consequences of behaviour and its forms are reviewed without reference to categories of conscious motive or fault. Instead of 'punishment', the correction or modification of behaviour is the remedy. In the place of punitive measures to coerce a calculating bourgeoisie subjectivity is the application of political judgement and social, psychological and medical science to the reform of conduct in the interests of socialist politics.

Pashukanis is opposed to *bourgeois* subjectivity – to the notion of the autonomous agent responsible for its acts. But he offers instead – in the implications of his programme – a new form of *subjectivication*: the object of these measures is 'socialist man'. All individuals who compose the 'people' are and must be mobilized towards the attainment of this end. This mobilization takes the form of mass practice and the imposition of 'popular' standards (Comrades' Courts), but for severe or more complex cases of deviation it must also involve specialist agencies (police, psychiatrists, pediatricians, etc.). Mobilization towards socialist construction of the sort Pashukanis supports means in practice mass surveillance and the adjustment of individuals to standards considered appropriate by 'mass' and state agencies. As Foucault argues in *Discipline and Punish* (1978a), there can be no system of 'discipline' – i.e. inspection of individual conduct and its adjustment to a norm – without definite forms of subjectivication. 'Social defence' is in substance nothing but a system of disciplinary surveillance and behaviour modification. If Pashukanis's conception were put into operation medical and psychiatric knowledge would be deployed by state agencies to serve the definition and enforcement of socialist 'normality'.

Pashukanis does not mention, nor did the practice of state institutions in the USSR devise, techniques of assessment and transformation of behaviour radically different from those in the 'capitalist' west. Psychiatry, pediatrics, penology and social welfare were and are derivations from the sciences and practices developed from the eighteenth century onwards by the European and American bourgeoisie. There is no distinctly 'socialist' policy or technique in matters of the medical or socially therapeutic manipulation of individuals. 'Socialist' policies, whether of reform through labour or behaviour modification, are restatements, resurrections or modifications of the programmes of 'bourgeois' reformers. The co-operative, socially pliable individual, capable of giving his full potential to the community, is no discovery of the October Revolution. Pavlov could add little to the practice of Pinel, Tuke or Rush, Makarenko nothing to Fry or Shaftesbury. The *techniques* of 'social defence' are in no sense specific to the *objectives* of a socialist society.[9]

This is no plea for Foucauldian libertarianism. It is not a plea against the inescapable oppressiveness of medical and psychiatric normalization. Medical and psychiatric intervention in compulsory forms cannot be dispensed with, except on pain of mass misery and pathology. We have no replacements for hospitals, mental homes and prisons – 'liberalizations' and 'domestications' of these institutions have been with us since *The Retreat*. *Red Bologna* adds little that cannot be found in our comprehensive schools or the NHS. Foucault challenges a carceral, 'gulag', a complex of disciplinary institutions to whose functioning law is conceived as a rubber-stamp. Pashukanis proposes in 'social defence' – for the very 'best' of motives, he is no spokesman for the stalinist police state – something that could only conform to Foucault's negative Utopia of 'disciplinary society'. Both are, from opposed motives, equally misguided. Medical, psychiatric and welfare institutions and practices cannot and do not escape from, could not exist without, the forms of definition and limitation imposed by law.

Foucault's notion of a 'disciplinary society', a total system of practices of 'government' based on 'normatizing individualization', is an absurdity. These practices have no unity of objective, content or effect. Foucault can assign such unity to them only by two dubious devices: the model of the Panopticon as the essence of all disciplinary power, and the 'body' as the common referent of all disciplinary surveillance and action. Without these devices the 'strategies' Foucault amalgamates into a single force are dispersed. Foucault does *not* derive the forms of government entailed in the 'microphysics of power' or the strategies these powers embody from a prior social origin. They are not an emanation of capitalism. Nor is there a single social support behind the disciplinary 'eye', an interest or agent whose servant these powers and strategies are. They are specific constructions in discourse and entail discrete techniques and practices. The 'solutions' to problems of social organization are neither given nor homogeneous. The 'needs' of economic relations are not known outside the definite forms in which they are constructed and met. The prison is first and foremost an 'idea in architecture', a specialist enclosure of space with its own conditions of conception, construction and management. So is the factory. As a form of organization it is not privileged or automatic for being 'economic'. Such forms had to be devised, campaigned for and introduced: other forms of organization are no less possible, a definite variety of policy 'lines' always confronts the agents involved in any decision about social organization. 'Capitalism' no more made the prison or factory necessary than they sprang fully armed from the head of Mr Bentham. Foucault's *Discipline and Punish* offers us this critical lesson; it insists on the specificity of forms of 'government', and yet it destroys the value of that lesson by homogenizing the powers thus created into a single oppressive disciplinary monolith.

In *Discipline and Punish* Foucault tends to counterpose legal and disciplinary regulation. Law is conceived as limit or prohibition, whereas disciplinary power transforms and magnifies the capacities of the subjects on which it works. Law is marginalized, legal adjudication becomes secondary to a mass of normatizing interventions in the form of a knowledge of individuals through mechanisms of surveillance. But there is no opposition between law and discipline, as the author of *The Birth of the Clinic* and *I, Pierre Rivière* should know. Law defines the status of the specialist practices and sets limits to the powers of the agents and institutions involved in forms of discipline, doctors, teachers, reformatories, hospitals, etc. For example, doctors are a legally defined class of agents with an enforced monopoly over certain classes of decisions and acts: part of their status is their capacity to assist the courts in evaluating the conditions of plaintiffs (whether insane, unfit to plead, etc.). 'Doctor' is a status in law, assigned public functions. Doctors make decisions sanctioned by law (e.g. whether an abortion is legal or not) and assist courts in making decisions. Legal regulation and the scope of legal rules loses nothing thereby. Without a publicly assigned position and legally defined exclusiveness in the performance of their role, the key institutions and agents of the 'disciplinary' region could not function: prisons, psychiatry, medicine, social work, and so on.

To imagine that these agents and institutions could operate without a specific instance of regulation, without definition and review, is possible for Pashukanis because he considers that administration can dispense with the form of law. Law is defined by him in such a way that the role of public law is a non-issue. Specialist, medical, psychiatric, etc., interventions are necessary and will remain so, whatever the form of economic organization. At the same time it must be accepted that there are no distinctly 'socialist' standards of conduct or 'socialist' techniques of social policy which might reform their practice. If 'civil liberties' are to be secured, definite formal limits on the action of institutions such as psychiatric hospitals and social security agencies have to be imposed to prevent them from serving as means for the suppression of political opposition. In the light of these considerations the idea that a framework of legal regulation and review be replaced by apparatuses of 'social defence' subject only to considerations of administrative objectives and effectiveness is disastrous.

The necessities of legal definition and regulation in the area of 'social policy' arise under a number of heads:

(1) The need to set standards of conduct and management for specialist institutions such as prisons, reformatories, mental hospitals, old people's homes, etc.: this involves competent agencies of regulation, inspection and disclosure independent of their immediate administrations; it also involves mechanisms whereby persons detained or undergoing treatment can obtain a review of their position according to definite formal grounds and conditions of admission.

(2) Equally necessary is the need to limit and review the powers and actions of 'mass' or communal organizations; there can be no free range for 'comrade's courts', co-operatives' committees, etc. Possibilities of maladministration and oppression of minorities in factories and communes are just as real as in institutions staffed by specialists like doctors. Again, access to tribunals on the part of individuals and capacities to oversee communal institutions by review bodies are a condition of protection of opposition and difference.

(3) The conditions of monopoly of certain forms of intervention need to be carefully set so as not to exclude significant possibilities of therapy, i.e. freedom to practise for psychoanalysis, homeopathy, acupuncture, etc., rather than a monopoly for conditioning therapy or conventional medicine (within certain limits).

(4) Involuntary commitment of individuals to therapy, the taking of children into care, etc., ought to be no less subject to judicial decision that it is in advanced capitalist countries.

'Social defence' can replace legal regultion only if *lower* standards of control of administration are accepted than pertain in the west. The same is true of any system that places reliance in matters of social policy on 'popular' democracy; mass practice has no spontaneous existence but always means definite organizations, which are no less in need of review or control than any other. Pashukanis and Foucault offer their respective visions of a regime of 'social policy' outside of law, the one a positive one, the other a negative Utopia, and both are equally impossible. These views reveal in their very defects why a framework of legal regulation is essential in matters of health, welfare and reform of conduct.

In the USSR Pashukanis's programme for the elimination of law and its replacement by 'social defence' was opposed in the name of 'proletarian law' or 'socialist legality'. These ideas have an odious parentage; no one would welcome standing on the same ground as state prosecutor Vyshinskii. The critical point of this opposition, that the state must take a definite legal form, while correct, is not at issue here. What is crucial is the nature and objectives of this legal framework. 'Socialist legality' is worthless if it means merely that there is a legal code and 'due process'. If that code and process are at the disposal of the Party and upper state echelons, by issuing orders to judicial functionaries through the Ministry of Justice *nothing* is thereby secured. The dictatorship of party leaders and state officials need not deviate one inch from strict legal rectitude (although Stalin's purges evidently did so). Unless the state machine is subject to practices of interruption, limit and control, legality and 'civil liberties' have no meaning: they are like a manufacturers' guarantee which excludes everything of value. 'Socialist legality' and 'social defence' amount to the same thing: the unimpeded centralization of state power in the proclaimed interests of social transformation. To *restore* 'socialist legality' in the USSR is to achieve precious little; the state has ample scope within the forms of law to hobble and repress its enemies. Its essays in 'illegality' are an unnecessary crudity born of long-acquired contempt for its own ineffective legal framework of control.

This contempt is no peculiarity of hardened Soviet party bosses. It is a common attitude of socialist Left and libertarian ultra-Left in the West. E. P. Thompson's impassioned appeal for socialists to accept the concept of 'rule of law' has had some effect in producing ritual acceptance of the notion that law and law enforcement are not purely oppressive expressions of ruling-class power. Thompson foolishly ascribes this view to imaginary 'structural marxists'. One of the few proponents of marxist theory to make this very point, which Thompson imagines to be a novelty, is in fact the target of his illiterate jibe – Althusser and his various followers. The need for Thompson's polemic arises within his own camp, the libertarian anti-communist Left. No one gave better expression to this conception of law as purely repressive than the authors of *The New Criminology* (Taylor, Walton and Young, 1973). To prohibit certain forms of conduct in law or by convention was conceived by them as an unacceptable limitation on 'healthy human diversity': how this anarchy of conduct was compatible with organized social relations or with the rearing of children as stable and socially acceptable personalities was not a matter thought worthy of explanation. Even they,[10] guided by mentor Thompson, have come to accept that law and its enforcement are not purely repressive. But there is no sign in all of this of any serious rethinking of the concept of socialism consequent on this valorization of law. Thompson and his epigones remain committed to the notion of socialism as the 'self-emancipation of the working class'. Socialism or communism means, as an ultimate objective, a society without complex differentiated organization, without irreconcilable differences or conflicts. I have tried to show that popular democracy cannot be the sole basis of organization, that 'mass' practice can be as oppressive as any other, and that the condition of political difference and debate of policy lines can be secured only by imposing limits on central state and mass organizations' capacities. To accept the necessity of legal regulations under socialism entails more than phrases about the 'rule of law'; it means changing the orthodox marxist conception of the socialist state.

RIGHTS AND THE SUBJECT

We have stressed the necessity for a framework of legal definition and regulation in socialist states. At the same time we have challenged the value of concepts of 'sovereignty' or 'rights' in the elaboration of this framework. This is for a number of related reasons:

(1) Categories of 'rights' and 'sovereignty' are generally presented as derivations of ontological doctrines in which institutions and laws are conceived as the expression or recognition of certain prior or privileged attributes of subjects. The support of these attributes is a unitary and constitutive subject. The 'sovereign' is the people or an individual, the monarch, prince, etc. 'Rights' are conceived as the attributes of individual human subjects deriving from their nature or essence, i.e. from their being free beings, ends rather than means, and so on. These doctrines, which are deployed to justify 'sovereignty' or 'rights', always lead to a conception of

social organization as expressive of a principle, a singular and homogeneous derivative of the will of subjects or individuals. Such doctrines are incapable of sustaining the complexity and heterogeneity of state institutions and social relations.

(2) It is precisely this complexity and heterogeneity that needs to be taken account of under 'socialization'. The defence and the limitation of the capacities of action of *organizations* are just as important an issue as those of individual subjects; this is why the notion of 'civil liberties' is inadequate to questions of effective organization, efficiency in decision-making and so on under socialism. To present the state as the homogeneous sphere of realization of a single will is to court all the dangers of non-recognition of its differentiation and to privilege in ideology certain institutions and organizations, classically the Party and higher organs of administration. Law as regulative of complex differentiated agencies can best be conceived not as the expression of the will of a single centre, but as a means of maintaining and yet limiting differentiation of decision-making by means of certain procedures and institutions.

(3) The capacities of public organizations are *constructed* rather than inherent; they have no single origin once the notion of a 'sovereign' is challenged. Organizations have no given nature or attributes, and the category of 'right' fits uneasily with the definition of their capacities of action relative to certain specific objectives.

(4) Human subjects are no more 'natural' beings with given attributes than organizations established in public law. The 'rights' of individual human subjects are likewise capacities and statuses constructed in law and convention. Subjects have no given nature of which 'rights' are the expression: the statuses and capacities of subjects are relative to the objectives of legislation and are differential (the statuses assigned to individuals are not homogeneous; viz. doctors, madmen, minors, etc.). The 'universal' statuses of civil rights establish very little; they always involve in order to be effective the specific construction and delimitation of the powers of institutions: thus 'freedom of speech' must be specified into specific and conditional limitation of police and municipal powers, conditions of access to media, etc. All the proclaimed 'civil rights' in the world are nothing beside the organization of institutions; 'civil liberties' are a codeword for certain *effects* of the control of institutions.

Pashukanis, as we know, challenged the validity of 'right' as a category in the public sphere; for him notions like 'right of parliament' were absurd and the whole structure of public law was an ideological illusion (albeit a necessary one). This challenge to the category of right is different from ours. It arises because, on the one hand, he considered the essence of law to be *private possessive right*, the recognition of the (socio-historically given) attributes of subjects as bearers of commodities; and, on the other, he conceived the state as in reality an *unlimited* instrument of class oppression. We have argued in an earlier work that, contrary to Pashukanis, law cannot be conceived as the recognition of prior attributes and that subjects have no given form in the relations of production independent of their specific construction in law (properly, right is not a mere recognition of possession; the form of property law conditions economic relations). We have also argued that state power is limited by the means of its exercise, that these means involve the organization of the state into differentiated agencies, and that this differentiation demands definition in public law. For Pashukanis the categories of public law are derivative of those of private law; law and the possessive rights of individual subjects are inseparable. Law must vanish along with the forms of real possession which generate 'bourgeois right'. Law and the category of 'right' are made co-terminous.

Pashukanis's position curiously parallels that of the most sophisticated representative of modern Anglo-Saxon analytic legal philosophy, Ronald Dworkin. Dworkin's *Taking Rights Seriously* (1977) is a critical challenge to legal positivism which insists that law does not consist in *rules* and their application alone. Legal practice must of necessity involve reference beyond the letter of the law to 'rights'. 'Rights' are categories pertaining to the attributes of subjects that condition the conduct of the legal process and provide means of settling difficult disputes where questions of the interpretation, applicability or validity of statuses arise. Legal practice constantly generates questions as to the 'fairness' of the law, whether 'justice' will be done to individuals if a statute is rigidly applied, and so on.

Dworkin is correct to argue that laws must involve reference to principles and objectives that go beyond statutes. Legislation involves extra-legal considerations of the objectives served by statutes, and practices of review by higher courts must involve principles of judicial procedure and of application of law to cases. But there is no reason, having said this, to argue that those objectives and principles must always take one form, that they express the philosophy of liberalism and involve reference to ontological questions (the attributes of sub-jects). Dworkin's brilliant argument is limited by the 'ordinary language' bias of the philosophical method he uses. It is a form of analysis of discourse which reviews certain bodies of statements that it selects by implicit rules of inclusion. It examines the distribution of statements within the universe created by such rules. It reaches con-clusions as to the conditionality of certain of those statements – that they make reference to 'rights'. But this can appear as a definitive analysis only by not questioning the limits of the distribution of the statements in question, by not examining the particular conditions of formulation and appearance of statements. It is a method that has traditionally shunned the questions reposed in a novel form by Foucault's *L'archéologie du savoir*. It tells us what a particular body of legal–political discourse and popular practices saturated by its categories tends to produce as statements. The conditions of possibility of other discourses of reference to the principles governing rules of law cannot become a pertinent question. It tells us how Anglo-Saxon lawyers and judges, within a definite range of discourses that organize a practice of law, are constrained to speak and write. It can tell us nothing about how the discourses organizing socialist legal practices should be constructed. This is not to dismiss Dworkin on his own terrain. His work is a powerful and necessary re-statement of the radical tradition of classical liberalism. He is fighting a battle for 'civil liberties' against state agencies *and* for legislation to promote social justice, protect oppressed minorities and so on. The discourse of 'rights' is a condition of argument he did not choose and cannot alter; it is a constituent element in legal and political debate in England and America. It cannot instruct us, however, in what socialist jurists should do; nor, for that matter, can it be more than a limited interven-tion in Anglo-Saxon legal debates. It tends to confirm rather than challenge certain of the dominant terms of those debates, *but there are others*.

I will try to argue that reference to 'rights', to the ontological attributes of subjects, by no means provides a means of deciding 'hard cases' or questions of what interests are to prevail in legislation. It can just as well make these questions insoluble or their solution arbitrary. I will argue:

(1) that laws can serve objectives of social policy, regulating the conduct of individuals, without interpellating subjects as bearers

of possessive right; I will take my example not from some existing
or future socialist state but from contemporary England, the 1967
Abortion Act;

(2) that to the extent that categories of right and ontological reference
are introduced into legislation and juridic discourse the result is to
generate the claims of rival ontologies, to parallel the rights of one
agent with the conflicting claims of those of another − a good
example would be the Baake case, but for our purposes a more
apposite example is the Paton case.

The 1967 Abortion Act serves the objective of decriminalizing,
under certain circumstances, abortion, thereby interdicting the
Offences Against the Person Act 1861. The Act does this by assigning
to doctors − a publicly defined status − the role of determining
whether an abortion is legal or not. An abortion is a legal act if
doctors acting in 'good faith' deem it necessary on certain specified
grounds. No one speaks of doctors' 'rights' in this matter; it is one of
the capacities and responsibilities as publicly recognized competent
agencies assigned to them under various Acts. No subject has a 'right'
to an abortion, nor is a special act of *consent* necessary. The Act does
not define any form of proprietal relation over the foetus: the father
has no 'right' to consent to or withold an abortion; a woman has no
'right' to one (indeed, in certain circumstances, abortions may be
performed *without* consent); and the foetus has no 'rights' in this
respect, although it is a *person* in law (e.g. under the Offences Against
the Person Act 1861). Paton sought to claim rights in respect of the
unborn child carried by his wife: he failed. Rankin, the lawyer hired to
represent him, demonstrated brilliantly that the law provided him with
no grounds to act. In reviewing the law on his matter Rankin assessed
the Act and was forced to question:

> whether the Abortion Act is talking about rights in the jurisprudential
> sense. In the Abortion Act . . . Parliament is dealing with the interests
> of the unborn child, in the context of eugenic permission for termina-
> tion of pregnancy and the interests of the mother and the unborn child
> in terms of danger to her life or danger to her physical or mental
> health. [*Paton v. Paton and Trustees* BPAS, p. 21]

Further, Rankin claims contrary to Dworkin a radical limitation of
the role of the discourse of rights in law:

> The rights with which the Courts are concerned, my lord, . . . are not
> after all natural or inherent rights. The law is not concerned with

natural law, but they are concerned with rights, which are the construction of the law itself, and the capacity which is conferred by law.
[*Paton* v. *Paton and Trustees* BPAS, p. 21]

Here we see a lawyer who, if the law permitted essentialistic arguments in this matter, has every reason to use them, meticulously
demonstrating that his client has no legal right or capacity to proceed
in this case. He does so by reference to the powers conferred by
statute, defining the subject as a person in law with a specific complex
of capacities determined by statute.

Rankin opposes the categories of 'rights' and 'interests'. 'Rights' in
law establish a capacity for a person to advance in the courts a claim
for relief or for an agent acting as legal subject for that person to make
the claim. 'Interests', on the other hand, are objectives expressed in
law that are secured by empowering certain personnel or agencies to
make decisions, in this case for doctors to determine the validity of
grounds for abortion. 'Right' is only one form by which legislation can
serve objectives, and this 'right' is a capacity to proceed as subject in
law to claim relief for some definite wrong; it is not necessarily defined
by reference to ontological attributes. 'Right' does not inhere in the
subject, but is the capacity assigned to it by law. Legislation,
therefore, need not necessarily create 'rights', even in the legal sense. It
may secure interests by assigning tasks to personnel or agencies; it
would be idle to think of this assignment as the creation of 'rights': the
determination of the legality of an abortion is not a doctor's 'right', but
a task he is deemed competent to perform by reason of status. Social
policy objectives can be served without endowing subjects with legal
'rights' and also without grounding on ontological doctrines. This is
the one great advantage of the 1967 Act, that it excludes questions of
possession, of 'right' to life, etc., rigorously: it closes a space of competing claims of the legal persons involved.

'Legal' rights are nothing but the capacities assigned to legal subjects; they can be transformed by legislation. 'Right' in this sense is
conditional on statute. The 'rights' Dworkin refers to exceed these
conditional capacities granted by law. 'Rights' in Dworkin's full sense
are part of a discourse of claims; they establish what it is the law *should*
recognize. These claims are founded on ontological doctrines, that law
must correspond to the nature of the subject in question. Ontological
claims can be advanced from two directions, for and against the form
of law. Law can be conceived as the recognition or expression of a
domain of 'rights', legislation as a process of realizing these 'rights'

and making law correspond to a more or less coherent or contraditory ontological field.[11] But ontological doctrines can also challenge law; as in the form of left-wing critiques in which law is conceived as a domain of abstract 'rights', a formal expression that is forever inadequate to the conditions of the concrete realization of what 'rights' signify: freedom, equality, etc.

Both these positions are evident in the debates on the law on abortion. Left and Right seek to challenge the 1967 Act in the interests of ontological doctrines. Anti-abortionists seek to advance the 'rights' of the foetus. The foetus – as human life from the moment of conception – has a right to life and the integrity of its person. This right takes precedence over consideration of the convenience of the mother, who must be obliged to carry the child to birth. Certain radical feminists privatize the 'right' of the mother to control her own body; the woman's body is 'hers' and she should have absolute disposition over it. This argument leads to a displacement of law; the 1967 Act is challenged because it makes abortion conditional on the doctors' decisions – it is not merely a matter of the woman's free choice. The woman should have unconditional control over her body, a control outside all legal definition and limit. This radical feminist argument is coupled with or parallelled by marxist arguments which seek to problematize the form of law. Greenwood and Young's *Abortion in Demand* (1976) exemplifies this coupling. Unconditional abortion is a revolutionary demand capitalism cannot meet. The 1967 Act is an example of a manipulative politics of population control in the interests of capitalist reproduction of a healthy labour force. It seeks to control 'social problems', to prevent the social costs of unwanted and deformed children. A woman should have an absolute right to choose how to control her own body.

Greenwood and Young's 'socialism' is the one form of society in which this freedom can be concretized and will be a freedom outside of law. Their stigmatization of the 1967 Act as eugenic manipulation is conditional on the notion that there will be no problems of 'social policy' in socialist states, that they will not be faced with the regulation of health, questions of population policy and so on. Unconditional abortion is a 'revolutionary' demand indeed; it transcends any possible form of organization of social relations in just the same way as Young's earlier unconstrained 'healthy human diversity'. Socialist states encounter certain necessities of regulation in the matter of abortion in a way no different from 'capitalist' ones:

(1) Abortion requires medical intervention which becomes increasingly complicated after twelve weeks; abortion is not a 'private' act but involves the consumption of medical resources, the provision of facilities and questions of alternative forms of provision. These questions of provision are not a matter of *a* woman's choice, but a general social question of health policy. Even if, as one would hope, abortion facilities are more fully and evenly provided, that is a matter of public policy and not 'private' choice.

(2) Doctors in modern capitalist *and* socialist states are legally defined personnel with a monopoly of certain competencies and who are empowered to use specialist discretion in their application and use. The demand for unconditional abortion, unregulated by law, implies a de-monopolization of medical competence. This is deeply problematic. De-monopolization would mean that anyone was free to perform abortions; there would be no limit to personnel, to methods or facilities. The possibility created by this *laissez-faire* is of a return to the era of the 'knitting needle', in the guise of alternative medicine and self-help. Even if one opposes permitting doctors to be a closed self-governing corporation, as with the BMA, and supports giving greater scope to nurses and other personnel, this means an enhancing of the legal controls over doctors and an extension of capacities to exercise skill to nurses and others. Socialist states should take the control of medical competence and the determination of means of intervention *more* and not less seriously. Compulsory preventative medicine, prohibition of smoking and so on imply a stronger legal framework in matters of health than we have today, whether in England or the People's Republic of China.

(3) The notion that abortion is a matter of 'private' choice is characterized by rationalism. It denies the realities of mental illness, neuroses, distress and just plain confusion that surround our competence to perform many commonplace acts, let alone whether to have a child or not. Socialist states should, one would hope, make competent and non-coercive counselling readily available and encourage people to make use of it. They would also be confronted with regulating the severely disturbed or subnormal; mongolism, psychoses and so on will not disappear because the forms of organization of the economy have changed.

A slogan like 'a woman's right to choose' may be an effective campaigning device, especially when it means the effective provision of contraception and abortion facilities, liberalization of grounds for abortion, etc.[12] But this slogan can be operationalized only in the legal definition of capacity and the organizational provision of means. The danger of such a slogan is when it signifies an absolute and unconditional 'right' outside of law; such a demand vitiates any attainable policy objectives. The danger of the discourse of absolute 'rights' is that rights are conceived as inherent in the subject, expressions of its nature. The subject becomes a constitutive entity independent of any social relations. Take the phrase 'our right to control our bodies', frequently voiced in this connection by radical feminists. It generates the notion of the subject as inherently possessor of itself, with an absolute right of disposal over itself. The implication is that there can be no limits to bodily conduct other than those chosen by the subject itself. Limits to bodily conduct are imposed by law in the interests of social policy objectives: one is prohibited from consuming opium or driving a motorcycle without a crash helmet, and one can be compelled to enter an isolation hospital if one has an infectious disease – the list can be extended considerably. In a socialist society such limits to conduct should not be reduced and prescriptive requirements about health and bodily skill ought to be considerably increased. For example, Chinese factories under self-management certainly have taken questions of fitness, occupational disease and so on very seriously, within the limits imposed by resources and technique, and workers have imposed norms of conduct on one another.

The danger in the derivation of 'rights' from some ontology of a constitutive and unitary subject is that the social relations in which they are to be realized become impossible. Persons, as social subjects, are the complex and differentiated terminals of distinct capacities and requirements imposed by rules of definition of states and acquired in social practices (see Adams and Minson, 1979, for an interesting discussion of this). The subject of 'right' is an originary and unitary entity: the 'rights' deriving from its ontological attributes are *unlimited* and also *unenforceable*; definite statutes will always make rights limited and conditional. Further, the problem with such ontologizations of 'right' is that they privilege a certain specific category of agents. A 'woman's right to choose' sounds unproblematic until one realizes that 'a husband's right to choose', 'a foetus's right to life', etc., can all be constructed by prioritizing different ontologies. A realm of absolute rights without contradiction supposes a realm of undifferentiated and equivalent subjects, but such ontologizations of 'right' are interventions in a complex field of differentiated subjects and agencies; they serve to privilege the claims of one such category of subjects. As such they are open to competing privilegings. Such categories of 'right' cannot assist in the resolution of complex questions of social policy.

The proprietal notion of 'right', as a possession of the subject, requires a unitary and centred subject as its support: a being present-to-itself, capable of 'possessing' itself and recognizing what is its own due. The notion of a *society* that does not constrain or limit the 'will' of this subject is possible only on condition that all subjects are identical, without differentiation of attributes and will, and by making the conditions of their interaction a matter of autonomous but mutual consent. This society of constitutive subjects is most clearly formulated in Rousseau's *The Social Contract* (1762). It may seem a long jump from the slogans of radical feminism to Rousseau, but the conception of 'rights' as absolute, as inherent to subjects, drives one towards the conception of the subject as an autonomous possessor-of-itself and to the general will as a condition of interaction of these subjects. Taking 'rights' seriously means taking the *fabliaux* of classical liberal–democratic political philosophy seriously.

If, on the contrary, 'rights' are conceived as nothing more than the specific capacities sanctioned by laws, then the discourse of unconditional claims becomes impossible. Legal rights reflect no inherent ontological attributes; rather, they serve certain socially determined policy objectives and interests. The rights sanctioned in law need not correspond to the forms of consistency demanded by an ontological doctrine of the subject; they have no inherent unity or a single point of reference. The composition of legislation can reflect distinct objectives and attempts to resolve competing claims. It is correct to argue that the composition of legislation must be discussed on grounds that go beyond the existing rules of law and that competing claims must be arbitrated between or reconciled. This becomes impossible when those claims are advanced in terms of absolute rights. The category of 'right', in any sense other than capacities sanctioned by law, generates difficulties in *any* legal system, as the example of the competing claims that can be advanced in questions of abortion shows. The fact that it generally involves reference to a concept of subject as inherently possessor-of-itself makes it radically incompatible with the objectives of socialist ideology. Those objectives involve the extension of the legal regulation of and practices of the social formation of individual human subjects.

ACKNOWLEDGEMENTS

I am grateful to Parveen Adams for first calling my attention to the Paton case, which she has discussed herself in *M/F* no. 3. This chapter is greatly influenced by seminar discussion; I am particularly indebted to Mark Cousins, Stephan Feuchtwang and Barry Hindess.

PART TWO

Contemporary Issues

CHAPTER 5

Men's Rea: A Note on Sexual Difference, Criminology and the Law

Mark Cousins

As a political force, feminism has always been engaged in struggles over the law. Precisely because it has not conceived the realization of its objectives as a matter for some future and decisive day, it has sought to transform laws in a detailed fashion. Particular forms of legislation have been demanded, and particular judgments denounced. The effects of laws have been monitored and assessed, and while the burden of this scrutiny has been to scorn the legalism of those who confuse enactment with effective provision, or who conflate provision with its current form of administration, there has rarely been a rejection of engagement with the law as such. It has been recognized that campaigns such as that to secure adequate provision of abortion or for equal pay entail an intimate concern with definite forms of legislation, struggles over the administrative means for its implementation, and a continuing political will to secure its enforcement.

This position may be contrasted decisively to a general approach to law, its enforcement and its transformation prevalent among sections of the Left. For if the law is conventionally designated in political argument as an instrument of class oppression or is the representation of commodity relations, it poses no proximate and general problems or possibilities. It is not that this position necessarily evacuates struggle over the question of law. Certain laws are strongly protested, others are suddenly supported at the prospect of their repeal. It is rather that a certain political distance from the question of law is maintained, and the question of legal reform is treated with a weary hauteur. A detailed support for particular legal reforms is tolerated at best as a benign and campaigning hobby, but one whose underside must be checked for signs of reformism or at least a confusion as to the proper objects of socialist politics. Hence the lack of socialist intervention in such matters as the proposals for the reform of company law or procedures of accountancy appears to many as self-explanatory. From this, feminism has sharply distinguished itself and as politics has counterposed the necessity of immediate engagement with problems of law.

Moreover, this political distinction has involved a practical distinction concerning law itself. Marxists frequently treat the law and the legal apparatuses as a homogeneous field, one that can be conceived as a general instance, operating in a unitary mode, singular in its source and punctual in its effects. It has frequently paid the law its full jurisprudential tribute, respecting it as a corpus lacking neither majesty nor rigour. But feminism has not, in general, treated law as this sovereign body. It has approached the law in different ways and with different objectives. The removal of civil disabilities, measures against forms of discrimination, and changes in family law have all required forms of political assessment and political argument that necessitate treating the law as a complex and divided field of intervention.

The question of conceptualizing the relations between sexual difference and the law might well be expected to have respected that political analysis, to have been wary of insisting upon a general and implacable relation. But it has frequently not done so. A number of texts have appeared which, if widely accepted, would make it increasingly difficult to articulate the political advantages of a position that refused to leave the law to its own devices, or to consider those devices all of a piece. And the plausibility of the position of texts may be enhanced for some by the fact that they proclaim themselves feminist; yet like many such events the invocation of a feminist sociology in fact entails the excursion of a humanist sociology rather than the incursion of a feminism.

Such enterprises usually begin by performing a general denunciation of sociology in general and a field of investigation in particular.

Criminology, or political economy or historical investigation is berated for having forgotten half of humanity. A proposal is then made to rectify this omission by remembering the other half. The objects of a conventional androcentric social science are to be gendered so that the startling oblivion into which half of humanity has been cast can be restored merely by the doubling of those objects. As a consequence a means is found for repeating the same sociology in the very moment that it is admonished. Remarkable and not very surprising consequences follow.

The text *Women, Crime and Criminology* (Smart, 1977) exemplifies this. It takes as its object female criminality while designating itself a critique. It does so upon the grounds that female criminality has been obscured, sometimes to the point of invisibility. So, from the first, female criminality as such is not itself questioned; indeed, it is retained as the necessary means for registering the mis-recognitions of female criminality that have threaded their way through criminology. To make such a critique, female criminality must stand outside the argument, real and waiting its analysis, waiting to be revealed and not obscured, waiting for the feminist research to disprove patriarchal ignorance. Yet it is an ironical homage to professional criminology that a critique that seeks to denounce it for its obfuscation of the question of women and crime should do so by repeating and respecting that traditional concept of criminology, criminality. At no point is the concept questioned as such, nor is its determination ascribed to criminology. It is merely repeated, for it is criminology's failure to deal with female criminality, not the concept of criminality, that is at fault. This position is required because of the grain of the argument. Presumably this androcentric criminology can correctly specify male criminality. In this way (and a similar movement of argument could be multiplied from various areas of research), in the name of analysing sexual difference, denunciation, followed swiftly by supplementation, protects rather than threatens conventional sociology.

For this text the sources of the occlusion of female criminality are twofold. First, there is traditional criminology – a series of texts that stretch from the nineteenth century to the present. This corpus itself observes female criminality in one of two ways: oblivion and error. Oblivion constitutes the charge that, like those other areas of research, criminology has left women out; that it has responded to oppression with amnesia; that what has been hidden from history is not likely to be found by the traditional historian. In sum, women constitute a great absence from the documented, the researched, and the surveyed syllabus of the visible. The charge of the blindness of criminology precisely follows the movement of denunciation and supplementation. It is at once a charge of oppression and incompetence, to be followed by projects of liberation and research.

But of course this oblivion is not held to exhaust criminology: what has not been ignored has been in error. In so far as female criminality has been addressed it has been with instruments of mis-recognition. The limitation of the majority of these studies arises as a result of a basic inadequacy in the perception of the nature of women and a reliance upon a determinant model of female behaviour. Such studies (cf. Lombroso and Ferrero, 1895; Cowie, Cowie and Slater, 1968) presume that an inherent and 'natural' distinction exists between the temperament, ability and conditionability of women and men, and recourse is made to the promise to explain female criminality (Smart, 1977, p. 176). It is thus alleged that from Lombroso onward criminology has assigned to women fixed physiological and psychological characteristics and that these characteristics are held to explain female criminality, in particular its rare and scandalous character. What is held to unify these series of texts is not that they conceive similar criminalities, nor that they concur in what its signs are, nor even how such signs might be deciphered. Rather, what is held to organize them into a unity, what absorbs their differences, is that they all rely upon one fundamental and enormous necessity: that it is possible to ascribe to women innate characteristics, and that these characteristics can be seen as the explanation of certain social phenomena, which can then be seen as their consequences. Such arguments are circular and reductionist; reductionist in that social phenomena are reduced to simple consequences of non-social phenomena; circular in that those non-social phenomena are not demonstrated but are arbitrarily deduced from social phenomena.

But what is strange is that these essentialisms, be they denounced as 'biologism' or 'psychologism', are confidently counterposed to a general category of the 'social'. The invocation of this category is considered sufficient to circumvent the reductionism and circularity of the explanations offered by Lombroso and his descendants. A 'social' explanation of female criminality can surely not be 'essentialist'? Yet one element of the essentialism of the contested arguments is that they all assume a unified object, in this case a population of women upon which a set of determinants can operate without demonstrating any mechanism by which this operation is affected, and without demonstrating a stable and uniform object upon which it is effected. It is this rather than the names of biology and psychology that lends weight to charges of essentialism. And it would be to demonstrate the avoidance of this in a 'social' explanation that would escape the charge of essentialism.

What this 'social' explanation is accounts for the second source of the masking of female criminality. It is indeed not solely criminology that has covered it over: it has already been obscured and distorted by the law and its administration. Law, legislation, adjudication, interpretation, the administration of trials, sentencing, the penal apparatuses, and the deployment of para-legal knowledges and practices – all work to fragment, divert and redirect female criminality in such a way that it is scarcely recognizable to a criminology, least of all to one already implicated in that process. This theme, although not formalized, is one that is required by the text by a condition that it has imposed upon itself. This is that in comparison with the treatment of male criminality a social process of discrimination against women is undertaken as an effect of partriarchal social relations in general.

This does not commit the text to argue that the discriminatory interventions all tend in one clear direction: on the contrary, they work in what appears to be different directions. But they are all systematic discriminations. On the one hand, girls are more likely to be cautioned than prosecuted when compared with boys; on the other hand, there will be a greater institutionalization of unconvicted girls in community homes. On the one hand, women are far less likely to be charged or convicted of certain offences than are men; on the other hand, women are more likely to have their crimes sexualized. But however the effects are differentiated they are all united by their relation to the common source of their distribution – patriarchal social relations. It is this that accounts for the reason why women are more likely to be placed in a mental hospital than thrown into prison, or, if they do go to prison, why it will be under a more medicalized regime than obtains in traditional forms of incarceration. And if there are more committed to prison it is more likely to be for shoplifting than for grievous bodily harm. Treated in one way or another, treated with relative leniency or with particular severity, the text requires that the mechanism that acts upon female criminality, and fragments it, is that of patriarchy.

It is this that dictates the confident jurisprudential axiom, 'Criminal laws, like civil laws, are man made in the interests of men in accordance with a paternalistic attitude towards women' (Smart, 1977, p. 8.). In local terms of the argument this proposition is brought to support the thesis of a female criminality distorted by patriarchal relations. Yet perversely this sets up male criminality as the norm by which reference is made to female criminality. For presumably patriarchal social relations permit male criminality to be adequately represented, even in court, whereas they dismember female criminality until it is lost to criminological observation, even to its most dilated pupils. What policy recommendations might be derived from all this is not clear, but it would be quite consistent with the argument to start transferring women from mental hospitals to prisons and to step up their prosecution.

But what far exceeds this local pattern is the axiom itself, that law is the law of patriarchy. Law grinds women and men rule the law. To such apodictic briskness it would perhaps be churlish to tack on exceptions – that perhaps others are ground or that perhaps sometimes no one is ground. And perhaps it would simply be quicker to suggest that the law as the instance of patriarchy is a paradox. For what would patriarchy be if it stood in absolute need of its regulation by the law? If the law of the Father braced the social into such a singular machine, why would it need to keep serving writs upon matter? What men would not be limited by a sovereign on another scene? For law is required to perform a definite task in producing patriarchal relations, or else it is merely the dumb repetition of these relations in general. If it is the latter then the law has no specific character; it is merely patriarchal violence upon stilts. If it is the former it remains to be demonstrated what its mode of operation is. Either way it essentializes the law, and in particular essentializes the relation between law and sexual difference by insisting that the relation is singular and operates within a homogeneous space.

It is this very characterization of the law and its effects that is the obstacle to the analysis of what can be loosely described as the relation between the law and women. Loosely described, that is, because it must be insisted that there is no singular, interior or essential relation between the law and women as such. It is the very concept of just such a relation that presents the analysis of the differentiated field of effects between the law and its objects, the things that appear before it, which is to say the things that appear within it. Those objects may also be organized by sexual difference and sometimes that sexual difference may be authorized and effective within the law. But there is no pre-given unity to such relations; they will be heterogeneous. The necessity of this heterogeneity can be bluntly stated to rest upon the fact that neither the category 'law' nor the category 'women' can be homogenized into unitary entities, capable of supporting a necessary and singular relation.

For, strangely, law defined as 'man made in the interests of men in accordance with a paternalistic attitude towards women' both essentializes the law and yet evaporates from it any specifically legal content. It assigns to it a function, that of realizing men's interests without any means for specifying what those interests are, how the law is to recognize them, or what are the means of realizing them. Doubtless this is because men 'know' what those interests are already and rule the law to secure them. But this is to confuse two quite different orders of specification. It may well be the case that legislatures and judiciaries are packed with men. It may well be the case that in sum the effects of legal regulation upon women can be held to have been both discriminatory and oppressive. It may well be that the sources of this will have included 'paternalistic attitudes'. Yet nothing licenses the stitching of these three propositions into the solitary truth of the law. For the propositions were drawn from a field of generalities that do not so much have to be contested as reminded that it is a field of a thousand other such generalities. But then it is an ingenuous compulsion of sociology to cast absurd truths from unexceptional commonplaces.

Only under definite theoretical conditions can the law be represented as a unitary entity. Certain forms of traditional jurisprudence can unify it as the expression of an unfolding rationality. Legal positivism could represent it through the unity of the command of a sovereign. Pashukanis could reply to this by making it the space of rights of the subject of possession. But each of these positions requires to be supported theoretically, and each of them will face analytic problems of where the boundaries of the unity lie, where law suddenly passes beyond itself. Each of them will draw the boundaries differently because their theoretical conditions differ. But in case of the assertion that law is man-made in the interests of men it cannot be stated what the theoretical conditions of the concept are, or how far the category of the legal is supposed to run, or how the law can be constrained to operate in this singular way. For presumably questions of commercial contracts or traffic offences are bracketed off as belonging to a realm of indeterminate indifference. But since no specification for this indifference would be given, the enterprise is circular. Law oppresses women and the rules of evidence for the proposition are contained within the proposition.

The second essentialization is of the categories 'women' and 'men'. This is ironic, since a major complaint against conventional sociology's conceptualization of sexual division is its recourse to elements of a natural division which is held to underpin a social division. In the discussion of female criminality traditional criminology is convicted of just such a lapse, of characterizing social relations by reference to some extra-social determinants, be they 'psychological', 'biological' or 'natural'. Against this is pitted the assertion that sexual division is the product of social relations and must therefore be accounted for at that level. But the project of a sociological explanation of sexual division is a paradoxical enterprise. On the one hand, the content of a sexual division is seen as an effect of social forces. Thus certain differential characteristics from levels of pay to crime rates are explained as the product of definite social practices. Yet, on the other hand, in such arguments the division itself, the fact of the division, always escapes, always appears to be beyond such explanation. And what was to have been an explanation of sexual division, which was restricted to its proper realm of social relations, turns out in fact to limit itself merely to offering explanations of particular contents of an always already existing sexual division, a division between men and women that then must predate its social existence. By men and women is meant here not a distribution of different anatomical and other characteristics between the population of humans, but that this distribution exists in a form capable of sustaining and indeed containing the principle of a 'division'. This principle must then be extra-social in the sense that it is a category that is assumed for the purposes of social analysis. Consequently the paradox of a call for the sociological explanation of sexual division is that, in order to support the concept of sexual division as such, its origin must be required to be prior to the forms of its social materialization.

Now this problem is insoluble only for as long as the pattern of the organization of sexual difference is posed in this way, in terms of sexual division. This is because the concept of division that is in play here is one that compels its terms to be mutually exclusive and jointly exhaustive. Men and women – the terms of sexual division – are being represented as different identities, and the difference must then refer to a difference anterior to whatever subsequent differences are added by the particular social relations. However sociological analysis chooses to fill out and detail those different identities, it cannot conceal that its argument requires that the origin and principle of that division is outside the social and must be so for social relations to be able to operate upon it as a stable entity. Thus a sociology of sexual division, of men and women, is logically compelled to promote a 'natural' difference to a discursive privilege. At the very moment that conventional sociology is denounced for this recourse, a variant of it is repeated. If that recourse is really to be avoided the concept of sexual division itself has to be displaced.

This can be illustrated by reference to the way in which much sociological writing proceeds as if what is referred to – men and women – is itself without any problems. In a conventional sense there is of course no difficulty. What is a problem however is when the terms 'men' and 'women' are used as definite categories within theoretical argument. There 'men' and 'women' are used as anchors for other categories such as 'male' and 'female', or even 'masculine' and 'feminine'. By this relay of connection it is finally required that the object of the analysis of the organization of sexual differences is persons – men and women. Thus discourses and practices are conceived ultimately as the way in which persons and things act upon other persons. It is thought that the entities 'men' and 'women' are possible objects of investigation for two reasons: they are human subjects in general, and in particular they share the characteristics of the entity to which they belong as a group. Things and persons can act upon them, and thus it appears plausible to speak of the action of men or law upon women. But once the pertinence of the centrality of persons is questioned, and once the category of sexual division itself has been displaced, this is no longer possible. There are no longer stable referents for the categories 'male' and 'female', 'masculine' and 'feminine'. They will be produced as definite forms of difference by the particular discourse and practices in which they appear.

In fact, the law provides a clear example of this, not only with regard to the categories 'men' and 'women' but to their parent, the person. This sanctuary of humanist sociology is crucially disrupted by the law, and cannot be made commensurate with legal personality. 'A person is such, not because he is human, but because rights and duties are ascribed to him. The person is the legal subject or substance of which rights and duties are attributes' (Pollock, 1961, pp. 61–2). Not all humans are necessarily legal persons, and not all legal persons are humans. Recently attention has been extended to the question of women at law in attempts to demonstrate the way in which women have been excluded from exercising certain rights or functions by means of excluding them from the cateogry of a 'legal person' (Sachs and Wilson, 1978). This has the advantage of drawing women and the law together in such a way as to avoid conceiving how one thing operates upon another, but rather of demonstrating how a discrimination is constructed. It demonstrates how judicial reasoning can determine a series of exclusions.

But a qualification must be entered with respect to this position. It can easily be made to appear as if men and women, that is persons, have their personalities recognized or denied by law: that what law does is to recognize or fail to recognize something that already exists. When the law fails to recognize a person as such or a person for particular purposes, then it can easily be assumed that this lack of legal personality is in fact in accord with a certain 'real' lack of personality, such as in a minor or lunatic, or that it is a failure of recognition, an unjustifiable exclusion. Thus a history of the exclusion of women from the status of 'person' in certain matters, and of the gradual 'reform' of the abuse, can appear as a moral critique of the functioning of judicial reasoning by reference to the simple truth that women were persons unjustly denied recognition.

The problem with this is that it assumes in common with a mass of jurisprudence and general theories of law that the process at stake is an act of recognition, the recognition of persons by the law. Thus a legal person is a subject to which are attached certain attributes which have been recognized in and by the law. This tends to support two related theories: first, that the personality that is recognized predated the act of recognition; second, that legal recognition is all of a piece – either you are recognized or you are excluded.

But legal personality is not so definitive as this; it is fragmentary. Obviously the women who were not persons for the purpose of taking a degree did not cease to be persons for other purposes. Nor was there a general exclusion of women from the term 'person' that would require, or could be repaired by, a singular reform. The Interpretation Act 1889 states clearly that 'unless the contrary intention appears . . . words importing the masculine gender shall include females'. And this was not a reform. Nor are the fragments of legal personality capable of being summed into a fully recognized person. It is not just a question of arguing that non-humans may be legal persons, though this is the case; it is rather that elements of legal personality do not exactly attach themselves to persons in the conventional sense at all, but rather to certain statuses which are supported by persons. Such might be 'husband' or 'wife', 'father' and 'mother'. And before it is objected that these titles are merely specialized functions of men and women, it is important to recognize that the categories can include 'spouse' or 'parent'. These statuses indicate a collection of rights and duties in respect of legal status of marriage and parenthood.

The heterogeneous collection of statuses and capacities in law, which mostly seem to bear upon the organization of sexual differences, cannot be made commensurate with the categories 'men' and 'women'. For men and women (persons) do not simply take on legal subjectivity as a rite of recognition from the law. If legal personality is not of a piece, and moreover if it is comprised of differentiated elements in respect to the type of legal action, then it is not a ticket that permits the holder to walk in and out of legal actions as a member of humanity at law. Rather, it is that law designates in particular actions what forms of legal personality are appropriate for joining or being joined in particular actions. What is important is what form of agency the law recognizes/constitutes as the appropriate subject. Sometimes this can be a person, a man or a woman as defendant, or plaintiff; sometimes it might be a man as father or a woman as mother; sometimes it might be a man or a woman as representative, agent or servant of a corporate body; sometimes it might be a female employee as in an action concerning equal pay; and it may of course be a woman who hails and prosecutes her subjects. But the point is that the materiality of these legal categories, of the distribution of types of agent that appear within the law, cannot be made reducible to men or women and their attributes.

This has important consequences for the way in which law sets terms for both analysis and for political evaluation of legal transformation. For it is not a question of registering what men or their law do to women, and therefore there cannot be any simple calculation of interests and the legal instruments needed for realizing them. It is a question of analysing what effects the law and the agents that appear within it have upon the organization of sexual difference, and of evaluating what legal reforms are necessary conditions for its transformation.

Such a position permits the political analysis of legal forms and of proposals for their change. This political analysis is always required by the very nature of political objectives. For the latter are never in principle capable of being realized outside the reformulation of definite forms of social agent. In particular, political objectives are not capable of being realized under the spacious rubric of the abolition or provision of general states of affairs, be they posed in liberal–constitutionalist notions of liberty and equality or in revolutionary–utopian doctrines of 'real' freedom. Political objectives will always require definite mechanisms for their realization, and those mechanisms must be capable of clear definition and must include the capacity to exclude other mechanisms.

With respect to sexual difference and the law, it means that analysis must engage with the law at a level that forswears the reductionist moralism of charging it with its past and present 'unfairness' (for this is hardly in doubt). It must analyse how particular legal forms of agency are more or less implicated in the organization of sexual difference and what effect they have upon that organization. After all, if what the law had done was to enforce a sexual division which persecuted women to the advantage of men, the implied political objective would be the rigorous elimination of all legal representations of sexual difference and a ruthless policing of agencies of legal enforcement in order to eradicate differential treatment.

That the relation between political objectives and forms of agency that are in part determined by the law is more various and complicated is supported by a current proposal. The Law Commission's *Report on Illegitimacy* (HMSO, 1979) argues that, since one-parent families remain 'a major social problem', the category of 'illegitimacy' can only exacerbate it. It therefore proposes that the distinction between legitimacy and illegitimacy should be discarded, and it details the legal consequences of this in the fields of guardianship, custody, inheritance, nationality and the establishment of paternity. In addition, it deals with the special questions of paternity of those children conceived by artificial insemination. But a report that is supposedly concerned with the problems relating to the illegitimate child is, it turns out, mainly concerned to establish a battery of new rights – for the father. 'From a strictly legal point of view, the father of an illegitimate child is today probably at a greater disadvantage than the child itself' (*ibid.* pp. 2, 11). Now it may be that the members of the working party judge the position of such a father to be disadvantaged, but from the 'strictly legal point of view' it is nothing of the sort. Fathers of illegitimate children simply do not have the legal rights of fathers of legitimate children. Strictly, it depends upon what point of view is upheld as to whether this counts as being disadvantaged. And yet the whole report is conducted as though the only effective way to abolish illegitimacy is to create a set of rights for fathers of children born out of wedlock. 'We tentatively favour the principle that the status of illegitimacy should be abolished and that the law hitherto applicable to legitimate children should apply to all children without distinction. No attempt should be made by statute to exclude any class of father from automatic entitlement to parental rights' (*ibid*. p. 14a).

What the report does, across a wide range of issues in family law and law of inheritance, is to abolish illegitimacy by drawing over all human reproduction, including artificial insemination, the general legal condition of wedlock. All forms of parenthood are to be treated as a variant of parenthood within marriage. In this way is the father brought back into all parenthood, with all his rights. Of course the report admits that this causes many problems but its commitment to the principle and its consequences is clear. Parenthood at law would be more closely bound to the rights and responsibilities of married parents, right down to its inevitable problem of the proper surname.

Others have pointed out the dangers of the proposals. But with respect to the arguments advanced in this paper two points can be made. The first is that, although it can easily be advanced as a legal proposal that could be oppressive to women, the assessment of that effect is made by tracing out the consequences of a change in the status of certain forms of parenthood that would be attendant upon altering the status of certain classes of fatherhood. What is at stake politically is a politics that advocates the possibility of different forms of parenthood as against the attempt to generalize the conjugal family as the sole legal model of parental rights and duties. The second point to be noticed is that the report is able to ally its proposals to a certain discourse upon equal rights. Certain classes of father are 'obviously' disadvantaged by having no rights. The problem with such a discourse in general is that it is remarkable both for its popular hold and for its polyvalence. At the very least it demonstrates the capacity for almost any legal change to be effected on the grounds that a right is in need of being recognized. Political opposition to the proposals is thus constrained by the fact that on the field of argument the space of 'rights' has already been partly occupied.

The report provides eccentric illumination of the problems of specifying the relation between sexual difference and legal regulation. It is concerned with the rectification of an 'inequality' between the sexes. It is concerned with the balancing of rights. And in the name of rights and equality it can propose the extension of one legal form and parenthood in such a way that certain current forms of single parenthood are threatened. This demonstrates that the problem of rights and equalities cannot be posed in an abstract and general way, for the reason that they will always appear within the frame of definite legal forms of agency and status. It is thus to those forms that both political analysis and the formation of objectives must be directed.

CHAPTER 6

Questions of Violence in Party Political Criminology

Frank Burton

Introduction: Eclecticism and Deconstruction

The ubiquitous experience of sadism and masochism informs us that the neurophysical and biochemical calculus of pain is one of avoidance and celebration. To premise explanations of the fear and pleasure of violence at the level of the economy of biological materialism is apparently to ground the subject of non-accidental pain in the discourses of bodily sensation. Violence in this familiar space is feared and revered because of its bodily effects; it is a means to a desired end. What could be more obvious: violence and the fear of violence causes pain, and pain, when not the desired end (revenge, retribution, atonement, pleasure, salvation . . .), makes possible other ends (submission, exchange, abolition, obedience . . .). But already, as the utilitarians calculated, and psychoanalysis emphasized, the discourse of bodily sensations has slipped into that of social relations. The mechanics of pain are not invoked in isolation from the social forms and functions of non-accidental pain. The logic of social relations infuses the logic of biology. The discourse's apparent innocent origin in physiology is read through a particular category of social stimulation. The immediate lesson: the intellectually deadening ease through which levels of knowing can be run together is the basis of eclecticism. And the study of violence is the study also of eclecticist

123

claims to knowledge. Eclecticism is one empiricist strategy that attempts to save the phenomenon. It does so by collating and conflating disparate discourses and the objects they realize into a given familiar, often commonsensical, rubric: 'crime', 'violence', 'terrorism'. These categories of ordinary language establish the license that eclectic empiricism thrives on. They are indeterminate and permissive categories whose very vacuity creates a space into which many discourses find their point of entry.

'Violence' is a particularly extravagant illustration of the indeterminacy of an empiricist category. The apparency of its object imbues the intellectual concerns of many disciplines: theology, anthropology, philosophy, sociology, psychology, ethology, psychiatry, medicine, law, international relations, history . . . In either isolation or conjunction these knowledges produce disparate objects of violence with variant effects and possible technologies. They generate a plethora of typologies, a multitude of themes and theories, a catalogue of programmes that constitute the raw materials, the discursive conditions of existence, for official policies on the containment and release of 'violence'. The complex patterning that this kaleidoscopic process of incorporation creates also renews the common-sense categories of ideology that define violence. Theoretical work attempts to analyse the formation of materialized discourses that realize the social technologies of control. To deconstruct the applied eclecticist effect upon knowledge is to raise also the possibilities of intervention into practices by theorizing forms of realignment desirable within theoretico-political conditions. The mechanisms of intervention promised by the tentative claims of 'genealogical' histories of the present remain, however, unspecified. The strategic possibilities that might emerge from deconstruction are obviously matters of political calculation. Reconstruction will be informed through strategies that can be theoretically justified as avenues to desired political ends. The appraisal of, and intervention into, current practices will necessarily be from another discursive place. In socialist discourse, and in matters of crime and law, what this place is and what the interventions should be are questions still remarkably untheorized within the metaphor of 'calculation'.

This essay sketches some of the dominant intellectual discussions of violence and then examines how these discourses (from philosophy, biology, etc.) are re-worked in party political criminology. The ultimate aim is to raise questions about their discursive realignment in public discourses on criminal violence.

Suspended then will be the desire to adjudicate between disciplines that speak of violence, to establish a hierarchy of coherence between them in terms of theoretical rigour or consistency. Suspended also will be the temptation to reject the study of violence as an impossible object. The purpose is to assess the effect of this licence in forming and reproducing technologies of violence. Yet, though the inquiry will refrain from celebrating classifications of forms of violence, and seek instead to investigate their forms of combination, it does not claim to specify the determinative mode through which plural, fragmented, partial and discontinuous discourses realize specific sets of administrative practices. This inability to reveal the discursive regularities and strategic coherences of contemporary criminological technologies points to the difficulty of deconstructing current practices. Those who speak of writing a genealogical history that opens up the formation of the present have yet to specify those con-temporary regularities that produce a mode of intervention into current practices. Historical archaeology, revealing as it is, has an absence in its own texts, an absence of a politics outside of an ambiguous programme that seems to both denigrate and elevate possibilities of reforms. As soon as analysis 'steps out' of history, out of the domain of relatively formed discourses, strategies and alliances and into present sets of technologies, the politics of contradiction become indeterminate. For the present is partly ongoing, partly cons-tructed by fragmented discourses that are barely intelligible, hardly formed, yet effective in unspecified ways. A political ideology will have difficulty in calculating intervention when its opposing object shows signs of continual indeterminacy and flux. One can speak of discursive strategies and alliances, points of entry and effect, moments of realignment and traversion more easily (and it is never easy) when the object is the discursive débris of past practices. But what of con-temporary criminological discourses and practices?

We learn from the histories of social administration to be sceptical of the rhetorics of humanist reform, to recognize that a change in technique is a modification to the disciplines of control. We learn that the policies realized are formations that are not reducible to the intellectual disciplines they draw upon. The limits of theory (and the strengths of empiricism) are embedded in materialized discourses that scoff at authorial intention. These reservations are kept in mind when matters of calculated intervention into contemporary practices and discourses are raised. But generalized orientations produce no political details. Genealogical analysis pales into an empty rhetoric when it dares to speak of the present, echoing only the promises of all other programmatic politics that fail to theorize the limits of theory. Perhaps there is no necessary political position, pessimistic or optimistic, derivable from archival description. In this non-determinate space political calculation will have to live with the contradictions of reform and produce a hierarchy of potentially progressive policies. The paradox of archival analysis is that, on the one hand, it optimistically emasculates those teleologies of power that put the present beyond reach and produce gestural politics. Yet, on the other, it demonstrates that power is a micro-physics that leaves no social relation unmarked. One can read off elements of a progressive or regressive politics; the analysis makes neither necessary. Nor does it articulate a mode of intervention. Politics is precisely the recognition of this contradiction.

The deconstruction of conventional wisdoms and the elaboration of their technical effects as power relations produces no guarantees in the field of political calculation. Criticism of leftist political culture (Donzelot, 1979) does not *ipso facto* produce a calculus of intervention. This non-correspondence between archival knowledge and political practice might also be the source of the gap between an elevated programme and its path of construction. How many texts end with exhortations about democratization of penal administration, decarceration and decriminalization, and community and workers' control) that are not immediately deducible from the presented analyses!

These problems are raised even in the most cursory investigation into the disciplines that speak of violence. Violence is a metaphor that resonates within a plurality of knowledges. The object of criminology's 'violence' is an interdiscursive site where several of these knowledges meet to be transformed. The criminal justice system materializes these discursive relations in technical policies. This paper is an excursion into some of the discursive conditions of existence of the contemporary criminology of violence together with an example of how this already refracted discourse is reworked again in party political pamphlets that seek to reform the technologies of the penal system. Finally, the paper attempts to raise problems about how best to intervene in public discourses on violent crime.

THE CRIMINOLOGICAL OBJECT OF VIOLENCE

Violence has frequently been the point of refutation or evaluation of criminological analysis. In those hopelessly ambitious crusades to theorize all those behavioural categories designated by the legalistic concept 'crime', violent crime has been something of an acid test. It forced marginal utility theory into the uncomfortable arena of psychic desire. Socialization and subcultural perspectives normalized it beyond recognition. Neuro- and psycho-pathology seemed to locate an insignificant residuum that only a strict nominalist could call crime. Subjectivist and naturalist appreciation left it silently uncelebrated. Critical criminology remained optimistically committed to its evaporation after the dictatorship of the proletariat and found the phenomenon of restricted short-term relevance. In Eastern Europe's 'socialist criminology' it is reduced to an ideological survival explicable in terms of a capitalist cultural lag (Bucholz *et al.* 1974). But, whatever the conceptual and methodological incoherencies in these grandiose etiological schemes, applied criminology has shared in the triumph of the administrative control and institutional containment of forms of violence. In that prolonged and detailed process of the politicization of the social and the statization of the civil through which many forms of violence are subjected to many forms of discipline, the creation of a criminology has helped sustain the management of the residuum. The welfare complex establishes acceptable norms of violence (in work, in domesticity, in popular culture) through the socialization to a legitimate order that is orchestrated by a balance of coercive and supportive policies. In its positivity subjects are held in order through a structure of rewards that found a stake in the social: the promise or reality of security, consumerism and off-spring mobility. In its negativity subjects are held in order through the disciplines of work/unemployment, the structure of indebtedness, and the orthodoxy of normative respectability. The primary institutions of the welfare complex create the power of the disciplinary norm. The secondary institutions of welfare are concerned to police the deviations from this norm and represent a domain of practices where social administration meets the criminal justice system. Criminology is concerned with the efficiency of controlling the minimal residuum that respond with perversity to normal modes of discipline in the family, school, work and community. Conceptions of 'efficiency' and 'control' are created in the changing specifics of criminological discourse.

Criminology, though articulated upon the triumph of administrative society, always appears in crisis as it strives to manage the marginalized failures of that triumph. Delinquent policy is an object of overt coercion, the exception that shows the rule of normalized discipline. Yet if the containment of the marginalized, de-politicized exception celebrates the micro-physics of power that Foucault (1978a) calls the carceral society, delinquency also reverberates as a threat. The ideology of penology resurrects the pre-triumphal era: it addresses the threat of an extensive criminality that problematizes social relations. And it is here that violence is the most eloquent of metaphors that signify ruptured social relations. Violence points to the space that administrative society has not succeeded in completely colonizing. In ideology this metaphoric site can set in motion chains of signification that connote a pre-social barbarity, escalations of vengeance and arbitrary physical force. Criminological discourse echoes the arguments of fear found in the liberal paradigms of political philosophy, which situate violence as a natural pre-sociality. The ontological implications of the argument are increasingly justified through a socio-biology and ethology that psychologize violence. Alternative paradigms (of an existential humanism and a sociology of violence) are also creatively re-worked into criminology, which is shamelessly eclectic in its mobilization of the human sciences in the formation of its object (c.f. Wolfgang and Ferracuti, 1967). Selections from this discursive universe that provide the criminology of violence with its raw materials will be briefly outlined.

DISCURSIVE ELEMENTS OF 'CRIMINOLOGY'S' VIOLENCE

Political and Moral Philosophy

Recent philosophical addresses to violence, principally from within variants of humanism, construct a reading subject weighted with the gravity of reality. The discourses appeal to the histories of Auschwitz, Hiroshima or My Lai. These realities of war, genocide, torture and possible global destruction create the effect that philosophical deliberations have serious intentions of appropriating the real in thought. For Arendt (1969) such litanies of carnage are both the source of the great legitimating force of violence and the representations of a massive intrusion of criminal violence into politics. Violence is *defined* as normal, undesirable and anti-political. Leftist teleologies of power, the saturated bureaucratization of political life, and the fraternal bonding of collective violence make future violence, more, not less, likely. For Arendt violence is part of the human condition but not a part to be revered as in the creative metaphors of Nietzsche. Violence is the enemy of political action; it is force without authority, coercion without power. It is increasingly physically instrumental and decreasingly dependent on support. It is, however, effective only in the short term and for specific reforms. The prolonged imposition of will without authoritative submission is fundamentally apolitical. The corollary is that all limitations on power (the concerted actions of groups) are invitations to violence. Arendt attacks the triumph of technicist politics which inhibit democratic accountability. At the same time she rejects leftist positions that, in embracing the ambiguity of insurrectionist politics, fail to theorize the antithesis of violence to power.

Arendt's non-optimistic advocacy of a political culture that realizes man's will to act, to power, to submission, remains a politics of critical humanism. Violence is theorized as a result of an unbalanced amalgam of state, will and power; reduced, despite the appeal to the real, to a-contextual moral universals. Nevertheless, such critical questioning of democratic pluralism has not gone unmarked within contemporary strategies of reform.

More radical are forms of humanism that indict liberalism for the humanism of its discourse and the structured violence of its practice. This politics of irony, which echoes within many critiques of official, institutional violence, is locked into the same imaginary space as the discourses of legitimacy it seeks to unseat. Most eloquent is Merleau-Ponty (1969) in his defence of the possibilities of a socialist humanism through revolutionary violence. Proletarian violence is justified if it is a violence 'which recedes with the approach of man's future' (Merleau-Ponty, 1969, p. xvii). In 1947 Merleau-Ponty answered Koestler's *Darkness at Noon* with an attack on liberal democratic violence and a still fraternal critique of Soviet Russia. 'It is impossible to be anti-Communist and it is not possible to be a Communist' (1969, p. xxi) because, while the communist critique of capitalism holds, communist practice seems to be moving away from the humanist intentions of marxism (classlessness, warlessness, freedom from decadence) to the violence of cunning politics. The dilemma of violence is that it is constitutive of decision and action; to choose is to prefer degrees and forms of violence:

> The Revolution takes on and directs a violence which bourgeois society tolerates in unemployment and in war and disguises it with the name of misfortune. But successful revolutions taken altogether have not spilled as much blood as empires. All we know is different kinds of violence and we ought to prefer revolutionary violence because it has a future of humanism. [Merleau-Ponty, 1969, p. 107].

On the same terrain as Arendt, we have here a modification only of the advocacy drawn from moralistic humanism. Ontologically condemned to violence: 'Life, discussion and political choice occur only against a background of violence' (1969, p. 109), Merleau-Ponty, with an earnestness never in doubt, surveys communist and liberal ethics to speak out against one-sided cold war evaluations. The specifics of his judgement is a comparative ethical analysis where capitalist institutional violence is balanced against the historical context of the party purges. Both are measured against a scale of actual and potential humanism. This now familiar mode of argument: 'violence as in the liberal state may be put outside the law and in effect suppressed in the commerce of ideas though maintained in daily life in the form of colonialisation, unemployment and wages' (1969, p. 163) – complete with all the conflations that produce a social theory through a universal ethics – reverberates through many of the paradigms of critique, including radical criminology.

Merleau-Ponty's qualifications of the necessity of violence in creating universal humanism are less cautiously expounded within the works of those writers most nearly associated with a political philosophy of violence: Sorel, Sartre, Fanon, Merleau-Ponty fears the contingency of history that denies guarantees to politics. Sorel (1941) rejoices in the hope of a spontaneous violence that will forge a proletarian epic. Workerist violence restores to a decadent bourgeoisie its former entrepreneurial vigour and aggression. Syndicalism is the energizing mythology that motivates the proletariat into a pure and brutal class war. Thus do the two great classes with their instinctual antagonisms aroused play out a sublime, heroic and immortal struggle. This same violence creates an ethic of the producer, a soldier–worker sustaining an eagerness to make a new civilization, and a free worker wanting to raise the levels of industrial output. Violence is a value, a form of Bergson's integral experience, an *élan vital* that purges the proletariat of parliamentary cretinism and dispels the prejudices of philosophy that equate force with barbarism. It is in the general strike that violence realizes the historical mission of the proletariat:

> Strikes have engendered in the proletariat the noblest, deepest and most moving sentiments that they possess, the general strike groups them all in a co-ordinated picture, and, by bringing them together, gives to each one of them its maximum of intensity; appealing to their painful memories of particular conflicts, it colours with an intense life all the details of the composition presented to consciousness. [Sorel, 1941, p. 137]

The mythology of the general strike activates worker solidarity, which is then gelled through the experience of collective violence. Mythology frees the imagination in a way that the more rationalist alternatives to transition through worker discipline and factory democracy cannot.

Sorel's *Iliad* is a fantastic narrative that draws on the metaphors of Nietzsche's master values, Bergson's integral experience and a romantic and utopianized marxism. Violence is a salvation, a purgative, a source of creative energy whose value has been denigrated by 'cleverness, social science and high flown statements' which associate it with barbarity:

> Proletarian violence not only makes the future revolution certain, but it seems also to be the only means by which the European nations – at present stupefied by humanitarianism – can recover their former energy . . . It is to violence that socialism owes those high ethical values by means of which it brings *salvation* to the modern world. [Sorel, 1941, pp. 90, 295]

These are the dominant paradigms in a text that is also a remarkable monument to ill-tempered political chatter and *ad hominem* attacks on parliamentary opponents managed through a syntax of discursive violence. Excesses, absurdities and incoherences aside, the signifiers of catharsis, bonding and transcendence have cut out a space for themselves in the languages of violence.

For Sartre, Sorel's 'fascist utterances' are of a separate order to the political questions that Fanon raises in *The Wretched of the Earth* (1967) and which he himself discusses in the famous preface. But Sartre's indictment of colonialization and Western liberalism and his support for the militarization of national liberation struggles is partly based, as is Fanon's, on the mythology of catharsis. The fracturing of colonial domination at the level of subjectivity is achieved in violence simultaneously with territorial liberation:

no gentleness can efface the marks of violence only violence itself can destroy them ... in the first few days of the revolt you must kill: to shoot down a European is to kill two birds with one stone, to destroy an oppressor and the man he oppresses at the same time; there remains a dead man, and a free man; the survivor, for the first time feels a *national* soil under his feet. [Fanon, 1967, pp. 18–19]

The jerky Sorelian prose is replaced with a relentless, controlled and incisive anger: violence restores a humanity to the degraded colons by substituting group cohesion for serial oppression. The constitutive retreat from freedom is temporarily assuaged. Sartre's ontology and social theory orders his polemic.

Fanon does something more than condemn colonial terror and torture, than mock liberalism's rhetoric, than rewrite another variant of a philosophical anthropology. It is true that his work is imbricated in a political and moral *philosophy*:

At the level of individuals violence is a cleansing force. It frees the native from his inferiority complex and from his despair and inaction; it makes him fearless and restores his self-respect. Even if the armed struggle has been symbolic and the nation is demobilised through a rapid movement of decolonialisation, the people have the time to see that liberation has been the business of each and all and that the leader has no special merit. [Fanon, 1967, p. 74]

But his reflections, through clinical case studies, on the relationship between psychiatry and criminology go beyond the desires of critical humanism. He examines the connection between colonial domination, generalized criminality (Algerian on Algerian) and mental disorders precipitated by the war. Here his discussion of violence is specific and he draws from psychoanlysis a repudiation of a psychiatry that essentializes the Algerian 'propensity' for violence, both criminal and political. He attempts to describe the manner in which psycho-pathological processes are structured within the socio-pathology of colonialized existence. He rejects a colonial psychiatry that attributes a semiology of Algerian criminality – the Algerian is a frequent, savage and irrational killer; he is predatory, aggressive, congenitally compulsive, melancholically homicidal; his superior and cortical activities are only slightly developed .. – to an etiology of psychic primitivism. His double rejection takes the form of articulating the social pathology of everyday life (for the masses enduring colonial repression) with a descriptive psycho-pathology that reveals the effects of violence on the mentality of tortured and torturer, victim and perpetrator. These notes temper the cathartic role of gratuitous, spontaneous and personalized violence and emphasize a socialized, revolutionary and disciplined form of party-controlled violence. But perhaps, more significantly, Fanon here confronts the pathological effects of violence while refusing to psychologize their origins. In facing this contradiction of the politics of violence he begins to question those facile conceptions of subjectivity implicit in humanist philosophy. This is a significant departure. Fanon's text touches discourses that are to be increasingly invoked by counter-insurgency: the discourses of criminality and psycho-pathology. Fanon's discursive effects are more normally traced within works that extend his analysis of the lumpenproletariat to the position of black Americans, but Fanon the psychiatrist also extends the discourses of politicized violence into the positivist knowledges of conventional social control. He takes his modified humanism into colonial criminology and begins to rewrite its conception of subjectivity.

Within these writers' texts can be found some of the more significant fragments that constitute the conventional wisdoms of the political philosophy of violence. They are predominantly moral critiques of political relations that inhibit, suppress or exterminate the conceptions of humanity inscribed in liberal theory: cold war discourses comparing the structures of official violence, national liberation arguments on the strategic necessity of armed resistance, tracts on the cogency of internal resistance through protest or terror. The authors' deliberations bristle with the argument, rhetoric and polemic that permeates the culture of 'progressive' thought: ideas of legalized, official, institutional violence (the wage, poverty, the criminal justice system), the suppression of substantive democracy through the technological *a priori* of bureaucratism, the violence of liberal humanist thought that eclipses reason, the determinism of historicism and positivism that free action from responsibility. These languages will find themselves selectively, partially and ironically re-worked in official, party political and other public discourses that incorporate and institutionalize intellectual productions. In the process of discursive slippage some of the rhetoric will be diluted, some of the 'excesses' will be pared and some of the omissions will be significant. But whatever form the contours of the discontinuity of authorial intentions take, public discourses, via perhaps the secondary texts of criminology, will install their own critiques of technical bureaucratism, structural violence and

lack of participatory democracy. The refinement of reform programmes has a moment in its logic whereby the critical edge of dissent is
discursively incorporated – or discursively abolished.

Variants of the Life Sciences: Biology and Psychology

The political philosophy of violence resonates *la grande peur* that civil
and international war threaten. In the quest for the origins of the
apparent universality of collective violence many explanations of
politics are reduced to a humanist ontology. Man's 'condition' is inscribed, in its negativity, in a will to power, a flight from freedom, a
'struggle over scarcity'; in its positivity, man is the creator, reasoner or
zoon politikon. These pre-given essentialisms make social conflict
either inevitable, or desirable, or pathological or eradicable, and
always the unitary effects of an original cause. Whatever the
particularities of humanist ontologies, they reduce politics to a drama
of critique, exhortation and condemnation that necessarily reflects the
protocols of their anthropologies. This closure of humanist reasoning
creates the possibility that the life sciences might produce a knowledge
that will create a hierarchy of credible moral universals. Into this
tautology is inserted one of the promises of biologism: that it can
puncture the philosophical universals to install a new set of scientific
ontologies. In particular, it is progressive humanism that is more frequently called into question by the discursive fracturing effected by
biologism.

Violence in biological materialism is grounded in the subjectively
recognizable phenomenology of anger, rage and frustration. The
empirical physiology of arousal – the acceleration of pulse rate and
rise in blood pressure, the increase in blood glucose, pupil dilation,
sweating, diminution of sensory perception allowing an increasing
tolerance of pain – is now more precisely redescribed in the language
of neurophysiology and biochemistry. The exact theoretical calculus
of the excitatory and inhibitory mechanism of the neo-cortex and
limbic system and their effects on visceral and other chemical
homeostasis remains unwritten. But the complex detail of both
medical and experimental knowledge has already produced a confident technology of intervention. Artificial electrical stimulation of the
hypothalamus and amygdala can induce rage; manipulation of other
parts of the limbic system results in pleasurable sensations. Removal
of part of the amygdala (stereotaxic amygdalectomy), hypothalamus,

cingulate gyri, thalamus or temporal lobectomy, lobotomy or frontal tracotomy can reduce levels of behavioural rage and aggression. Similarly, iatrogenic manipulation of endocrinological reactions associated with aggressive behaviour, particularly with the male hormones (androgens), can affect the desire and capacity to partake in aggressive and/or sexual behaviours (Laborit, 1978; Elliot, 1978).

Psycho-surgery and drug treatment are the applied medical knowledges for pathological conditions. The continued refinement of medical diagnoses and 'cures' is the source of a constant intrusion into criminal discourses on violence. The variety of pathologically aggressive subjects created by brain lesions owing to traumas, infections and congenitality or those caused by endocrinological or metabolic imbalances have established a crucial significance within criminology. This is so despite their empirical insignificance, and it is a triumph of the essentially nominalist conflation of behavioural into legal and medical categories. The violence of the pathological subject is elevated to a position of discursive privilege within many of the criminological anthologies of violence. The resulting medicalization of penal programmes has now reached a stage where an agreement to an implantation of the drug Oestradiol can avert a prison sentence for a persistent paedophiliac (*The Guardian*, 25 May 1979).

As well as having specific effects at the level of the pathological subject, biology is constantly present in theorizations of subjectivity that seek to adjudicate between a given individuality and an acquired sociality. The biological capacity for agonistic behaviour is, for example, made the point of departure for tracts on the inevitability of 'aggression and violence', 'rage and frustration', 'anger and hatred'. In ethological accounts animal sociality is the result of the functionalism of agonistic relations. In the paradigms of socio-biology the reading subject is invited to collude in the possibility that the engaging details presented represent a natural sociality. Close to nature, but in 'society', the mechanisms of intra-species aggression are normalized into teleologies of bonding, ecological spacing, adventitious sexual selection and orderly status hierarchies. Moreover, aggressive violence attributable to territorial distributions, status realignments or sexual competition frequently *appears* cultural because of the ritualized submission signalling that imposes limits on injury within conflict. Behavioural psychology's effect on ethology has been to demonstrate that certain learning practices (maternal care, group discipline, experiences of combat) have a significant determination in mobilizing instinctual aggression. Thus ethology with its apparent normativity is more easily elided into the socio-biology of human societies via its popularizers – Ardrey, Morris, Lorenz. One recent re-working of ethology into contemporary criminology has been through the concept of 'defensible space' (Newman, 1973). Animal ecology thus adds its weight to the universal condemnations of postwar, high-rise public housing. Notwithstanding the disclaimers of ethologists that the facile conflation of ethology into sociology be resisted, public discussions on property violence frequently show the marks of such an interdiscursive alignment (Clarke, 1978; Maymen *et al.*, 1978).

Ethology's effect is achieved through the silencing of the symbolic, language and ideology; its normativity is purely gestural, the direct result of a biological agency. In psychoanalysis the relation between the coercion of biology and the coercion of the symbolic has been the specific object of inquiry. Freud's speculative biology led him to a self-consciously tentative assertion ('What follows is speculation, often far-fetched speculation ... a fantastic hypothesis'; Freud, 1955, p. 24) that a death instinct might exist. Its end would be to inhibit all excitation towards the ultimate inertia of an inorganic state. Beyond the sexual instincts that result in drives for pleasurable satisfaction, beyond the partially libidinized ego-instincts that seek the reality of self-preservation, might lie a further force of a desire for the inert quiescence that the inanimate brings. Continuing to play the 'advocatus diaboli', Freud posited that: 'sadism is in fact a death instinct which under the influence of the narcissistic libido, has been forced away from the ego and has consequently only emerged in relation to the object' (Freud, 1955, p. 54). Non-pathological aggression and violence are constitutive of the antagonism of the dual instincts. Many variants have been re-worked.

For Lacan (1977), aggression is the correlative tendency of the narcissistic structure of the formation of subjectivity. Aggressive competition emerges from the contradictions established in the mirror-stage when the subject forms an ideal image of its own body. In the next phase of development the child erotically fixes his self on this ideal image that awakes in him an internal tension for a desire of the impossible object of the Other that is him and is not him. This rivalry with an alienated, impossible self is sublimated in the oedipal complex via a rivalry with the identification of the imago of the parent of the same sex. The entry into the symbolic partially transcends primary narcissism and aggressivity by giving the subject an I, an ego. The subjugation of the subject into culture is only ever partial in the sense that the narcissistic moment and aggressive tensions appear in all the genetic phases of the individual. It was Freud's 'audacity' to portray the paranoiac structure of the self through the metaphor of the death instinct. Both, however, would seem agreed on the impossible conception of an altruistic self being inserted into the ontologies of moral and political philosophy.

Re-worked into a criminological ego-psychology, the homicide/ suicide becomes an actualization of the death-instinct. Modified by the frustration/aggression hypothesis and fleshed out with the differential psychology of the violent offender, criminology has sustained an almost perfect fit between criminal violence and personal psycho-pathology:

> From the Rorschach test studies of the murderer, especially when compared with normal subjects, emerges a personality characterised by egocentrism and a lack of emotional control. He can also be described as an explosive, immature, hyperthymic person who is unable to establish social contact. He displays a deficit of conscious control and a strong need for the immediate gratification of impulses. [Wolfgang and Ferracuti, 1967, p. 217]

> [an] emotionally shallow and highly suggestible personality who appears narcissistic, immature, impulsive, socially retarded and whose general behaviour, when faced with tension, stress or frustration, is very unpredictable. [Perdue, 1964]

Thus, social psychology is able to link relative deprivation to frustration and aggression via a learning theory of socialization. The final ensemble makes possible the presentation of the ecological and cultural transmission of deviant psychologies through the pathological normative structures of criminal areas.

PUBLIC DISCOURSES ON CRIMINAL VIOLENCE

The first part of this chapter has dealt with some of the discursive elements that are invoked in public discourses and materialized in contemporary penal strategies. As practices they are realized within the welfare complex and contribute to the continued legitimation of the monopoly of state force. The control of collective violence and the marginalization of individual violence is not the exclusive concern of the criminal justice system but is one object of all the institutions of socialization. To speak, then, of continuing or channelling forms of violence (criminal/political, social/individual), is to speak from the kaleidoscopic ensemble of technicist politics that over-determine the minutae of social relations. This politics of administrative control has as one of its conditions of existence a collusive and parasitic relation to the knowledge process. The discursive regularities that adhere within practices are as much matters of strategic calculation as intellectual coherence. The calculus of a practice will thus show the tension of its theoretico-political conditions of existence.

It is not surprising that the phenomenon of violence dissolves into a plurality of etiologies and typologies as soon as it is discussed. Part of this indeterminism is the limits of knowledge, part is the eclecticist effect of the relationship between power and the knowledge process. Anthologies on violence demonstrate the intellectual incompatibility of the classificatory systems they celebrate: disparate epistemologies, contradictory concepts, mutually exclusive facts. But the paradigms all make claims to a knowledge that justifies modes of intervention. The criminology of violence espouses as knowledge eclecticist anthologies and presents the criminal justice system with maximum discursive license to forge tactical alliances that result in pragmatic technologies. To trace the process of this articulation of knowledge and power relations within the domain of criminology is to theorize the discursive regularities realized in programmes of penal control and reform. One aspect of such work involves a theoretical description and interpretation of the dominant arguments and modes of appropriation evidenced within public discourses on law and order (cf. Burton and Carlen, 1979). The particular texts examined below are not the rigorously researched and competently argued documents that receive the state's official imprimatur but are the overtly partisan productions of the political parties. These truncated, marginal and partial texts are significant for the clarity with which they proclaim the party's refor-matory intentions. They are pamphlets that openly connect the intellectual productions they draw from to the penal technologies that they offer to the professional and lay electorate. They run together the continuing strengths of traditional discourses with fashionable ones. Intellectual hesitancy and qualification is lost in the zeal for forming pragmatic proposals. Party political criminology is a distillation and condensation of the multiple themes and theories of the many disciplines it draws upon. In seeking to refine the politics of criminality these texts run together the metaphoric ambiguities of knowledges that speak of crime and violence. They ignore the empty pleas of the anthologists (Gunn, 1973; Wolfgang and Ferracuti, 1967; Storr, 1968; Tutt, 1976) to separate out forms of violence and levels of analysis – to grasp the essential eclecticism that is encouraged in the body of these general discussions. Party political criminology is of interest because it employs, in a crudely economic fashion, the contemporary *bricolage* of the arguments of reform. The fabric of a party pamphlet is woven from the conflicting paradigms available to it. The following analysis indicates some of the combinations that have resulted in the discursive alignments of the reform programmes of the Labour and Conservative political parties.

Conservative Variants

> We have urged that magistrates be given back the power to lock up the really delinquent and violent minority. A Conservative government would operate a 'glass-house' system of detention centres for some of those youngsters – so that they receive a short sharp shock treatment which I hope will deter at least some of them from getting enmeshed deeper into the mire of crime. [Whitelaw, 1978, p. 27]

To suggest a sense of discursive movement from the above sentiments, it is instructive to examine a 1946 Conservative pamphlet on delinquent youth: *Youth Astray* (Conservative Party Committee, 1946). The tone of this text has a Fabian optimism and is as imbued with social democratic reformism as a Labourist document. We are instructed that crime and violence have declined in the last 100 years because conditions of employment, public housing, health and education have constantly improved. Prosperity alone, however, does not create a moral commitment to legalism; state penal policies are also of crucial significance in legal socialization. Penal policy should balance retribution, deterrence and reformation and not only reflect the state's duty to its citizens but also create the conditions that encourage laws to be obeyed by the subject's own free will. The recalcitrant might respond better to compulsory re-education than to flagrant retribution, and, although deterrence remains essential, contract theory learns from history that supervision and re-education are required ingredients for the control of the under-socialized.

Moreover, we learn that the state has a parental duty to those denied a good home and who fall into crime. While every opportunity should be given for the young offender to demonstrate his innocence (*sic*), after a finding of guilt a full social, psychological and economic report should be prepared by a probation officer describing 'the happenings that caused him to be charged'. These reports should then be used to place the offender in a suitable institution. For the under-seventeens this should be either a non-punitive remand home or a more disciplined approved school. For the over-seventeens a borstal institution should be used. Prison should be restricted to the over-twenty-one population. These classificatory decisions are essential. In particular they discriminate between those in need of care and protection and those who are depraved. Without thoughtful classification and vigilant supervision there is every opportunity for moral contamination: 'of the neglected child by the accomplished gang malefactor; of the first offender ... by the persistent law-breaker ... of the girl who is sexually innocent by the girl who is immoral' (Conservative Party Committee, 1946, p. 14). Successful discrimination requires a supply of adequate places in remand and approved schools; bottlenecks are fatal to 'any scientific classification'.

Within the institutions a pedagogy of citizenship training should be installed. Instruction in social history, current events and (for girls) commercial training should be encouraged and communicated, when possible, through the new techniques of group discussions and documentary film. After release a comprehensive back-up system would be undertaken by compassionate professionals: 'effective after-care can only be achieved by the personal touch of those who care, and care deeply, for the welfare of young people' (p. 42).

Echoes of Benthamite taxonomies merge here with the latest modes of correctly identifying classes of delinquency. Subjects are then re-educated with the beginnings of a crudely applied psychotherapy and a faintly traced supervisory welfarism. The final didacticism is to circumscribe these technicisms with a predominantly sociological etiology and a moral determinism:

> The misbehaviour of boys and girls is merely the outcome of conditions social and economic and to some extent hereditary for which they themselves cannot be blamed. The blame — for blame there is — rests largely upon society. [p. 42]

A political generation later, the paradigms of ' liberal' Toryism have seemingly been pre-empted. Postwar reconstruction and rising living standards have not prevented an apparently rising crime rate. More pertinent is the emphasis given to increases in violent crimes. All four elections in the 1970s saw the connotative association of public disorder and violent crime. In the Tory campaigns robber and 'mugger' are discursively aligned with 'flying picket' and 'demonstrator', and all with 'terrorist'. Political and criminal violence came to signify a general malaise of society in Tory manifestos. Hall *et al.* (1978) have described this phenomenon as part of a hegemonic shift from consensus to coercion that reflected attempts to re-structure a declining British capitalism into a more efficient corporatist form. Increased use of legal restrictions on organized labour, political dissension and expressive life-styles represented moments of disciplining forms of resistance precipitated by economic crises and the policies of recession. Within this process, violence is the 'key signifier' that, in the writings of state functionaries and political and moral entrepreneurs, metaphorically associates disparate modes of resistance. These are broad contours, but certainly the apparency of the shift has surface plausibility. 1946's *'Youth Astray'* has been displaced by a new stridency:

> At a time of rising crime it is essential that we do all we can to deter people, especially young people and children, from joining the growing band of those who are robbing and attacking our fellow citizens .. I support the group's recommendations to substitute for some offenders a short sharp shock treatment on a more firmly disciplined basis, rather than longer sentences in an over-relaxed environment.
> [Whitelaw, 1977, p. 6]

But to talk of a shift from consent to coercion within the criminal justice system itself would be to overwrite the new discursive and technical configurations. We are, perhaps, more nearly dealing with a rhetoric of coercion expressing a transformation that is a rationalization of the administration of justice. Longer prison sentences and harsher regimes are to be reserved for the dangerous, persistent and violent offender; for the masses a policy of supervised liberty is, progressively, to replace incarceration. The seeming reversal of welfarism and the accompanying elevation of coercion is founded on the strategic extension of the administrative society which has been stabilized by all postwar governments. While the rhetorics of a coventionally authoritarian penology permeate the recent texts of the then Conservative opposition, these discursive effects are very much a syntactical veneer which belies the continued elevation of the paradigms of reform made possible by the applied human sciences. This is not to minimize the material consequences that, for example, the attacks on the Children and Young Persons Act 1969 might realize. Nor is it to ignore the significance of a free vote on the re-introduction of capital punishment ('These vicious young thugs who go out and murder people ... should not go out in the knowledge that their own lives cannot be forfeited': Thatcher, 1979, p. 15), but it is to specify such developments within the wider strategy of conservative penology. The following discussion does not examine those arguments that connect the texts (through the tactics of parliamentary oppositional electioneering) with the metaphoric resonances of violence and lawlessness. Instead it examines arguments that centre policy implications in the continued strategy of carceral specialization, supervised liberty and passive community discipline: that is, to rationalized administrative reformism.

The first persistent paradigm in these party pamphlets concerns the selective decarceration and de-criminalization of the marginal offender. The overcrowded prisons (in 1976, 5,709 prisoners were three to a cell, 10,726 two to a cell: CPC, 1977) have led to a severe breakdown in inmate discipline and staff morale culminating in protests and riots. The removal of the mentally disturbed, alchoholic and drug addicts and the 'inadequate' petty offenders would relieve some of the tensions. These inmates would be re-classified in secure mental hospitals and detoxification centres, and for the inadequate 'basic lodging houses with the simplest of amenities should be established for inadequates, that is, weak-willed and immature persons, to provide a place where such people may be sent or seek refuge according to their need' (CPC, 1977, p. 11). Prison remains for the violent and persistently anti-social criminal, but this carceral specialization requires a slightly modified humanism:

> No society can be sustained without a respect for order and justice. One of the chief functions of prisons as we see it is to foster this respect by providing a punishment for crime, which all can understand and fear, and by giving society a protection, which all can share against the persistent and violent offender ... If we are right in our view that the reformative effect on prisoners is minimal ... then it must be accepted that at present the main practical value of prisons is to punish serious or repeated crimes, and where necessary to protect society from dangerous criminals. [CPC, 1977, p. 7]

Here the conventionally powerful arguments of deterrence are reaffirmed while simultaneously a rationalization of the potential inmate prison is proposed. That the arguments for selective de-criminalization have been ceded does not provide grounds for optimism that such reforms will not involve a long struggle or that their realization might somehow escape the intensified strategy of non-carceral supervision. Perhaps it is true that the success of the tactics of Mathiesien's (1974) 'unfinished', the calculation of competing contradictions, is premised upon the contingency of a new discursive site being already in place within the penal system. But it is a confidently pessimistic politics that can assert that all such reforms always strengthen the micro-physics of power.

Violent crime, within the party texts, becomes the focus for policies of severer regimes, lengthy sentences and the object of the Conservative 'Beat Crime '78 Campaign'. This very emphasis allows, however, the pursuance of the continued shift to non-custodial sentences for the vast bulk of crimes. Humanist critiques of the ill-effects of imprisonment are invoked to justify a more discrete form of categorization. On the one hand we have an advocacy of selective coercion, because

> Crime is not only becoming more serious it is also becoming significantly more violent ... The typical serious crime of the 1970s is robbery all too often combining the use of violence and the carrying of weapons with careful planning and the promise of high untaxed profits. [Fowler, 1973, pp. 9, 18]

But on the other hand,

> The prison should not be used as a social dustbin for petty offenders and drunks but should be confined to the serious and persistent offender. [Fowler, 1973, p. 19]

And it is precisely the minimization of the use of prisons that the texts seek to legitimize:

> The violent offender, the armed robber and the terrorist should, however, expect nothing other than a severe and lengthy prison sentence. Such offenders would be the exception in a policy of moving towards shorter sentences and the use of alternatives to prison. [Conservative Research Department, 1978, p. 139]

The policy of shortening sentences within severe regimes will therefore maximize the psychological effect of deprivation before it normalizes into familiar contempt or into institutionalization. After release the subject's supervision will be continued through the use of custody and control orders: 'essentially a sentence the first part of which is served in prison followed by a term outside prison which is subject to close supervision in the community' (Conservative Research Department, 1978, p. 14). Similarly, all suspended sentences should be supplemented with supervision and the automatic prison sentence for breach of suspended sentences should be permissively reviewed. Community service orders should also be widely extended, and although this would result in an increased failure rate it would provide information on the categories of offenders more likely to respond to this economical and promising policy. Other existing alternatives to prison, such as adult and juvenile attendance centres, should be made more efficient and be more frequently used. This supervised liberty requires a substantial expansion of the probation services: 'there is hardly a facet of reform, inside or outside prison, that can succeed without a dedicated, expanded, efficient and well paid Probation Service' (CPC, 1971, p. 5).

Beyond the immediate supervision of the offender, but within the same strategy of the statization of the social, is the third discursive tactic, that of advocating the paradigms of the co-operation of neighbourhood resources. Extracted from the attacks on a non-participatory, formally democratic political culture is the possibility that non-professional local associations might act as a passive form of policing. Vandalism, for example, owing to the 'social isolation of vast soulless housing estates' (CPC, 1978, p. 2), might be contained through the creation of a community spirit. The corollary of this tactic is that the various agents dealing with crime should be brought into closer working arrangements with each other and with voluntary community associations. This extension of professional influence into lay associations might require retraining and would certainly invoke a more rigorous vetting of potential teachers and social workers to determine if they would always 'set a good example' (Conservative Women's National Advisory Committee, 1978, p. 6; see recommendations 6, 13, 15 and 16).

The policy orientations of these manifestos cannot be appraised as simply being attacks on a social democratic treatment or welfare model of penology. They are partially selective attacks (on the violent, persistent or political offender), but within a wider policy of community-based control for the 'normal' offender. Their lines of reasoning are frequently based upon the more complexly argued official inquiries (cf. Younger, 1971; Seebohm, 1968), but they advocate their recommendations with less qualification and reserve.

This discussion of Conservative texts will end with an outline of one of the most shamelessly cavalier examples: *'Delinquents at large?'* (Conservative Women's National Advisory Committee, 1978), which is the contemporary equivalent of the first pamphlet examined, *'Youth Astray'* (Conservative Party Committee on Policy and Political Education, 1946). Its analysis is drawn from a survey of the opinions of professionals in the administration of law and justice systems, and it reads like a litany of popular causes. Delinquency springs from an unspecified combination of broken homes and a shortage of love, security and discipline, qualities that themselves are products of mental stress, inadequacy, poor education and selfishness. These existent conditions are aggravated by a normative crisis characterized by the erosion of respect, the decline in the stigma of criminality, the climate of violence and the lack of individual purpose. The 1946 paradigms of social deprivation have been modified to emphasize psychological deprivation and normative crisis. The institutions under scrutiny become the ideological formations of family, school, church and media. The stridency of the report's recommendations endorse the duality of the punitive and supervisory strategy. Parents of offenders under the age of criminal responsibility should be liable for prosecution for the 'criminal' acts of their offspring. Parents of under-eighteen-year-old offenders should be mandated to attend the criminal trials of their children; fines for such offenders should reflect parental income. In the schools potential child delinquents should be noted and full inquiry reports be prepared. The Bench should have restored to them the power to make a residential care order in secure accommodation for second offenders. Also among the twenty-seven recommendations is asserted the need for a greater liaison between the more carefully selected agents of control as well as the orchestration of a continued campaign against lawlessness. The traditional censorious instincts of Conservatism are thus firmly embedded within the administrative techniques of supervision and surveillance.

Labour Party Policy

The most striking omission in Labour Party texts on questions of crime is the absence of polemic. The party's intellectual fabianism does not draw upon the more arresting arguments of a marxist or even a radical humanist jurisprudence. There is no equivalent to Sir Keith Joseph's vituperative attack on the 'rule of law': 'We must earn our continued good fortune. Can our generation consider giving away its birth right for the very thin stew of social justice?' (Joseph, 1975, p. 5). In its place we have a more vapid form of meritocratic social democracy:

> The growth of crime has many causes, which are closely related to the social and physical environment and must be tackled through policies on housing, education, the economy and the social services. Labour's objective is to protect society by a just and humane criminal policy seeking to rehabilitate the offender and to give reparation to the victim of crime. [Labour Party, 1978, p. 3]

There are occasions when the party's pamphlets have been more speculative – that (e.g. Labour Party, 1965) capitalist ethics generate criminal motivations, because they promote acquisitive and competitive values which also sustain resentment in failure; or that crime is connected 'to the breakdown of a sense of community, the commercialisation of values, the cult of violence, the impact of war, and the threat of universal destruction' (Labour Party, 1960). However, the overwhelming weight of analysis has been in terms of a social democratic contract theory that can deduce citizen compliance from the juridical and political relations of a meritocratic state (Callaghan, 1970).

Labour's position has been overtly to retain a theoretical commitment to the progressive refinement of the welfare state in the continued belief that crime and violence are the likely but not necessary results of the absence of 'care, guidance and opportunity'. The increase in reported crimes together with the general advances in living standards has led only to a more sophisticated appraisal of the intellectual arguments of deprivation. The party emphasis on inequality and poverty is still evident, but:

> we believe that since there are two aspects to deprivation, we can perhaps point immediately to two groups of deprived children. Those who, with their families are living in poverty; and those whose family life has broken down, perhaps as a result of the death or other loss of one or both parents, or through the total inadequacy of the parent to cope. [Labour Party, 1966, p. 27]

By 1973 the party is talking about multiple deprivation in income, housing and family relations which lead to the domino effect of labelling failures and reproducing cycles of deprivation. In the schools curriculum contents orientated to middle-class values and mediated through bourgeois linguistic structures are geared against the working-class child. The policies of selective, positive discrimination are embraced:

> In this context, the Labour Party is tired of seeing vast sums of money spent on social programmes aimed at improving the life-style of those in need but which in practice help first those who already have enough and only second those for whom the programmes were devised. [Labour Party, 1973, p. 3]

The etiologies expressed within social democratic criminology show here their indebtedness to some of the more popular paradigms of the sociology and psychology of delinquent motivation.

But if the absence of an aggressive rhetoric and a more candid celebration of liberal social science distinguishes the Labour variant, their penal strategy looks increasingly bipartisan. Indeed, Tory pragmatism, having occupied the terrain of supervised liberty, has forced the Labour authors into a defensive posture. Labour, too, supports alternative sentences to prison except for the persistent or violent offender (Labour Party, 1978, p. 17). Labour encourages the activation of community involvement in the new politics of passive control: 'management policies towards a higher level of tenant involvement in the design and running of estates are encouraged' (Labour Party, 1978, p. 30). And Labour also is committed to an applied ecology that creates an environment more resistant to property damage: 'The introduction of the concept of "defensible space" is now being encouraged in the design of council estates to avoid impersonal and unsupervised areas' (p. 30). With little principled policy differences to emphasize, the current Labour texts engage in rebuking Tory appeals to authoritarianism and thereafter demonstrate how police manning increases under Labour and how growing crime rates are not respecters of either party's rule.

These sketches of party political criminology reveal that both parties are committed to the power relations of socialization as well as segregation. The policies of supervised liberty through non-carceral modalities of pacification, regulation and reformation are firmly implicated within the welfare complex. The constant refinement of these practices is achieved through the productive utilization of selections from the eclecticism of criminology. Penal politics is well schooled in the applied human sciences.

In matters of violence we have seen how the metaphoric ambiguity of its connotations is mobilized within the party texts. Both the rupturous politics of collective violence and the asocial nature of individualized criminal violence are separated off from the constrained and measured coercion of penal administration. There is no need to conflate the party positions or to minimize the material effect of Tory rhetoric by pointing to the strategic symmetry of penal politics. Both share in the triumph of the welfare complex that has succeeded in controlling the historical sources of violence. Both hold up contemporary violence as the menacing, even if faint, echo that is the evident measure of political success. Violence in these discourses has a double moment: as a functionality of failure it can simultaneously embellish the impoverished rhetoric of technicist politics.

STRATEGIES OF INTERVENTION

Intervention into the network of discourses and practices that realize state strategy is inevitably haphazard and without guarantee of effect. Every theoretical and political innovation is capable of incorporation in some form. Recognition of this contradiction might be the first stage in theorizing intervention in terms other than of utopian optimism or pessimistic closure. Some modes of intervention are clearly more pertinent than others. In intellectual work there have been recent attempts to penetrate the academic progeny of criminology with the radical humanism of symbolic interactionism and phenomenology and the even more radical humanism of a form of marxism. The latter's attempt at intervention in matters of criminal violence was vacuous because it displaced such questions to a realm of historical anachronism once a successful transition to socialist legality and diversity was achieved. But this transition was part of an assumed and untheorized teleology whose discursive effect was merely to invoke a future against a present. The moralisms generated from these critiques of capitalism influenced the pedagogic fringes of criminology but went without impact on the more rigorous empiricist human sciences that are dominant within the practices of legal administration. Common-sense criticisms of radical criminology's more obvious contradictions were soon to be raised: for the specifics of theorizing transition, for explanations of 'socialist' failures (cf. Downes, 1979; Cohen, 1979).

To question the unexamined conditions of existence of radical criminology would be to deconstruct the absent but determinant conception of capitalism as a monolithic entity that underwrites its texts (cf. Taylor, Walton and Young, 1973; 1975). This monolithic entity has as one of its (minor) *necessary* effects a crimogenic mechanism that emanates from the structure of its economic, politico-legal and ideological relations. The metaphor of progress that accompanies the supersession of the monolith predicts the collapse of crime as a social phenomenon. In such analysis questions of transition are thought at the level of a benign futurology: the closure of utopianism circumscribes the rhetorics of a crime-free society. To disavow the notion of capitalism as an immanent structure with necessary laws of motion and inherent tendencies of supersession, and to question therefore the unity of socialisms is to emphasize a new pertinence: what are the specifics of struggles within contemporary British capitalism? (cf. Cutler, Hindess, Hirst and Hussain, 1978). The emphasis that such an orientation gives towards the detailed conditions and possibilities within a particular conjuncture is an invitation to fill the space of the present, a space vacated by leftist futurism. It might also begin to displace common-sense critiques. In conditions of a stable parliamentary democracy socialist strategy might be more effective by working towards the possibility of transition inherent in the existent political culture:

> The basis for support for socialist politics is whatever issues and struggles from which it can be made. These issues are diverse and always specific to the economic and political conditions of definite nation states. The key question of the issues from which socialist politics can be made is whether they further the struggle for non-commodity, co-operative, popular and planned forms of production and administration. The answer to this question depends on political calculation; on the context and the forces involved. [Cutler *et al.*, 1978, p. 258]

In penal politics the scope for organizing forms of resistance to legal and welfare policies is extensive. Already civil rights groups, professional associations and community organizations are pressing for reforms that may have a progressive moment. These and other campaigns should not be forestalled by a rationalist illusion that their histories are pre-written. This paper has shown how not totally unsimilar reform proposals might emerge in the party programmes of supervised liberty. Penal politics are implicated in the contradictions of strategies of co-optive reform and strategies that seek to increase the democratic control of the welfare complex. Decarceration, decriminalization and the activations of community resources are three of the paradoxical possibilities that are raised in current political criminology. If the politics of the correct line are to be replaced by a politics seeking to transform the popular elements in the existent political culture, then the first theoretical task will be to analyse how this site is already colonized by establishment reform programmes:

> It is no accident that the state initiates its own attempt to solve the con-tradiction of welfare through the Community Development Projects (CDP) at the very same time that there emerges spontaneously throughout the country, in a scattered and un-coordinated fashion, community organising projects. Both are responses to the problems generated by the state's massive intervention into the areas of housing, health, education and welfare. [Cowley *et al.*, 1977, p. 225]

Cowley's text is an informative account of some of the problems that are created in theorizing a climax of demand and the limits of reforms while simultaneously politicizing a community – problems such as political satisfaction with minimal successes, establishing elitist divi-sions (e.g. between the working class and the 'poor') or becoming unpaid state workers in the social sphere.

It is within the efforts towards democratization at the professional and community level that questions concerning the control of the administration of justice and the politics of legality can be raised. At a theoretical level intervention into questions of violence can be made more pertinent through a continued deconstruction of official criminology. From here the attempt to punctuate the reform program-mes and to defend established rights might be more readily theorized. In matters of criminal violence this may well involve invoking the established discursive *tactics* of: (1) recognizing the crime problem for the working class (Greenberg, 1977a); (2) relativizing and historiciz-ing claims of increasing levels of violence (Stedman-Jones, 1971; Tilly, 1969); (3) undermining empiricist claims with empirical facts (e.g., most violence is domestic or between acquaintances; capital punish-ment does not have a demonstrable effect on the murder rate: Morris and Hawkins, 1970; Morris and Blom-Cooper, 1979); (4) normalizing reforms through comparative analysis with more progressive regimes; (5) exposing the violence of new technicist forms of control; and (6) demonstrating the encroachment on liberal ideology that attacks on civil rights entail.

To end by being categorical: in present conditions of a stable parliamentary democracy there can be no discursive place for celebrating, no matter how ambiguously, any forms of violence.

CHAPTER 7

Questions of Juvenile Justice

Mike Collison

INTRODUCTION

This chapter is concerned with the form and effective administration of the contemporary system of juvenile justice in England. However, some of the points I wish to consider are not exclusive to the UK, in that they correspond to similar problems facing progressive politics in the USA, Western Europe and, to a limited extent, in existing socialist administrations. My focus will be on state practices and juvenile lawbreaking/misbehaviour in a period when crime and practices of discriminatory criminalization have become an important area for political and ideological intervention by the Left. In considering the problems of political calculation raised by such intervention it will be argued that an effective politics always operates within a number of theoretical and ideological contradictions. That is to say, the engagement in existing penal politics can be neither simply read off from general theories of crime or law, nor be content with the ironical disclosure of the class-discriminating effects of existing patterns of criminalization.

The conventional form of representing the problematic relation between theory and calculation in penal politics has been to talk of a *short term* and *long term* always in a relation of ambivalence and contradiction. For example, in *The Politics of Abolition* Thomas Mathiesen (1974) argues for a politicized criminology whose origin lies in the spontaneous politics of the incarcerated. Such a spontaneous politics is able to recognize the imaginary relation between crime and criminalization, and, through its marginal status, is expected to ironize the *rule of law*. The concern of this politics is to realize the decarceration of the majority of the prison population; its strategy involves the insertion into penal politics of demands that cannot be accommodated as reformist. The form of these demands is continually dictated by their refusal of existing modes of representation (for example the assessment of rehabilitative effects) in order to avoid co-optation. At the same time such refusal could realize a long term whose motive is socialist relations and socialist legality. The idealism and essentialism of this argument have been both adopted (Cohen, 1975) and eroded (Taylor and Young, 1979; Young, 1979). This is not the place to engage with it except in so far as it is necessary to question a politics that is *not* condemned to its insertion in, and calculation of, existing modes of representation of a common-sense of crime and criminals. I would argue that it is difficult to calculate the possible effects of political and ideological intervention within theory, and therefore difficult also to construct a penal politics that always already avoids the 'errors' of left idealism and reformism/gradualism (Young, 1979).

JUVENILE JUSTICE

That the notion of juvenile crime is an important signifier of a general malaise in morality, discipline, economy and freedom makes it (along with the presentation of violence – see Burton's chapter in this volume) of critical importance for the analytic deconstruction of a coercive penology. This importance lies not only in the need to confront techniques of regulation whose impact rests significantly on the young and unemployed working class, but also in the real problems raised for the regulation of youth in any (future) transition to socialism. There is nothing to suggest that the problems of regulation will disappear with the construction of a socialist mode of production; neither is juvenile crime of no concern to the working class now.

Current arguments (whether right or left) about possible changes in the structure of juvenile justice recognize an asymmetrical relation between law and practices of criminalization/socialization and a symmetrical relation between juvenile crime and those practices. Conceptions of juvenile crime are constructed in common sense to be used discursively; they present the necessity and naturalness of changes in techniques of power. The task of theory is to specify the conditions of such discourses; the task of politics is to challenge such ideological common-sense notions of crime and criminals, the effects of which notions lie in the incorporation of specific categories of individuals in state practices of coercion and help.

Given the extensive literature on juvenile justice, it would be unnecessary to consider in detail the history and structure of the law, the juvenile court, family social work, etc. (see Packham, 1975; Morris and Giller, 1979; Pinchbeck and Hewitt, 1973). Therefore in the first section I intend, rather cursorily, to outline some of the important theoretical, political, and ideological conditions underpinning the Children and Young Persons Act 1969 (hereafter CYPA 69). In the second section conventional arguments constructed in criticism of the act will be examined in order to reveal a series of contradictory effects of the demands of *welfarism* and *legalism*.

LEGISLATION

The CYPA 69 has been seen as a frustrated revolution in child legislation revealing ambiguities in its conflation of arguments of need and guilt. That its effective administration has changed the practice of socializing and controlling the young is seriously in doubt. Nevertheless, when taken together with the products of a sustained period of questioning the efficacy and legitimacy of criminalization, the intent of the CYPA 69 was the decentring of power relations away from the judicial to professional administrations. Essential need replaced essential guilt as the condition for state intervention. Of course, the categories of guilt and need have a long history of conflation and difference in discourses of punishment/treatment, and it is claimed that this history bedevils the act in its conservatism (compared for example with Longford: Labour Party, 1965), in its inability to break with dualistic conceptions of *causation*. This dualism appears under a number of rubrics: need/guilt, responsibility / non-responsibility, custodial / therapeutic, welfarism / legalism, prevention / deterrence and so on. The CYPA 69 needs to be sited as part of the history of criminological discourses that desire to discover both crime and punishment in reason (classical) and yet express embarrassment at the lawbreaking of the young, old, mad.

What does the act suggest? I propose to discuss this under four headings: youth crime, criminal responsibility and the family, social work knowledges, and philosophical dilemmas.

Youth Crime

The problem of youthful misbehaviour, and juvenile lawbreaking in particular, has at various times been presented as a serious threat to social order and the rule of law. While for the nineteenth century and the greater part of this century the initiative of regulation resided either in penal (public) or assistantial (private philanthropy) domains, since the last war the movement has been towards an alliance between the penal and assistantial (as public responsibilities) with the co-ordination and concentration of state-sponsored social work. This has resulted in the interpenetration of the assistantial and penal domains in a range of state practices concerned with youth. In part this can be seen as the outcome of postwar economic reconstruction, with its attendant demands of selection and specialization in the distribution of labour skills in turn resulting in an increased period of childhood dependency. Thus we have seen the progressive raising of the school-leaving age creating, more than ever before, a period prior to work (with its own forms of discipline) yet after childhood (and the distribution of parental responsibilities) that has engendered its own particular problems of order and control. The phenomenon called 'youth crime' thus exists within, and in relation to, the much wider concern of responsibilities *for* and responsibility *of* youth in general. Postwar social policy has been fully cognizant of the interpenetrations of socialization and criminalization.

From presenting the problem of youth as one of reconstruction (HMSO, 1946) to presenting some youths as possible objects of penal coercion (Whitelaw, 1977), there have been repeated attempts to con-stitute an ideologically effective relation between crime and interven-tion. 'The main and deep-seated causes of juvenile delinquency are hardly in doubt', suggest a confident Home Office in 1949 (HMSO, 1949, p. 4). These are 'unsatisfactory home conditions (bad and over-crowded housing, family conflicts, neglect, lack of affection and parental interest) . . . and the widespread influence of changing moral standards' (HMSO, 1949, pp. 4–5). The strategies of prevention obviously follow: 'there must be a recognition of what every child needs in the way of affection and secure environment . . . [and] every endeavour must be made to maintain and reinforce in the minds of

both parents and young people the standards of good conduct'
(HMSO, 1949, p. 5). In other words, the subject of crime is socialized
and moralized. Not only are social conditions held to account, but
also the conduct of parents is held up for scrutiny and re-education,
within an overall programme of prevention (see Ingleby: HMSO,
1960, pp. 1–9). The dualism of, on the one hand, determination by
social conditions and, on the other, the failure of the family *despite*
these conditions recurs throughout official arguments about juvenile
crime and child neglect in the period 1946–68.

Thus official reports express a dismay at rising statistics of
publically recorded lawbreaking among the young (particularly within
the fourteen to seventeen age group), and an optimism with regard to
prevention and treatment: 'A high proportion of adult criminals have
been juvenile delinquents, so that every advance in dealing with the
young offender helps also in the attack on adult crime. The prospect
of success, and its rewards, are greatest with young offenders'
(HMSO, 1965, p. 3). Despite a hesitancy (at the level of theory) to
prescribe the causes of delinquency, in common-sense terms these are
obviously located in deterministic practices of socialization (HMSO,
1965, p. 3). However, this simple reduction is not enough; there remains
a residual category of subject for whom no such 'excuses' apply: this
subject cannot be broken free of the capacity for criminal intent. In
common law the principle of *doli incapax* required proof by the
prosecution of intent (i.e. knowledge of wrongfulness) among children
between the ages of seven and fourteen. In political discourses
articulated around law and order there is a tendency for proof to
reside, not in the mind, but in the nature of the offence. The inability to
endow the not fully adult subjectivity with consistent capacities has
produced juridical confusion and the political opportunity for the
creation of an (empirically) obvious 'hard core' of delinquents.

More directly, this duality creates a system of juvenile justice that
raises seriously the question, often begged or suspended by radical
analysis, of *rights*. It is typically suggested in reflections on process
that the facts of offence are rarely in dispute in juvenile courts. The
policy intent of juvenile justice makes this a formal and negotiated
effect of the determination of disposal (there are nevertheless considerable differences between the practices of various courts; see Anderson,
1978). Yet given the dualism in discursive representations of subjectivity and the dualism in strategies of disposal (penal–welfare,
custodial–assistantial), the partial abandonment of due process (i.e.

the attempted transformation of function of the court) also abandons some of the safeguards in the adversorial determination of guilt. In the USA subsequent to the Gault decision it was recognized that 'the interests of the child' were not sufficient conditions for legal rights. In this country, while for example legal representation is available (although not widely used), the formal and interactive structure of the courts seriously questions the protection of *legal* rights by such means (Anderson, 1978, pp. 37–44). This question will be referred to again in the second part of this chapter.

The CYPA 69 and its previous White Paper *Children in Trouble* (HMSO 1968) sought to marry the judicial and welfare functions of state agencies dealing with the regulation of youth. They suggested that, first, the child or young offender should be investigated as a case of *need*, and only in exceptional circumstances, once a series of safeguards have been met (discussion and liaison between recognized agencies), should this result in criminal prosecution. For the under-fourteens criminalization was not seen as appropriate to the object of intervention. For this group an offence was not to be a sign for intervention *unless* the conditions for care proceedings were also met. If they were not, informal methods of cautioning should apply. It is trivial to point out that this is circular (i.e. offending is a presenting symptom of deprivation), but it is important to recognize that (1) the wider use of cautioning by the police, and (2) the liaison imperative (if fully implemented) can result in an increasing number of juveniles being brought to court (Ditchfield, 1976). For the fourteen to seventeen year group again criminal prosecution should be avoided for all but a small minority; the major form of disposal was to be the care order.

In the forms of disposal there was to be shift from the penal to the assistantial. Care and supervision orders, intermediate treatments and family support were to replace borstals, detention centres and attendance centres, and there was also to be a reorganization of local authority institutional provisions under the community homes scheme. Consequently, jurisdiction would be displaced (partially) from the judicial to the professional (social work). The form of the Act's implementation under a hostile Tory government demonstrated that the dual picture of the offender could not be denied (Bottoms, 1974). The logic of social reform philosophies was to replace the judicial, as a knowledgeable place from which to speak of crime, with social, educational, medical and fiscal knowledges which speak of incapacity. The short history of the Act's use, and, in particular, the increasing use of the fine, detention centre and (on commital to the Crown Court) borstal, has indicated that the two approaches can be combined in conflation and difference to provide a discretionary social control (HMSO, 1978).

Criminal Responsibility and the Family

The family is the principal mechanism through which the young are socialized and regulated. It is assisted in this task by the various institutionalized practices of social work, schools, medicine, law, social security and so on. In other words, according to Donzelot, the family is the point of location of a matrix of social practices that seek both to constitute it and to regulate it (Donzelot, 1977). The profound importance of the family in the postwar period can be seen in the connection made by official reports between types of family and juvenile crime. With the development of social knowledges which challenge legal discourses confident in classicist principles the family again significantly becomes the location of *crime*. In the past censured for its failure to impart a bourgeois morality, the family is now assisted in the recognition of its own needs (see for example the attempts of social work to theorize its practice in relation to need).

The reason why the family has been important in this period is that it is called upon to extend its competence, that is to be responsible for the child for longer periods prior to work (or unemployment). Official reports of the period 1946–68 address and admonish the family for its repeated failures in the mirror of normality. This failure is not conceived as a fall from grace, a comparison with the past, but an obstacle to the constitution of new relations within the family (Hodges and Hussain, 1979). The 'family charter' period of legislation attempts to support the failed family at the same time as it redistributes public and private responsibilities. The effects of such a strategy have fallen predominantly on the working-class family. This strategy is represented as a triumph of welfarism.

Welfarism as a general programme for the coercive and didactic reproduction of social relations entails a contradiction in responsibilities (George and Wilding, 1976) in that the public and the private intersect at the point of responsibility and freedom. By this I mean that a private (individual) responsibility is opened to a public scrutiny (as part of a collective responsibility) in order to be reinserted in the private. This will become clearer if we consider the particular

relation between the family and youth crime. While postwar consensus politics proclaims proudly an equal opportunity in economic
growth, education, housing and health (and incidentally unemployment!), it was recognized that the ability to seize such opportunity was
unevenly distributed. Some families were not indeed normal, generating a concern for the family (Curtis) and for a fabian morality
(Callaghan). This concern coincides with sociological positivism
(Taylor, Walton and Young, 1973, pp. 10–30), which theorizes the
origin of criminal careers in upbringing. 'It is the situation and
relationships within the family which seem to be responsible for many
being in trouble ... and it is therefore with family problems that any
preventative measures will largely be concerned' (HMSO, 1960, p. 7).
The family therefore becomes the site of a double economy: of labour,
and of crime. Arguments of juvenile crime require an intervention that
is progressive and interrogatory; it is necessary to *detect* neglect and
to work *with* the 'inadequate or substandard family' (HMSO, 1960,
p. 8). The right of such interrogation and intervention depends not on
a legal right of punishment but on projecting certain *needs* on to
families or individual family members. The particular form of
representation of needs or interests makes clear the displacement of
responsibilities mentioned above.

Formally official arguments about crime and deprivation register
social conditions beyond the individual (or family), such as housing,
unemployment, amenities, etc., as conditions for behaviour. Yet this is
an unhappy situation, as varieties of positivism would find if they
attempted to explain why all the inhabitants of areas of urban deprivation are not before the court. The answer to why certain youths break
the law, why certain families fail in their responsibilities, has entailed
an analytic reduction; in social work this is variously called the psy-
choanalytic reduction – or the client relation. By a process of analytic
and practical reductions the problem of differential opportunity under
welfarism is divested of its structure in order thus to be transposed on
to various psycho-social capacities of individual subjects. Once arguments concerning *crime* have displaced its juridical origin from an
individual subject it is relocated in family agency. Thus 'support the
family' also says 'prevent crime'; the family is held to account for its
members' deviance. This displacement of responsibility and intervention on to family agency is neither necessary nor without challenge
(for example, that coming from radical social work which seeks to
overcome the coercive reduction of psycho-analytic case work: see
Chapter 8 below by Clarke, Langan and Lee).

Another important condition of policy documents and the CYPA 69 was the unification of the practices that act on the family within a common strategy of investigation and assistance. The Curtis report called for a unification of authority (Home Office) and a professionalization of practice. Ingleby recognizes that the task of discovery is dispersed among agencies but should be co-ordinated; Longford proposes a family service; and so on. In other words, the general movement is towards a sharpening of surveillance, and its displacement over as wide a field as possible.

> Arrangements for the detection of families at risk should extend over the widest possible front. Many different sorts of agency and worker will function in this role. Neighbours, teachers, medical practitioners, ministers of religion, health visitors, district nurses, education welfare offices, probation officers, child care officers, housing officers, officers of the National Assistance Board and other social workers may all spot incipient signs of trouble. [HMSO, 1960, p. 17]

Such a system of police would have done credit to Thomas Cromwell's administration (Elton, 1972), or would do credit to our worst fears of totalitarian control if it were not for the mode of its legitimation: the interests of the deprived. The purpose of the irony is neither to trivialize the nature of social work functions, nor to 'transcend them', but merely to recognize the *extension* of a normative surveillance.

The CYPA 69 recognizes the need for a wide-ranging investigation prior to court appearances, privileges social work as the major co-ordinating agency, and prescribes that the family situation should be the source of knowledge of the case. If one member of the family is in need of care or before the law, then this becomes the condition for the right to intervene in the social management of all familial relations. It has been argued that the displacement of responsibilities and the extension of concepts of interest has put the family on trial through the non-judicial mechanism of the social inquiry report. I shall return to this question, later, for it raises a number of problems connected with the desirability of freedom and privacy as progressive demands within the existing legal structure.

Social Work Knowledges

While the family has been the effective location of coercive and didactic institutional practices since the nineteenth century, the major movement since Curtis has been for the state to take over directly what previously had been the terrain of private philanthropy. The demand for systematized strategies for the family created the space for the development of a service that could claim privilege in arbitrating between the various knowledges that impinged on the family. Social work has developed a particular knowledgeable discourse about the nature of social problems. This knowledge is eclectic, in that it seeks to appropriate (speak for) all the knowledges previously brought to bear on the family (sociological, psychological, medical, fiscal, moral). The condition of privilege lies in the client relation, or the ability to represent problems and solutions in a unique form. This privilege is at present under attack both from within social work itself (radical social work) and from government-imposed financial restrictions. The immediate history of the CYPA 69 depended to a great extent on the shifting balance of strength of senior social work and its ability to shape policy (Bottoms, 1974). This process has often been recorded as an opposition between social work and magistracy, between social and judicial, between Right and Left, and so on. However the dichotomies were not clear-cut; a middle ground was conceded in both arguments. This middle ground was constituted in the dual form of representing reactions to crime in the dichotomy of punishment/treatment.

The collapse of arguments distinguishing between the child who comes before the court charged with an offence and the child in care proceedings (from 1927 to 1968) entails a unity of practice for the young person. Offending is one (among many) presenting symptoms of need. This is the condition for the claim of social work responsibility for the management and treatment of the offender. This is regarded as the shift to welfare philosophy in the CYPA 69. However, while Longford proposed the abolition of the juvenile court (embracing thereby therapeutic rather than penal determination), the current act *retains* the court, thereby retaining both neglect and intent in an uneasy relation. The unease of this relation occurs at the level both of penal discourses and of court strategies (Anderson, 1978).

Most commentators suggest that the act and especially its implementation created this unease (Morris, 1978), leaving open the discursive possibilities for presenting the carceral as a natural response to some lawbreaking. Proponents of a welfare orientation claim a failure in the continued judicial categorization of offender/offence while simultaneously 'giving' to social work the dubious role of advisor

(SER) and therapeutic mechanic (once this disposal has been decided on by the court).

Philosophical Dilemmas

Here we return to the question of youth crime because it has been suggested that the CYPA 69 sustains a philosophical problem of representation. Penal discourses attempt to construct a symmetry between crime and punishment; the origin of the latter resides in the former. Penal discourses that seek to talk of juvenile crime are incoherent, yet ideologically effective. So, for example, representations of a commonly shared knowledge of juvenile crime constructed within law and order discourse are caught continually contradicting themselves, yet at the same time they have an ideological und political effectivity. The problems begin with the desire (of jurisprudence and philanthropy) to represent difference in juvenile crime, to sustain the coherence of difference in penal practices. In the nineteenth century the law begins to interrogate different subjective categories of responsibility of the young, the old, the mad, etc. (Taylor, Walton and Young, 1973, pp. 7–10), and to develop a new range of penal practices (the hulks, industrial schools, reformatories, etc.). In other words the movement is towards the segregation of young from adult in state practices of discipline and surveillance. Today this complex of contradiction and coherence remains in children and young person legislation as a series of contradictions of *jurisdiction* and *objects*. A policy statement:

> The juvenile court remains a *criminal* court . . . . The weakness of the present system is that a juvenile court often appears to be trying a case on one particular ground and then to be dealing with the child on some quite different ground. This is inherent in combining the requirement of proof of a specified event or condition with a general direction to have regard to the child's welfare. It results, for example, in a child being charged with a petty theft or other wrongful act for which most people would say that no great penalty should be imposed, and the case apparently ending in a disproportionate sentence. [HMSO, 1960, p. 26]

That the sentence appears disproportionate (removal from home, for example) seems to be little assuaged by the incorporation of parent and child into alliance with the law (CYPA 69). Criticism therefore suggests that criminal and welfare jurisdictions are not coherent.

However, they are made coherent by the professional and common-sense productions of the juvenile court system. If the designation of capacities resides in judicial decision (with varying degrees of intervention by social workers), then the calculation of treatment based on this judicial determination resides with the professional knowledges of social work, psychiatry, etc. In an important sense this is little different from the adult system.

JUVENILE JUSTICE AND RIGHTS FOR CHILDREN

This second part of the chapter deals with a variety of arguments that have been made which seek to raise discussion of the form of the CYPA 69 and suggest possible changes in the way the state responds to lawbreaking by juveniles. The most powerful arguments, that is to say those arguments that are likely to be ideologically effective, have been made by the Right (Tory Party, Magistrates Association, Police Federation, etc.), in such a way that a common-sense public knowledge of juvenile crime (and prevention) has been formed. Any argument proclaiming itself 'progressive' must therefore be cognizant of the power of such common-sense notions, yet must intervene in order thus to deconstruct them. When such 'progressive' arguments are examined it will be seen that the means of intervention in a penal politics directed towards juveniles creates a number of contradictions where Right and Left meet on a common (although unwanted) terrain.

At present juvenile justice (at least for the fourteen to seventeen year age group) mirrors closely an (apparent) ambiguity in contemporary systems of criminal justice: that is, that penal strategies move towards the strengthening of carceral regimes (longer sentences, secure accommodation) while at the same time seeking no-custodial penalties and intermediate treatments (Mathews, 1979; cf. Scull, 1977). The first movement concerns itself with the *violent*, the second with the *socially pathetic*. Demands for the strengthening of custody depend on the ability to represent a hard core of criminals and a socially dangerous category of offences (e.g. violent offences). The penological discourse, which predicts the necessity of change, invokes *danger* and *defence*. On the other hand, decarceration programmes originate in financial accounting (overcrowded prisons, lack of building programmes for specialized institutions, etc.) and crime theories that suggest that institutional segregation realizes little of therapeutic/correctional value for a broad range of offenders. The dualism of aetiologies of the hard core and the pathetic, while creating an area of dispute over numbers and relative dangerousness, nevertheless remains a common ground for 'progressive' and 'conservative' penal politics. Even a romantic criminology faces the problem of what to do with the hard core, not only in existing society, but also in any (future) socialist society.

The hard core and the pathetic occupy a significant place in the politico-ideological discourses into which the problem of juvenile crime is inserted. While the general historical movement in the penal system has sustained decriminalization and therapy (need) as leitmotivs of practice (theoretical and judicial), the subject of classical thought remains ever-present, ready to be invoked against the tide of 'liberalism'. Some, at least, know what they do. Current arguments about juvenile lawbreaking thus point to the increasingly violent lawbreaking of the young as an index of the capacity to know right from wrong. Welfare discourse's ability to represent both capacity and cause for this kind of lawbreaking is seriously questioned by a right-wing reaction to past liberal reforms. Thus in a circular argument (which nevertheless is ideologically effective) statistics of disposal can be invoked as proof of this serious category of crime and knowing criminal subjects (conversely the same statistics may be used as an argument that the magistracy, with successive government's complicity, have circumvented the CYPA 69 by applying inappropriate sentences). The dualism in common-sense knowledges of crime legitimates a dualism in adjudication and intervention. The adopted strategies are presented as obvious and set the grounds on which we may talk 'sensibly', of penal measures. While it may be both possible and/or desirable to represent the subject of crime and the subject of regulation in a different form to that hitherto existing, nevertheless it remains the case that we are constrained to talk within the existing, yet incoherent, dichotomies *and* be aware of their effects. Thus at the present time we are witnessing the displacement and symbolic dispersion of categories of violence to embrace juvenile crime and to redeploy carceral strategies for the young. Since 1970 right-wing arguments have sought to introduce security and defence as increasingly necessary adjuncts to a 'soft' welfare jurisdiction. Of course, security has never been absent from the system; i.e., the court has available to it the detention centre, junior borstal, and attendance centre, as well as many community homes which adopt 'protective security'. But specific recent proposals have called for such measures as secure care orders, a move that would entail a conflation and displacement of the boundaries of the assistantial and the penal. Similarly, the 'short sharp shock' has come to symbolize a new war against juvenile crime, even though the rhetoric masks a principle that has been part of the system for some time.

These are the issues that any progressive penal politics has to confront. The problems of *how* to engage in such a debate are enormous. That these problems *should* be confronted has always been recognized by a liberal penology but frequently denied as a 'correct' (theoretical or otherwise) strategy of the Left. Part of the ambivalence to a direct intervention in short-term penal politics resides in the inability to transcend both pre-constituted dichotomies and the effects of those dichotomies in forming a public common sense of juvenile crime. Any argument that seeks to disclose the circularity, for example, in calls for harsher penalities because of an increase in serious offences also has to address (1) the reasons why such calls are unproblematic to an existing public knowledge of crime, and (2) that the effects of crime in existing society fall most heavily on the working-class inner city population. Recognition, therefore, of the complex determinations of lawbreaking (and its distribution) and criminalization practice (and *its* distribution) poses certain limits on political intervention, these limits forestalling either support for existing systems of control or the over-romanticization of deviance.

Again returning to the constraint of opposites, arguments raised against right-wing proposals for juvenile justice fall into two broad, and apparently contradictory, theses: *welfarism* and *legalism*. The first suggests that an extension of welfare programmes for dealing with young law-breakers would prevent the worst effects of criminalization. The second suggests that, in rushing to embrace need as an orchestrating category for state intervention in the control of youth, certain fundamental rights (which adults are able to claim at law) have been subsequently denied by welfarism. The two arguments are contradictory in the sense that they are bound up with the dual representations of lawbreaking behaviour mentioned earlier. However, they are not necessarily contradictory when considered as a calculated form of intervention into conventional penal politics. Contradiction and coherence in arguments that may have progressive effects will now be examined briefly under the two broad characterizations of welfarism and legalism. The particular arguments examined are not exhaustive of the arguments that have been and may be made.

WELFARISM

A conventional argument made by social workers and sociologists is that punitive strategies may be confronted by claiming a betrayal of the 'philosophy of the Act'. The failure to implement certain pivotal sections of the Act, and, more importantly, to provide sufficient resources to maintain and expand a wide range of treatment techniques, has, it is suggested, led to a situation in which the welfare orientation is criticized for failing to do what it was never allowed to do. Punitive strategies are then easily inserted into the space (of regulation–prevention) that welfare was never allowed properly to occupy. Contrary to such attempts to produce a shift to an increased penal jurisdiction, social work etc. claims that rising rates of official lawbreaking, rather than signifying a failure of social work practice, actually demonstrate a failure to allow social work to adequately 'do the job'.

This 'betrayal' is compounded by the structure and practice of the juvenile court which, as Ingleby pertinently observed, *is* a contradiction in that it remains a court of law. Decisions of guilt–innocence are arrived at from different psycho-legal premises to ones of need–incapacity. The professional and personal role of the social worker has remained ambiguous in the juvenile court in relation to determination of legitimate agency (law or welfare) and appropriate capacities (guilt, need). Thus social work feels that the claim of impotence by the magistracy is illusory; the magistrates have retained control over the young, leaving to social work a residual competence.

If a punitive shift in juvenile justice is to be forestalled then, it is suggested, social work must reconstruct its role:

> If social workers wish to develop their role in working with juvenile offenders and retain their social work emphasis they must be as involved in the issues of process as they are currently in issues of treatment. [Morris and Giller, 1979, p. 30]

However, given the present discursive and institutional structures within which social work operates, claims for an increased role of social workers in the process as well as treatment of juvenile law-breakers raises several problems. First, the extension of social work into fields previously represented as legal relations and regulated by judicial reasoning would carry with it a number of 'sinister' effects. Second, the nature of social work discourse itself as a therapeutic normative discourse must be questioned in a progressive politics. And finally, the denial of the appropriateness of the legal representation of social relations and social action raises the problem of the form in which social work practice may be open to interrogation and regulation itself.

Extension of Practice

'Need', 'neglect', 'deprivation' and 'substandard' are the operating categories of social work, attaining meaning with their articulation in specific discursive relations. It is assumed that what social work does is 'good' in so far as it responds to interests and demands outside itself. These external interests provide the conditions for social work intervention. Arguments for the extension of the field in which social work may operate depend then on suggesting both that there is undetected need, and that the needs already cognizant to social work are not properly represented. The practice that is predicted involves an increase in mechanisms of detection *and* a proliferation of techniques of welfare. This practice would continually be open to demands for prevention, a demand that will exist in spite of internal criteria adopted by social work to evaluate success and failure.

I quoted in irony the proposals in the Ingleby report for the range of individuals that should be involved in the detection of need, and I think that here we have to take it seriously because a return to the 'philosophy' of the Act as a demand would entail just such a *police*. Moreover, given the structural location of social work, this would be a *state police* without legal regulation. The post-Seebohm restructuring and co-ordination of social work was a move in this direction. In official reports the connection of agencies *as* a social policy would sustain an 'obvious' agreement *of* social policy; or, to put it another way, the criteria for intervention are absolute and not imbricated in the professional knowledges and institutional protocols of particular agencies. For example, juvenile liaison schemes, when articulated with a broad range of other agencies as a progressive attempt at circumventing criminal proceedings, have also been used as an explicit

coercive mechanism in areas previously excluded from police surveillance. Within the paradigm of 'legalism', intervention by the state,
though discriminatory in its effects, in *form* assigns more than a
rhetorical importance to rules that are legally enforceable (judges'
rules, rules of arrest, rules of evidence, regulation of entry). These
rules, while circumvented in many concrete practices, remain as a
possible area of ironic struggle for individual rights and protection by
the law! To suggest an extension of the field of operation of social
work as a strategy *against* the criminalization of the young
unemployed working class by presenting the existence of 'undetected
need' can actually suspend such rights (both formally guaranteed and
concretely denied) in favour of imputed interests. Civil liberties
become subordinated to interests interpellated on to the client subject;
the individual subject thus can be constituted as the point of intersec-
tion of both personal and bureaucratic demands.

Similarly, the proliferation of techniques of welfare poses a range of
possible effects which *may* be appropriated as either progressive or
repressive in the context of existing penal politics. In a sense this
suggestion converges with a questioning in this country and the USA
of the rehabilitative ideal (Allen, 1959). A proliferation of the techniques of welfare is at the same moment a proliferation of the semio-
techniques of power, in particular the power to constitute and
reproduce categories of normality. Even adopting a position of normative consensus, there is considerable empirical doubt as to the efficacy
of various techniques. The proposed shift to a welfare orientation with
the attendant social work emphasis on worker–client individual relations would merely provide for the increased denial of (previous) legal
rights (which are positive as well as negative) instead legitimating a
variety of interventions by reference to represented needs.

What is being suggested here is that certain progressive welfare
demands are ambiguous in their possible effects and open to serious
challenge from Left and Right. For example, current proposals by the
Home Secretary for the institution of secure care orders *can* be
represented as a displacement from the penal to the assistantial as well
as a change in the technique of punishment.

A Normative Discourse

Already the problem in arguments for the shift to welfarism of
accounting has been raised. It can be dealt with briefly: intervention

by social work in the management of social relations operates on sets of criteria that are, almost metaphysically, inscribed in the interpersonal relation of social work itself; i.e., every need is different! It can be argued that the existence of a system of co-ordinated social work now is both a recognition of inequality and an extension of the policing of social relations: it is both victory and defeat. This is a conventional point, always made in general arguments which seek to comprehend the welfare state form and the problems faced in even talking of a *radical social work* (e.g. Corrigan and Leonard, 1978).

But the problem of accountability is more specific than this. It is a problem that resides within the circle of arguments that speak of individual capacities, care and rehabilitation, that is, the discretionary sentence. It is difficult to speak of 'sentenced to care', but there is nothing in the effects of care to distinguish it from a punitive disposal except in so far as it represented as originating in a different motive. It remains a particular form of the denial of *liberty*. However, instead of this denial being the product of the legal determination of guilt within a welfare orientation, it becomes the outcome of definite, but discretionary, professional knowledge. This of course does not entail the romanticization of the rule of law as an ahistorical ideal, but it does recognize the potential of formal rules which appear independent of class determination (Picciotto, 1979). I have already noted the desire of juvenile jurisdictions to incorporate the tried (family and offender) into the process of legitimation of the trial as part of the individualizing of determination. This becomes, in concrete court practices, a gestural attempt to secure legitimacy for discretionary sentences based on the premises of an individualized caring. Many youths however are not to be 'fooled', expressing surprise at distinct arguments for disposal, some invoking the gravity of offence, some the incapacity of the offender (with which the offender is ideally meant to agree, as the tortured are meant to agree with the work of the devil). The decisions on how long an offender (also in need) is to serve within a welfare jurisdiction are wholly internal to the social work agency. It is at this point that the effects of arguments from the Right contradictorily coincide with the effects of arguments calling for justice for juveniles. Punitive proposals from magistrates and politicians call for the increased power of the judicial over the discretionary practices of social work under care jurisdictions, providing legal regulation of both the form and the length of therapeutic intervention. This is also a possible argument for progressive intervention in juvenile justice. It would recognize both the gestural attempts at forming an alliance of legitimation with those before the court *and* the mechanics of social work power over social relations. The extension of welfarism would systematically *increase* this mechanics of power, thus denying the possibility of a legal struggle which attempts to forestall (at least) some of the effects of criminalization in the contemporary juvenile justice system.

Regulation

In order both to extend the area of operation of the rehabilitative/therapeutic and to guarantee rights, it has been suggested that social work should be supervised and regulated by an independent tribunal. However, it is impossible to conceive at present of rights that are not *legal* rights. A tribunal would necessarily operate with the criteria of need/interest, which I have already argued are internal to social work knowledges (as well as existing in common sense and in social democratic theories of sociality). The challenge to social work practice therefore, would have to appeal to the misrecognition of need or the misrepresentation of interest from *within* social work discourse, *or* deny the privilege of that discourse by constituting a (more) privileged site from which to speak of juvenile crime. The denial of social work discourse (in other words, the way social work represents its own practices) is precisely the desire of right-wing arguments that seek to represent the necessity of change in Children and Young Persons legislation (as obvious) and to shift the balance of power in juvenile justice back to the judicial (if, indeed, it was ever 'lost').

However, the choice of political/ideological strategy cannot necessarily be reassured by theoretical coherence. In the desire to regulate the activities of rehabilitative agents it seems possible both to question the internal criteria of practice and to deny the privilege of the discourse whose effects are realized in that practice. Yet such a strategy would have to recognize its openness to incorporation in arguments that suggest a return to judicial authority and thus the 'rediscovery' of law and order.

LEGALISM

In this final section two areas of concern in the present system of juvenile justice will be described, pointing out the possible contradictions entailed in certain progressive demands.

The first area of concern is directed towards the existence in quasi-penal establishments of large numbers of children between the ages of twelve and seventeen. These children, recipients of care orders, are deemed to require a secure form of accommodation broadly similar to some adult penal establishments. If it were not for government spending economies, secure accommodation would be one of the heaviest areas of investment in the control of youth. The formal logic involved is therapeutic; i.e., it is necessary for rehabilitation that these children are locked away – the practical protocol admitted to is that institutional 'dustbins' have to be resorted to for 'difficult' children when all else fails (*The Guardian*, 25 August 1979).

The second area of concern deals with the *form* of the juvenile court. Despite official exhortations to adopt a welfare-caring approach to the disposal of cases before the juvenile court, it remains effectively a criminal court. Indeed, some courts have been little affected in their practices by the CYPA 69. Therefore if the juvenile court still operates ambiguously as a criminal/assistantial institution, then some form of legal advocacy is required to assert and represent the rights of those before that court. In many instances the need for legal representation is either unrecognized (by the participants) or actively discouraged (by the court).

The two demands generated by these concerns of 'rights for children in care' and 'legal advocacy for children in court' are paradoxical when inserted into current political and ideological arguments. I will argue schematically that both demands may produce effects that can be progressive and/or conservative in existing penal politics.

This ambivalence of effects resides in, and expresses, an ambivalence in notions of the 'rule of law'.

> The case for the rule of law ... expresses either a demand for the application of coercion in social relations, or for the control of such coercion ... [Picciotto, 1979, p. 164]

The notion of the rule of law served a particular function during the transition from feudalism to capitalism as a mechanism for the regulation of arbitrary power and as one of the general conditions for the political and ideological representation of a social class: the bourgeoisie. But the rule of law cannot be reduced to a simple (class) origin, either empirically (Hay, 1975) or theoretically (Hirst, 1979b). This is not to suggest that the rule of law is an abstracted morality (Thompson, 1975), but merely that, despite the class privilege realized in the application of this 'rule' to practices of criminalization, the existing constitution of social relations as legal relations is a limiting condition for any political engagement with its product: the working-class criminal. Thus, while the Right unites under the slogan of a return to the 'rule of law' (as a law and order society), it is *equally* possible to raise the issue of the rule of law as a progressive demand. Juvenile justice is a good example.

RIGHTS FOR CHILDREN

One of the more disturbing effects of a shift to a welfare-orientated system of juvenile justice has already been mentioned. Children and young persons are finding themselves locked away for longer periods in varieties of secure/penal establishments which increasingly are called upon to do no more than simply contain. Although this extreme involves only some 300 children (the actual numbers are likely to increase substantially under Tory policies), as an extreme it represents the limits of a continuum where the liberty of the young is denied in one form or another for long periods as the result of *caring*. Such a motive, and its practical effects, is not unproblematic. As a response to this situation organizations such as NACRO and Justice for Children are fostering demands that entail the protection of the rights of children. These rights are seen to be systematically denied by the discretionary professional practices of social work (and the juvenile court), practices orchestrated by the principles of need and deprivation. A range of needs are interpellated on to the juvenile subject simultaneously to be the condition of legitimation for the restriction of that subject's actions. The claim for the protection of rights is, therefore, also a questioning of the legitimacy of social work practice.

The formulation of a demand for the rights of children, and the calculation of its possible effects, raises a number of practical and theoretical problems.

As a result of the CYPA 69 magistrates are faced with a range of possible disposals, the major ones being: the fine, a detention centre, a borstal (on commital to Crown Court), and the care or supervision order. The fine, detention centre, and borstal disposal are all determined by magisterial decision and governed by determinate rules (i.e., what the magistrate may decide). The care and supervision order, on the other hand, is merely a general decision to give responsibility to a non-legal agency for the control of the young offender. Under the present system appeal may be made only against the original care order and *not* against how that care order has subsequently been administered. Therefore, to make sense of the demand for an appeal to protect the rights of children either (1) the non-legal agency would have to be open to independent interrogation of its conduct in particular cases, or (2) that conduct would have to be open to legal scrutiny in court. If the latter were the course to be followed a number of effects, not all of which may be desirable, would result.

Most importantly, to be able to hear a question of the conduct of particular care orders magistrates would have to have increased powers of surveillance over care orders in general. This is precisely the desire of right-wing opposition to the CYPA 69; that is to say, to provide an extension of the competence of legal knowledge and argument over a field partially denied to it by that Act. Similarly, to open the conduct of the care order to judicial scrutiny and possible control would result in a serious challenge to the discursive privilege of social work in representing both the cause and prevention of lawbreaking. It is a short step from such a challenge of social work to the judicial control of care orders *per se*, the erosion of the basic tenets of a therapeutic stance, and the concession that judicial determination is appropriate to the object *qua* subject of need.

If the conduct of social work in determining the form of care orders, etc., were open to interrogation (and claims of rights independently of the court) by tribunal or review panel, then a problem of power and knowledge is created (see pp. 160–2 above). Social work discourse is such that the derivation of practice in individual cases is arrived at (often) ambiguously from a range of general criteria, the needs of each client being different. To challenge such discourse is to challenge that which is ever reducible; i.e., arguments for the continuance of care orders can always invoke either the peculiarities of the client or the privilege of the particular client relation involved. This is one of the principles of therapy diagnosis (whether psychiatric or social) that remains as an obstacle to any proclamation of rights, fairness, etc., by a tribunal. However, the 'right to care' must not be confused with personal claims of legal rights and civil liberties.

Briefly, to claim the rights of children either by reference to the court or by the protection of an independent tribunal entails a number of contradictions. The former would bring an apparently progressive argument in consonance with that emanating from the Police Federation, Magistrates' Association and William Whitelaw; the latter would be an impossible project without seriously challenging the privilege of social work knowledge. In turn this challenge would be welcomed by political and judicial opinion, which seeks to erode the social work role in the administration of juvenile justice.

LEGAL ADVOCACY

The presumption of children and young persons' legislation is that the appropriate form with which to deal with juvenile offenders is not that of accusatorial trial but that of interrogatory discovery. In other words, the juvenile comes before the court having indicated by certain actions (which may include breaking the law) a case of need which the court then proceeds to remedy. The social worker ideally plays a pivotal role; (s)he is given the task of discovery, reporting, and recommending. The court responds to such reports by common endeavour to reach a satisfactory conclusion (to both the court and client(s)). This is the idealization of the juvenile court. However, existing practices in court depart significantly from such a caricature. The discovery and representation of needs has already been questioned: the representation of need is internal to the professional knowledge that constitutes it as meaningful. And yet the social worker is viewed as a more or less adequate representative of the child's 'interests', speaking both for and to the child (it is not presumed that child or family can adequately represent their own needs–interests; in fact, the converse is frequently held in principle to be the case).

Similarly juvenile courts do not unilaterally embrace the welfare jurisdiction given them by law. For some courts the presence of the social worker becomes an unnecessary impediment to the professional and bureaucratic demands of court process. While within the idealization offending (and the nature of offence) is a secondary concern to the clients' background, life-style, emotional stability, etc., in many courts the opposite occurs; i.e., there is a tendency for a greater focus on the nature of the offence. Crudely, examples are being made that address the juvenile population with the severity of punishment, and address the general public to reaffirm ideological arguments which suggest a breakdown of law and order.

It is in response to the concrete practices of the juvenile courts that go against the intentions of the CYPA 69 that calls for an extension of legal advocacy are made. I would want simply to suggest that such an extension of legal advocacy may face certain obvious problems and entail both positive and negative effects. A major problem would result from the contradictions and conflations in discourses of juvenile crime and court practices (mentioned earlier).

In a recent interactionist account of juvenile court practice Richard Anderson describes how two courts can operate on different principles, one being predominantly welfare and the other legal in its orientation (Anderson, 1978). The insertion of legal advocacy in the first engenders problems of competing professional knowledges. In the second legal representation, while nominally protecting legal rights, nevertheless reinforces the appropriateness of legal reasoning to questions of juvenile lawbreaking.

In a situation where decisions on appropriate disposal are arrived at through principles of welfare and pathology, legal advocacy has been found to be anachronistic and redundant. The reason is clear. Legal argument cannot (nor would it wish to) embrace the determination of needs; except those internal to criminal law. The juvenile court under welfarism does not seek guilt or innocence but a social rather than legal knowledge of the offender. The legal representative in this situation either constructs arguments that are out of place or defers to the other client representative: the social worker. In cases assumed to fall within the competence of the welfare pathological model the engagement (by family and juvenile) of legal representation and the subsequent questioning of the social 'diagnosis' would itself provide further arguments of need and therapy. It is axiomatic to much social work practice that the client (juvenile offender) should recognize in the social worker the capacities of privilege, authority and help. To engage a legal representative would therefore deny those capacities to the social worker. In other words, the insertion of legal representation in such a court would, in interactionist accounts, attempt to reconstitute already fashioned sets of interactive and professional relations necessary to the functioning of that particular court.

Legal representation and advocacy within juvenile courts constituted as places of judicial reasoning and penal determination would apparently be less problematic and more desirable. Legal arguments can be used effectively to protect certain rights and to fight against certain practices of criminalization. However, the situation is not entirely clear. We are talking of legal advocacy for a predominantly working-class clientele under a legal aid provision which itself has been seriously questioned as a guarantee of rights (Bankowski and Mungham, 1977; see also studies of court professionals, e.g. Carlen, 1976a). Two problems arise: first, the ability to obtain legal aid in cases before the juvenile court, and second, the actual nature of the legal representation that may result. Both problems derive from the practical effects of a piece of legislation that, in formally denying guilt or innocence as appropriate categories for the juvenile court, pragmatically provides for a practice where guilt is *presumed*.

This leads to the second area of problem with legal advocacy in such a court, which is a more general one. That is that juvenile courts subsequent to the CYPA 69 operate with a circle of arguments of need–guilt and a confusion of conditions for therapy–punishment. The ambiguity remains even in those courts that, both by their dominant form of argument and by the nature of disposals (fines, detention centre, etc.), are criminal courts. Thus to imagine a legal representation that was competent would be also to assume a form of trial that was accusatorial. In other words, the juvenile court would revert to the form of the adult criminal court. Simply, legal argument would discover guilt subsequently to argue mitigation and or be replaced by social inquiry reports. Such a result would be consistently challenged by social work, yet be acceptable with current right-wing arguments of *juvenile responsibility for lawbreaking*.

CONCLUSION

This chapter set out to describe the conditions on which the current system of juvenile justice in the UK is based. In particular it drew attention to the forms in which responsibility for social behaviour has been reinforced as properly residing within the *family unit*. The inclusion of conditions within the family in the knowledges available to the court, and the physical inclusion of parents in the secret trial of the juvenile court, have created a situation in which state agencies are able increasingly to supervise familial relations in minute detail. This supervision falls predominantly on the working-class family, the young and the unemployed. Further, it was conventionally pointed out that the manner in which social work engages in its own task tends (in the short and long term) to dissolve concern with the wider conditions that tend to expose (predictable) categories of families to supervision, regulation and criminalization.

The second part of the chapter argued, by caricaturing certain positions, that certain demands when inserted into the realm of penal politics could have contradictory effects. In other words, it was suggested that the desire of certain arguments could consistently be both supported and eroded when considering them as matters of *politics*. It seems clear therefore that traditional dualities adopted in conventional arguments may not be sufficient guarantees for their success as penal strategies. Thus it would be possible, when confronted with recent right-wing proposals that seek to alter the practices of criminalizing and socializing the (deviant) young, to argue for *both* welfarism and legalism. To do so would be to engage in a politics that is always in contradiction (whether theoretical or practical).

Penal politics has often itself been seen as marginalized. However, in recent years it has become a central element of the system of symbols invoked to represent order and chaos, government and anarchy. In common-sense any left politics is, and will be, challenged with the demand of law and order from the very audience it seeks to represent as its own. Simply, juvenile lawbreaking *is a problem* for the inner-city population, and *any* penal strategy will be asked the embarrassing question of its regulation. However, the present system of regulation produces a number of effects that can be said to undermine liberal notions of civil liberties, to be discriminatory in their impact, and to be ideologically effective in general right-wing arguments of order and control. In the short term, therefore, it can become a site for political intervention. In the long term it will continue to be a site for political intervention and calculation despite certain theories that suggest a simple and unitary origin to lawbreaking and, therefore, an idealist politics of transcendence.

Social Work: The Conditions of Crisis

John Clarke, Mary Langan and Phil Lee

In this chapter we have attempted to come to terms with the present situation of social work in Britain by focusing on its political conditions. At this level, we are conscious that it says nothing new – indeed, given that it has been possible to write it only on the basis of the many discussions and arguments we have had with many people over the last few years, it would be surprising if it did. What it does represent, however, is an attempt to put together those different elements about the development of social work in a systematic way, and to understand how they act in producing the current crisiss of social work.

The article was written in the belief that it is not good enough in the present situation (if it ever was) to produce analyses of social work that are simply collapsed into a general theory of the capitalist state. This sort of analysis deduces the political character of social work from more general and abstract statements about the class character of the state. Though such concepts form an indispensable starting point for any adequate analysis, specific instances such as social work cannot be derived directly from them. The relation between these general concepts and specific instances can be properly established only by grasping the sets of particular historical determinations and struggles that constitute those instances.

THE CONSTRUCTION OF SOCIAL WORK AS A STATE AGENCY

It is important to emphasize that the practice of social work pre-dates Seebohm in a variety of specific forms; but it is the major reorganization and consolidation of social work in social services departments that provides our starting point. For it is here that social work takes its place unambiguously as part of the centrally directed state apparatus. This reform is also, in our opinion, one that underpins many of the tensions and contradictions currently confronted by social workers.

It is essential to remember that social work was not originally a part of the planning of the welfare state. The creation of social work in the form of a 'family and community service' must be seen as a consequence of a reappraisal of the workings of the welfare state since 1945. This reappraisal is conducted within the changing ideological and political composition of social democracy in this period.

We have to begin, then, from an understanding of the changed character of social democracy that follows on from the so-called 'postwar settlement' of full employment, rising standards of living, and a welfare state financed by progressive taxation. This provides the ground for a revisionist social democracy based on the belief that the tasks that classical social democracy had set itself had been accomplished by such a settlement; that is, that the problems of material inequalities had been largely resolved and removed from the political agenda. The new political agenda that was constructed was to focus first on the quality of the technical supervision of the managed economy by the Labour Party, and second on the improvement of the quality of social life. This centred specifically upon improving the capacity of certain 'residual' social groups to cope with and benefit from the new social opportunities created by the postwar settlement. What was *not* lost in this revision was the overall social democratic commitment to accomplishing political solutions through the machinery of a 'neutral' state, apparently above and outside particular class interests and taking the concrete form of technical and administrative machineries. The new direction involved an intensification of this commitment to technical solutions by taking for granted the accomplishment of a technically managed crisis free welfare economy. This meant that the political agenda became a matter of identifying emergent problems as minor internal malfunctions of this system, requiring only further corrective technical strategies.[1]

This redirection of social democracy was reflected in the shifting social composition of active Labour Party membership towards precisely those groups of state professions busily engaged in operating these technical corrective strategies (Hindess, 1971).

The development of social work is embedded within this redirection, and we can grasp this relationship through three main elements. First, it involved an argument that, although the welfare state was largely successful in its operation, some problems remained. In part, these were seen as arising from the second element, that of bureaucratic inefficiency and disjunctions between different welfare agencies. The remainder were accounted for by reference to the incompetence of certain residual social groups, often in the guise of the ubiquitous 'problem family'. These appeared in a variety of forms. Most usually, they were defined as having a general inability to cope with 'the new technical apparatus of life',[2] but also, they were seen as a problem owing to their inability to find a way through the new bureaucratic provisions of welfare. This was identified in the observation that certain families required assistance from a variety of welfare agencies, thus involving an unco-ordinated duplication of effort and resources. Social democratic debates in this period began to centre on 'a family based social work service' as the means of improving, through the medium of personal relationships, the coping capacity of these groups, and of co-ordinating and improving the connections between such groups and the welfare bureaucracies.

It has often been argued that the so-called 'rediscovery of poverty' in Britain in the early 1960s was an acute embarrassment to this variant of social democracy. Far from this being the case, it was precisely the dominance of this social democratic paradigm that ensured that the first rumblings of the economic crisis came to be interpreted in such a way. This paradigm facilitated the containment of evidence of the beginnings of a major capitalist crisis within definitions of poverty as generated by bureaucratic problems in the delivery of services, the lack of economic resources to make the services technically efficient, and the stubborn personal incompetence of certain groups of the population.

It is these elements that delivered the Seebohm solution, a reform that provided the 'magical resolution' of all these problems. First, it proposed that the new social service should act to co-ordinate aspects of the other welfare agencies, to improve the delivery of services, and particularly to assist those clients who, for reasons of bureaucratic inefficiency or personal incompetence, were failing to benefit from welfare state provision. Second, it proposed that the social services should provide the personal arm of the welfare state, creating more efficient co-ordination and rationalization of services for the 'perenially incompetent' (such as the blind, the elderly and the disabled), and for the socially disadvantaged. Third, the service was to take on the task of improving the social functioning of those groups who suffer from problems of personal and relational disturbances and malfunctioning.

The effect of this conception of the new role for social work for those who came to staff the new social services departments was the absence of any clearly defined 'social work task'. The 'task' for the new social workers was in fact a complex assemblage of a variety of different elements – a mixture of parts of work taken over from the old specialist occupations (e.g. the children's departments and the psychiatric social workers); parts taken over from other state agencies (for example, the work of the probation service in the juvenile courts) involving a whole range of both permissive and statutory duties, together with the broader injunctions to co-ordinate relations between clients and other state agencies (e.g. housing, supplementary benefit, the health service and so on), as well as providing advice and assistance to the family generally.

In addition to these intended relations to, and appropriations from, other state agencies, social services also became involved in tasks that Seebohm naively failed to anticipate. Because of Seebohm's belief in the potential adequacy of other welfare agencies, it could not appreciate the extent to which the systematic impotence of those agencies would lead to further expansions of the range of social work tasks.

The core of this new social work agency was then a sort of 'empty centre' – just a collection of jobs, duties and responsibilities hung together in the person of the new 'generic' social worker. What covered this 'empty centre' and gave it apparent coherence, what made it 'generic', was the insistence that all of these bits in some way involved the 'personal dimension', and could best be dealt with through personalized means – the worker–client relationship. This covering was to be enforced through an insistence on the vital importance of trained and qualified social workers, whose training would provide the whole series of knowledges through which this personal dimension could be best achieved and managed, and at the same time construct the appropriate professional identification.

THE INTERNAL CRISIS OF CONFIDENCE

It is hardly surprising that the creation of the new social services departments was very soon followed by expressions of doubt about their role from social workers working in them. These doubts covered a whole spectrum of problems – professional, organizational, personal and political. We want to argue here that the crisis of confidence and the expression of doubts and cynicism are not accidental fantasies. Nor are they due to social workers' lack of maturity or failure to come to terms with authority: rather, they are rooted in the organization of social work, and the tensions and contradictions involved in that organization.

The first point here relates to what we have already said about social work as an agency located within the terms already established in other state apparatuses. What emerges from this is a *structural subordination* of social work to the other agencies to which it is connected. Social work derives its tasks and its orientations from these other agencies; its operational world is permanently defined in relation to their policies and practices. In some aspects of their work, social workers operate on the margins of other agencies, negotiating their clients through the definitions and practices of these agencies, but almost always in a situation where those definitions are the central ones (e.g. in relation to housing, supplementary benefit and in the court room). In other areas, social workers are required to work alongside 'colleagues' from other professions (e.g. doctors, psychiatrists, etc.), but again, almost always in a position of relative subordination where the element of social work practice is defined within the frame of reference of the other professions. This is also indicated in the eclectic nature of social work theory, with its constant gleaning from these other fields (e.g. medicine, psychiatry, pscyhoanalysis).[3]

Terence Johnson (1972) has written of the 'mediating professions' of the state, suggesting that one of their characteristic features is the task of mediating client demands (or client definitions of need) to the agency's administrative definitions of what those needs are and how they can best be met. Clearly, in social work the task of translating client definitions into administrative ones is not solely a matter of the accommodation of the client to the agency's definitions, but of social workers having to mediate client demands to the more powerful definitions provided by other state agencies outside social work itself. Johnson also suggests that this double requirement of both representing the client and operating the administrative definitions provides one of the key structural sources of tension and conflict for such professionals. It is through this concrete form of purveyor of second- and third-hand mediated state definitions that the social worker confronts the client. It is this reality that is suppressed in the professional rhetoric of the social work task as the connection of the individual and society.

The second aspect of subordination that we want to deal with is of a somewhat different order. It involves the internal organization of social work itself, that is, the bureaucratic structure of the social services departments. There is more at issue here than the usual condemnation of bureaucratic inefficiency, or the irrational expansion of the 'chiefs' over the 'Indians'. Bureaucracies have a more significant role than these superficial criticisms would suggest. They provide a rigorous and hierarchically structured system of control and supervision, and they offer the possibility of a systematic mechanism of policing and scrutiny of subordinates by superiors. The organization of social work within such a structure involves the installation of a sort of 'mechanical' or 'organizational' conscience on the front-line social worker. This can be operated if it appears that the professional conscience of the trained (and therefore supposedly mature and self-regulating) social worker is not functioning properly. This organizational conscience can also act to fix the broad tenets of 'good professionalism' to the more tightly defined prescriptions of the bureaucratic administration itself. More mundanely, the system of supervision operates to ensure some minimum of conformity on the part of the social worker, and to reproduce the client–worker relation of assessment, analysis and guidance (and the personalizing effect of that relation) between the worker and her supervisor. This appropriates older professional and paternal forms of supervision which pre-date Seebohm, and organizes them through a more rigorous hierarchical structure.

This is not to suggest that the bureacratic system of control 'works' successfully in any complete sense – like other systems of control and regulation it has its limits and builds its own sources of resistance and opposition. Some of the limits of this mechanical conscience are, we believe, visible in the increasing demands from senior officials in social services for the provision of social work training which is more task-oriented, and which may build greater 'organizational loyalty' in those being trained.

The bureaucratic control of social workers is one of the key mechanisms in the crisis of confidence within social work itself – inducing and continually reinforcing a division between basic grade workers and the management. This divide can take a number of forms – for example, hinging around the gap between those who have to deal with the 'real world' of the clients and those who merely administer. But whatever the form they take, this organizational structure of control produces its own set of internal tensions.

Finally in this section we have to confront the doubts that emerged among social workers about their relationship with clients. Expressions of these doubts were the questioning of the care or control element in social work, and a growing concern about the use of social workers as 'soft cops' to contain and individualize social problems.[4] This represents a real double dilemma within social work. First, in however distorted and constraining a form, the creation of social work involved an attempt to intervene in real social problems and provide some form of social assistance. The social worker's task has been to manage the gap between the real problems that clients encounter and the definitions of how their 'needs' can be met. This process of adaptation often requires an attempt to 'conform' the clients to the established patterns of provision.

Second, this task of managing the relation between the client and the administrative controls is one that involves both 'care' and 'control'. *That is, 'care' is not the opposite of control, but one of the mechanisms through which control can operate.* Control is exercised through the machinery of the capitalist state not only in the most visible form of physical repression and coercion, but through other more apparently neutral means, such as the operation of administrative criteria and decision-making (in housing allocation policy, for example), and through the personal relations involved in social work and similar 'caring' roles. In social work, this exercise of control through the medium of care involves a doubly exploitative relation. First, it attempts to exploit the assumed willingness and 'need' of clients to engage in more personalized relationships. This alternative to strategies that operate through bureaucratic or authoritarian relations is constructed because of the resistances that such strategies generate. Second, it involves the state's exploiting the social worker's personality – requiring her to use it and her willingness to 'work with people' as the resources of control. Like the bureacratic form of control mentioned earlier, this intention is not uniformly successful in practice. It, too, produces its own specific forms of tensions and resistances – distrust and resentment on the part of some clients, and the feeling of 'conning' and manipulating people on the part of social workers.

THE SOCIOLOGICAL CRITICS OF SOCIAL WORK

These problems received a somewhat different expression in sociological attacks on social work. The emergence of new 'radical' strands of sociological thought in the late 1960s and early 1970s, based particularly in the sociology of deviance, involved a sharpening focus on the exercise of social control in advanced capitalist countries. In many ways, this focus on social control had a sort of 'revelatory' style – identifying the operation of control in apparently progressive, humanitarian and benevolent initiatives by the state. Social work became one of the key examples of this hidden control masquerading in a humanitarian guise. In part, this analysis depended on what now seems a naive assessment that 'reformism' had won the political day, and that consequently there was a substantial shift taking place to more subtle forms of social regulation, from the 'old', more visibly coercive mechanisms. At this level, it is obvious that there was a sort of congruence between the emergence of the sociological critics and the growth of doubts and disenchantments among practising social workers themselves.

But this apparent unity of interests had less to do with sociologists' ability to identify the central issues affecting social workers, and more to do with political conditions common to both groups. One of the effects of postwar social democracy, discussed earlier, was to narrow the political arena around a limited agenda. This narrowing was challenged by an eruption of alternative forms of politics – sexual, counter-cultural, student- and community-based politics, together with a resurgence of the traditional revolutionary Left. These movements both reasserted political issues omitted from the agenda, and posed politics on new terrains. These were political developments to which the new generations of sociologists and social workers were exposed.

The congruence between sociology and social work has never really developed into an alliance of any strength. The two groups have not substantially managed to overcome their different orientations to the problems of theory and practice.[5] Although there have been attempts, both jointly and on the separate sides of the divide, to do so, these have never achieved the sort of alliance projected in the nightmares of the commentators of the social work and academic right. In these the charismatic and persuasive pronouncements of the sociologists have been held responsible for leading naive, immature and gullible social workers away from the paths of good social work into the labyrinths of political theory and organizational subversion (Lewis, 1977). As in all nightmares, there is a work of displacement being accomplished in which the material and organizational sources of the doubts and difficulties experienced within social work practice are masked through their transference on to the machiavellian figures of the sociologists. In fact, the accomplishments of the sociologists have been much less grandiose than this!

Our argument here centres on the failure of several varieties of radical sociology to produce useful and progressive knowledge in relation to social workers. The initial concern with questions of social control, exemplified in labelling theory, attempted to proffer advice in the form of strategies of 'radical non-intervention', coupled with the advocation of tolerance for different life styles. Intervention itself was seen as producing and compounding the problems it claimed to solve, particularly in the field of 'victimless crimes' (Schur, 1973). This approach alerted social workers to the ways in which clients were defined, and to the possible effects of such labels. However, the simple moral relativism of this approach failed to offer social workers any political grasp of the structural problems they encountered in client groups or of their own position in the state apparatus.

One attempt to move beyond the 'empty moralizing' of sceptical deviancy theory took the form of the development of a marxist criminology, in which crime and social control were located within the structural arrangements of capitalist societies. Though important analyses have been produced from within this tendency, its politics have largely been abstract and rhetorical – for example, in summoning up the vision of a crime-free socialist society as a political goal. Thus, one of its limitations has been the inability to generate more concrete and interventionist connections.

Some of the elements of this tendency are also visible in the move from the analysis of social control to its location in theories of the capitalist state. Though such theories have provided more analytical purchase on the problems of social control, they have been politically debilitated by slides into functionalist analysis. The attempts to provide more complex analyses of the state in capitalist societies have often produced conceptions of the state as a monolithic unity and tied by too compelling a logic to the needs of capital's development. The effects of this are to neglect the role of class struggles and their consequences for the state's development, and to close the possibility of understanding contradiction within the state as sites of particular struggles (e.g. Marx's classic analysis of factory legislation).

The final version of these marxisms that we want to mention is the movement into theoreticism. We have in mind here the preoccupation with generating ever more elaborate epistemological guarantees of theoretical certainty. This introspective cycle of theorizing upon theory has the effect of removing theory from any deeply connected guiding role in political action. This dissolves any stress on a mutual relationship between theory and politics.

There is a recent attempt to find a path between these two positions, one that defines itself explicitly against, on the one hand, the collapse into moral relativism, and, on the other, the excesses of abstract marxism. While having its roots in the former and allowing that the latter has made some limited advances, it defines its own project as constructing a middle-range criminology connected to systematic interventions into policy and practical issues. It argues that these should be based on a 'back to justice' model.

Though some of these authors begin from a sensitive analysis of the dilemmas of crime and crime control in capitalist societies, there is a reluctance to follow this through into a marxist analysis. (e.g. Cohen, 1979). Generally, the possibility of developing a marxist analysis is foreclosed by the well practised ploy of equating marxism with the spectre of Eastern Europe. There is no attempt made to explain the particular structural conditions that produced stalinism and the regimes of Eastern Europe; rather, they are conjured up as a vision of the inevitable consequences of marxism.

The equation by these authors of marxism with Eastern Europe means that there can be no possibility of making interventions from any class political basis – what replaces this standpoint is a return to the problematic of classical reformism. Some inhabit this space with an uncomfortable but 'realistic' acquiescence, while for others it is their natural home. Their critique, however, gains some contemporary relevance, because it attacks some of the bastions of revisionist social democracy – often in the right places, but from the limiting vantage point of classical social democracy (cf. Downes, 1979, p. 14). These problems are focused in the demand for a return to the principles of justice and legal rights as the only viable principles on which intervention can be made. Despite the analysis and understanding of the class character and repressive nature of bourgeois law offered by the more sophisticated proponents of this position, conceptions of law and justice appear to be the only available 'independent' guarantor, because of their apparently 'universal' character.

The effect of this development is to return us to where the new sociology began – the problem of reformism. But here, under political conditions where reformism appears to be in retreat, state reforms, instead of being seen as the most sophisticated instruments of capitalist control, are represented as advances that need to be defended. This problem of underestimating the complexity of reformism is not one that is peculiar to sociology, but also appears as one of the dilemmas in the current situation of social work, and we shall be returning to it later in this chapter.

RETRENCHMENT AND THE ATTACK FROM THE RIGHT

If the first and most vocal attack on social work was launched from within left sociology, the second and more powerful assault has come from the Right, launched from the middle of the fundamental economic crisis of British capitalism. This crisis has had three main effects on social work. While social workers have had to confront the consequences of the crisis for the individuals, families, and groups that they encounter, this crisis has also expanded those apparently marginal groups of 'problems' – the unemployed, the homeless, the poor, and the forms of personal destruction produced by such conditions.

These conditions have been exacerbated by having to confront this expansion within the context of the attack on state spending. The series of cuts, began under Labour and now pursued with greater vigour by the Conservative government, exacerbates the task of social work by closing down the resources of other agencies (for example, housing and the NHS) through which it negotiates its clients. The production of 'solutions' then comes to require an intensification of the labour of social workers. As the material resources of assistance are reduced, the 'personal' relation itself becomes increasingly central. For example, the proposal of 'community care' solutions, supported at one level as one part of a critique of the effects of institutionalization, has become state policy in a number of areas (for the aged, the mentally ill, children and young people). They have become policy because they require less capital expenditure, and only the greater work of community supervision and monitoring by social workers.

This pattern of cutting state expenditure is felt as much within social services as it is in the other state agencies. The reduction of capital expenditure and the freezing or abolition of posts (particularly those that are politically 'sensitive', as in Wandsworth or Tower Hamlets, for example) are some of the current expressions of this. Here too it has the effect of requiring the intensification of social workers' labour by removing alternative 'solutions', such as spending on homes or hostels.

This attack on social work has not occurred just at the economic level; it has also taken the form of a sustained ideological offensive. This has focused on the 'softness' and incompetence of the social work profession. The attack has been articulated through a series of *causes célèbres*: social work cases, particularly those involving children as victims of violence and of inadequate supervision, that have apparently 'gone wrong' through the incompetence, inexperience, laxity, excessive liberalism of the social workers. This is coupled with a demand for a return to more traditional and coercive forms of discipline.

It is precisely such attacks and demands that connect with central themes in the rise of Thatcherite populism (Hall, 1979b). This is well illustrated in the Thatcherite attack on excessive state spending, and in particular on state 'interference' in private matters. Here it proposes that people (and families, in particular) should be left to develop their independence rather than be reduced to a position of dependence on state support and state expertise. This also involves the attack on liberalism – the form in which 'creeping socialism' inserts itself into the state – as a set of values that has eroded and undermined traditional moral certainties. It is these virtues that must be reasserted. The resemblances to Thatcherite populism (and particularly its anti-state elements) are vividly depicted in some of the responses to the social workers' strike of 1978–9. Who needs these 'experts', particularly if they can be shown to be immature and incompetent experts? After all, it is clear that many of these problems require only the application of a certain amount of 'common sense', which, as we know, is a capacity that liberal professionals lack by definition. All the more persuasive is that 'common sense' in this guise conveniently involves a much cheaper solution in terms of state spending – either by getting people to 'help themselves' or by the 'non-expert' means of providing more auxiliary services to the community (e.g. home helps).

This external attack has its parallels in the internal world of the social services departments, involving a greater tightening of the controls and checks on social work practice. The most visible signs of this are in the greater demands for organizational loyalty and commitment, and in a greater degree of 'routinization' of the most sensitive social work tasks. For example, the public concern about social work's role in cases of non-accidental injury produced the response of sets of detailed procedural guidelines which social workers were to follow in such cases. These guidelines were provided both by the professional body and by the local and national organizational structures. As well as providing for greater routinization, these guidelines also involved the subjection of the basic grade to greater scrutiny and control by the other levels of the hierarchy – the demand for 'accountability'. These are part of a systematic attempt to produce greater 'conformity' among social workers to the agency's definitions of the social worker's task. This involves attempts to push back even further those marginal areas of 'professional autonomy' within which some social workers have found space to manoeuvre (cf. Pearson, 1975).

This is accompanied by growing demands for the 'rationalization' of social work education to equip social workers better for the agency task. In large part this hinges around removing or reducing the influence of the less practical elements of the curriculum (with more 'troubling' ones such as sociology in mind) and the expansion of the more practical and skill-based elements (Kornreich, 1978).

Social work is not alone in being subjected to this attack, for the same processes are visible across a number of state agencies. Attempts are being made to reorganize and conform these agencies to the requirements of the new 'iron times'. Thus, for example, the 'great debate' on educational standards, and more specifically the reorganization of technical and business education, have as one of their key elements a commitment to relate education more closely to the needs of the economy (i.e. of the employers). Similar tendencies can also be seen in the proposals for reorganizing supplementary benefits, in the initiatives to cope with the youth unemployment problem through preparation for 'work experience' (i.e. work discipline), as well as in the more obvious proposals for trade union law reform. These are all parts of the reconstruction of the agencies and mechanisms of the state in directions that ensure that they play their part in producing a capitalist solution to the present crisis. This is to be accomplished not just through the cutting of public expenditure, but also through changes in the mode of operation of state agencies.

CONTESTATION AND CONSTRAINT IN SOCIAL WORK

We have attempted to establish what the material conditions of the crisis in social work are by considering the development of social work in the last decade. We now want to turn to some of the ways in which these conditions are lived out and responded to by practising social workers. Our aim here is to insist that these conditions do not produce, of themselves, one simple response or solution on the part of social workers. We can only indicate something of the range of those responses.

We can begin with some of the key internal inhibitions and constraints. A central role is played by the construction of social work as a largely privatized and individualized practice. The effects of this in producing social problems as a series of individualized and disconnected 'cases' are reproduced internally in the tendency for case loads and social workers' assessments to become individualized. This militates against attempts to define problems as collective ones and to construct collective solutions to them. This privatization shapes the character of some responses to the crisis of social work, producing them in individualized forms.

One of these we would call the 'retreatist' response – those for whom continuing in social work is so intolerable that they give up. This is indexed in social work's high labour turnover, as well as in the more temporary 'withdrawals' reflected in illness and absenteeism. Second, there are more instrumental accommodations, which withdraw personal commitment from the social work task. This involves a more cynical and disenchanted conception of it as a job that provides money. Personal, social or political satisfactions are divorced and sought elsewhere.

The pressure to individualism reappears in a slightly different form in the tensions between unionism and professionalism, with the professional orientation laying greater emphasis on individual standards of competence, training and performance. Professionalism operates against attempts to organize the occupation collectively, on however limited and defensive a front. It also obscures and clouds the questions of power and domination, both between the social worker and client, and within the social work hierarchy. These elements are obviously ones that do not go uncontested. A variety of radicalisms, not all of which sit comfortably together, have been developed as solutions to these problems – unionization, anti-bureaucratic struggles, and attempts to develop new forms of practice.

We now have to return to the structural subordination of social work within the state itself. For this poses problems of which issues social workers have to struggle over and to what extent these are within their own keeping. The subordination of social work to the definitions and practices of other agencies acts as a permanent constraint on the possibilities for organizing solely within social work. This subordination sets limits within which many of the specific questions of social work practice are posed. This is no revelation, for it is precisely on these boundaries that many of the daily struggles of social workers take place. But these tend to be in the form of individual struggles to win through particular cases – to manage, cajole, con and negotiate on the margins of these definitions.

A further series of inhibitions lies in the external conditions of social work, and involves the problems of working with marginalized and disorganized sectors of the population. The accusation that social work operates to individualize social problems is only part of the story, for the problems that social workers encounter often confront them as individualized cases. They operate primarily among sections of the population that have already been marginalized from the central relations where collective strength and organization exist (the elderly, children, the mentally ill, families, the unemployed sections whose problems are structurally produced as well as merely 'labelled' as individual ones). Additionally, these problems are often received in the form of 'pre-packaged' individual cases from other referring agencies. There are some real grounds for optimism here, for the last few years have seen the growth of organizations both nationally and locally built around these 'marginal' issues and groups. Some have involved social workers, some have been constructed within the client groups themselves, and these act as a reminder that the political possibilities themselves are not fixed and eternal, but are open to movement and development (e.g. Claimants Union, Programme for the Reform of the Laws on Soliciting, Mental Patients Union).

The Classic Constraint: Social Work and Social Democracy

We now want to return to our earlier argument about the creation of social work within revisionist social democracy, and consider its legacy for the current crisis. The commitment there to finding 'technical solutions' to social problems through the creation of a new group of state experts is one that suppressed the question of constructing social work with any sense of popular political support. The construction took place through an alliance of state expertise – politicians, administrators and the professionals themselves – rather than being connected with any broadly based 'external' working-class demand or support. Unlike many reforms introduced by social democracy, this is not constructed as a response to any organized working-class pressure. Nor is there any attempt made to educate and develop working-class support for this as a necessary or 'progressive' measure which is in the class's interest.

The absence of any attempt to construct popular support is characteristic of a series of 'liberalizing' reforms introduced in the 1960s in the arenas of welfare, penal policy and education. Rather, social democracy's efforts become increasingly fixed on the construction and management of the *economic* unity of the nation. That is, the Labour Party attempted to contain working-class demands in the guise of the 'national interest' within the economic confines set by a deepening capitalist crisis (e.g., the Social Contract and the Concordat). One of the key forces in the current crisis of social democracy is its economically determined inability to deliver the economic concessions that make this particular form of managing a national unity possible. This, coupled with its failure to develop popular support on other terrains, has created a particular crisis of political authority – to which Thatcherism attempts to offer a new solution.

The neglect of a popular basis around these 'liberalizing' reforms constructed through the 1960s has meant a situation where the new conservatism, with its appeal to traditional values, has been able to define and dominate the debates around these areas almost uncontested. It has been able to draw on and cultivate the regressive elements of 'common sense' which the reformism of the 1960s ignored, to present these reforms as excessive interference, excessive government expenditure, the erosion of traditional values and so on (Hall, 1979b). It then attempts to utilize these elements as if they were a popular will for an assault on the welfare state as a whole. The specific elitist character of the reformist solution has left this arena vulnerable to colonization by the new right populism, and has left social work without any substantial political basis from which it might draw working-class support. The search for a solution to social work's problems in the crisis is shaped by these two forces: the failure of revisionism to develop any defences for social work, coupled with the Thatcherite assault. One major solution that has emerged is the defence of existing levels of state provision and welfare rights, allied to a commitment to the principles of universalism and the accomplishment through state provision of social justice. There is a clear parallel here with the 'back to justice' movement in sociology discussed earlier – what unites them is their commitment to universal principles, particularly as embodied in the notion of justice, and to the state as the means of achieving these. Both of these involve an attempt to revive and refurbish the principles of classical social democracy.

The key error of this position is to forget the similarities between revisionist and classical social democracy. The central similarity is that both act as political mechanisms to manage and contain working-class struggles, and to produce consent through the work of containment and concession. This error leads those who would return to the principles of classical social democracy to misunderstand the character of its state reforms. They assume that the achievements of universalism and welfare in the postwar settlement were the progressive accomplishments of the state itself. What this omits is any understanding of the basis of these reforms in class struggles, and the vital role performed by social democracy in coupling working-class demands to state-provided and regulated solutions. To be more precise, the political work of social democracy involves two accomplishments. The first is the separation of the content of what is provided from the forms of its provision and control. What is accomplished here is the exclusion of any working-class democratic control of this provision by its organization through an apparently neutral state machinery, whose bureaucratic, technical and expert mechanisms operate within capitalist logics. Second, the concession of real advances in material provisions allows the mobilization of working-class political consent to this overall capitalist logic, by representing these gains as if they were major incursions into or transformations of capitalism on the road to state socialism.

This predictable lemming-like rush back to classical social democracy, conditioned by the failure of revisionism and the threat of the Right, simply misrecognizes the location of progressive forces –

it identifies them with the social democratic formula rather than with the class struggles on which that formula works.

Our argument so far should make it clear that we see social work as a child of social democratic revisionism, but it should also be clear that we do not see any solution to its problems within the revival of classical social democracy. Consequently, we cannot argue for any simple politics of defending social work institutions in their present form, however attractive such a limited strategy may appear in the shadow of the Thatcher axe.

We accept that it is vital to develop trade unionism within social work, and to build links with other sections of the labour movement both within and outside the welfare state. We would also want to insist on the importance of developing community organizations and struggles among the users of state services. It is important to recognize that social workers occupy a potentially privileged position in being able to connect these traditionally separated areas of struggle.

Such struggles are essential to defending the material gains that the working class have wrestled from the state. But while these struggles are treated as merely defensive, what is being defended is both limited provision and the form in which that provision is organized and controlled – the state bureaucracies. The only possible escape route from this reconstruction of the social democratic scenario is when these struggles develop as a challenge to the forms in which provision is organized and controlled. These are the means by which popular conceptions of, and strategies for, welfare and its organization could be developed. For social work, such developments would be important as the basis from which the questions posed within radical social work could be answered. The questions of what purposes social work exists for, who controls it, and is controlled by it, and how it is to be organized and practised can only be resolved in any progressive direction from such a political understanding.

Notes

CHAPTER 1

1. According to Marcel Mauss (1979, p. 84), the conflation of the notions of law, right and *persona* proceeded rapidly from the second century BC.

> a moral sense [was] increasingly added to the legal sense; a sense of a conscious, independent, autonomous, free, responsible being. The moral consciousness introduces conscience into the juridical concept of right.

I am not arguing that these conflated relationships between law, right and constituent modes of subjectivity are either necessary or peculiar to the capitalist mode of production, only that within the capitalist mode of production they have a major, determinate effect: the successful obstruction of any arguments that would conclude that state criminalization processes have less to do with guilty intent and more to do with capitalist social relations.

CHAPTER 2

1. It should be made clear that Rajah was only one of a number of prisoners engaged in this action. He is singled out in this article because his case was taken as a 'test case' by the NCCL and because of his agreement that all details of the proceedings relating to him might be freely used in order to establish the full significance of the case itself and the eventual verdict.
2. Merlyn Rees addressed himself to this problem during his period as Home Secretary. In a classic piece of double-think he declared that: 'I have concluded that this independence [*that is, the independence of the Board recommended by Jellicoe*. L.T.] and the Board's present functions are compatible.' In other words, he had completely rejected the Committee's central argument. But that in no way inhibited his final comment on the

matter: 'I have however accepted much of the general argument in the Jellicoe Committee report.'

3. The final point to be made in such a piece as this, of course, is the contrast between the initial judicial treatment of the Hull prisoners and that accorded to the Hull prison officers who were charged with conspiracy to beat and assault them and their fellow inmates. The following summary makes most of the necessary points.

> The prison officers were alleged to have beaten, kicked, abused and humiliated the prisoners ... Initially the Board of Visitors found the prisoners had no cause of complaint against them and a Home Office enquiry found them not guilty of maltreating the men. They were only brought to court as a result of a relentless campaign by P.R.O.P. [the prisoners' union] and a remarkable persistence on the part of the investigating police officers. When arrested and charged they were allowed full legal representation and trial by judge and jury. They were found guilty and allowed to go free. [*New Statesman*, 13 April 1979]

CHAPTER 3

1. See *Kuruma* v. *R.* [1955] A.C. 197; *King* v. *R.* [1969] 1 A.C. 304.
2. *Jeffrey* v. *Black* [1977] 3 W.L.R.895. See *Mapp* v. *Chic* (1961) 367 U.S.206.
3. See *Miranda* v. *Arizona* (1966) 384 U.S.436.
4. The judgment of Breitel JP in Matter of *Rockwell* v. *Morris* (1961) 12 App.Div. 2d 272 (Supreme Court of New York) states strikingly the American approach:

> A community need not wait to be subverted by street riots and storm troopers; but also it cannot, by its policemen or commissioners, suppress a speaker, in prior restraint, on the basis of newsreports, hysteria, or inference that what he did yesterday, he will do today. Thus, too, if the speaker incites others to immediate unlawful action he may be punished – in a proper case, stopped when disorder actually impends; but this is not to be confused with unlawful action from others who seek unlawfully to suppress or punish the speaker.

5. (1939) 30 U.S.496.
6. None more so than the crucial decision of the Divisional Court of the Queen's Bench Division in *Duncan* v. *Jones* [1936] 1 K.B.218, a case to contrast with the statement in Rockwell, cited above, n. 4.
7. *Alderson* v. *Booth* [1969] 2 Q.B.216.
8. Criminal Law Act 1967, s.2(6).
9. See the cases cited in n. 1 above.
10. *Chic Fashions (West Wales) Ltd* v. *Jones* [1968] 2 Q.B.299; on this particular point a warrant issued under the Theft Act 1968, s.26(1) may now specifically authorize the seizure of such other goods.
11. In *Jeffrey* v. *Black* [1977] 3 W.L.R.895, the defendant had been arrested for stealing a sandwich and an illegal search of his home without a warrant produced a quantity of cannabis.

12. *Garfinkel* v. *Metropolitan Police Commissioner* [1972] Crim.L.R.44.
13. *Jeffrey* v. *Black*, n. 11 above.
14. Leigh (1975), referring especially to *Chic Fashions (West Wales) Ltd* v. *Jones, Jones*, *Ghani* v. *Jones*, n. 15 below, and *Garfinkel* v. *Metropolitan Police Commissioner*.
15. As in *Ghani* v. *Jones* [1970] 1 Q.B.693.
16. *Elias* v. *Pasmore* [1934] 2 K.B.164.
17. The word 'wilfully' included in the Police Act 1964, s.51(3) in defining the offence of obstruction and therefore some knowledge that the constable is acting in the course of his duty is required. In *Willnott* v. *Atack* [1976] 3 W.L.R.753 it was held that an intent to obstruct was necessary. The defendant pushed a policeman who was struggling with another man and did so in the belief that he could handle the situation better himself. The Divisional Court held that intent and hostility (?) were required. If the constable is assaulted the offence is one of strict liability and no such intent need be proved: *R.* v. *Forbes* (1865) 10 Cox.362. Since pushing is an assault the result if assault is charged will be curious.
18. *R.* v. *Fennell* [1971] Q.B.428.
19. The words used in *Donnelly* v. *Jackman* [1970] 1 W.L.R.562 were that 'it is not every trivial interference with a citizen's liberty that amounts to a course of conduct sufficient to take the officer out of the course of his duties'. In that case a policeman was trying to persuade the defendant to stop and answer questions and twice tapped him on the shoulder as he walked on. On the first occasion the defendant made it clear that he had no intention of stopping and when the policeman tapped him again the defendant assaulted him.
20. *Squires* v. *Botwright* [1973] Crim.L.R.106.
21.   It is a fundamental condition of the admissibility in evidence against any person, equally of any oral answer given by that person to a question put by a police officer and of any statement made by that person, that it shall have been voluntary, in the sense that it has not been obtained from him by fear of prejudice or hope of advantage, exercised or held out by a person in authority, or by oppression.

Practice Note (Judges' Rules) [1964] 1 W.L.R.152, approved as a correct statement of the law by Lord Reid in *Commissioners of Customs and Excise* v. *Harzand Power* [1967] 1 A.C.760.
22. *R.* v. *Ovenell* [1966] 1 Q.B.17.
23.   Every person at any stage of an investigation should be able to communicate and to consult privately with a solicitor. This is so even if he is in custody provided that in such a case no unreasonable delay or hindrance is caused to the processes of investigation or the administration of justice by his doing so.
24. *R.* v. *Allen and others* [1977] Crim.L.R.163; in *R.* v. *Lemsatef* [1977] 1 W.L.R.812, the Court of Appeal upheld a judge's decision to admit a confession when a request to see a solicitor and a request by the solicitor had been refused: 'This court wishes to stress that it is not a good reason for refusing to allow a suspect, under arrest or detention, to see his solicitor, that he has not yet made any oral or written admission.' But where is the sanction?

25. In *Lemsatef*, n. 24 above, the Court of Appeal said

> It must be clearly understood that neither customs officers nor police
> officers have any right to detain somebody for the purposes of getting
> them to help them with their inquiries. Police officers either arrest for an
> offence or they do not detain at all. The law is clear ... If the idea is
> getting around among either Customs and Excise officers or police
> officers that they can arrest or detain people, as the case may be, for this
> particular purpose, the sooner they disabuse themselves of this idea, the
> better.

Strong words, but the appellant's confession was admitted in evidence, its
admissibility was upheld and the appellant's conviction upheld.

26. The shouting of abuse at one's neighbour in a public place was held to be
an offence under the section in *Ward* v. *Holman* [1964] 2 Q.B.580.

27. *Brutus* v. *Cozens* [1973] A.C.854 – disruption of play in the Wimbledon
lawn tennis championships when a white South African player was on
court.

28. [1963] 2 Q.B.744.

29. Glanville Williams drew attention to the absence of an authoritative
definition in 1954: 'Arrest for Breach of the Peace' [1954] Crim.L.R.578.

30. See e.g. Williams (1967), Chapter 5; Brownlie (1968), pp. 17–22; and
Daintith (1966).

31. (1864) Ir.C.L.1.

32. *Piddington* v. *Bates* [1961] 1 W.L.R.162. In these days of mass picketing
and violent clashes on some such occasions it seems remarkable that this
case concerned a specified number of pickets as the maximum (according
to the police) that would be consistent with preventing a breach of the
peace. The statement in the law report that a recalcitrant picket 'pushed
gently' past a policeman and was 'gently arrested' has a certain period
charm.

33. [1963] 2 Q.B.561.

CHAPTER 4

1. Edward Thompson, in the conclusion to *Whigs and Hunters* (1975),
defends the notion of the 'rule of law' and conceives it as embodying
certain values – fairness, equity, etc. These values are, however,
problematic: law follows from certain procedural rules. The ideology of
'rule of law' is double-edged; it unifies *all* laws as equal parts of that rule.
Every statute, every bit of judge's bodging to cover 'gaps' in the law, is
valid and binding: the Industrial Relations Act 1971 as well as the laws
proscribing acts that are universally condemned, like murder and rape. No
wonder it is so popular with characters like Paul Johnson or Lord
Hailsham.

2. This may seem a harsh judgement on two of the most original thinkers on
questions of socialist organization, and two leaders most willing to recognize the specificity of organizational questions and the means to tackle

them. However, neither Mao nor Lenin could break from the conception of a single-party state or the need to assign powers of strategic decision to the centre. In both cases the notion of a unitary 'working-class' or 'popular' interest capable of expression in a single centre vitiated their own specific innovations. Lenin's last texts took an immense step back from the Bolshevik 'forced march' conceptions of socialist construction, but his organizational solutions – the Workers' and Peasants' Inspection, for example – respond to the problems of control of party and state by further valorizing the *social origin* of the personnel. Regrettably, his token 'toilers' could have been no match for skilled party and state functionaries. The problem was thought in terms of the 'deproletarianization' of party and state. This was nothing but a disaster. Actually, many of the higher state administrative bodies and official functionaries – Rykov, Torsky, Frumkin, Gosplan, etc. – were more capable of managing affairs and devising a viable strategy for socialist construction than either the party rank and file or the various 'Lefts' (including Stalin after 1928). 'Stanlinism' was, among other things, a *coup d'état against* competent state administration, and socialist specialists were its chief victims.

3. Lenin's *State and Revolution* (1964) obliterates the analysis of the specificity of the political he derived from Kautsky and further developed in *What is to be Done?* (1963). We are not simply endorsing Kautsky. Kautsky did not abandon class essentialism; he continued to conceive socialism as a necessary consequence of capitalist class antagonisms, but he did radically qualify the political conditions of its expression.

4. For Cole the condition of association and of the interrelation of associations was fellowship; he assumes an essential harmony on the basis of which associations act. A systematic legislative government was not necessary; co-ordination problems could be resolved by a 'constitutional judiciary' (Cole, 1921, p. 137), but one free to make *ad hoc* decisions.

5. The promulgation of the 1936 Constitution at the beginning of the terror was a gross and vulgar joke played by Stalin on the Soviet citizenry and the able and honest men who helped to draft it – Bukharin and Pashukanis among others. But the excesses of a Stalin cannot hide the worm in the bud. Bukharin and Pashukanis were almost as far from conceding the need for checks in the capacities of central state agencies, for a radical differentiation of the functions of state agencies, and for the necessity of erecting effective means to review and proscribe, if nessary, policies and actions.

6. The same considerations apply to courts as bodies of review, supervision and definition of limits. Adjudication and legislation are not separate; courts can be both makers and arbiters of rules. A condition for effective courts is that judges and lawyers are not officials of or under a ministry of justice, receiving orders from higher echelons of the administration and using their judgement only within limits established for them in advance. Specialist jurists are necessary, but the danger of a corps of judges is evident. Non-specialist members of courts, elected or called at random,

election of judges, etc., are mechanisms to supplement juridic competence with considerations of wider interests and prevent the formation of a closed corporation of specialists.

7. The fact that there is no distinctly *socialist* conception of nationality, age of majority, conditions of socio-political competence, etc., is not a point of criticism of the practice of socialist states. Only those who believe socialism is a society–totality conferring its distinctive features on every aspect of life will be disturbed by the absence of distinctly 'socialist' positions on social policy questions. Socialist states may differ in these matters, and it is an open question of debate whether different solutions to social policy problems are better or worse. The fact that certain solutions resemble those of 'capitalist' states cannot in itself be sufficient grounds for criticism.

8. The slogan of abolishing the division of 'mental and manual' labour goes hand in hand with a conception of social organization as the couple to popular democracy and the centralized expression of common 'interests'. This slogan is inadequate because specific organizational forms and competencies cannot be dispensed with if complex activities are to be administered *and* the consequences of authoritarian centralization challenged. Basic administrative skills are a condition for broad political involvement, and for an informed and politically competent populace. But they are merely a starting point. Specialist skills of administration and organization – economic management, engineering, medicine, etc. – are also necessary; these must differentiate the population into distinct occupational competences which are not at par with one another. Likewise, decision-making must be performed by and be accountable to definite specialist bodies, not the 'people' as a whole. This is not a problem if forums for the debate of the decision on policy issues, forms of limitation and interdiction of action, and means of inspection and review are developed appropriate to the control of the differentiated agencies of decision.

   In an earlier work, *Social Evolution and Sociological Categories* (Hirst, 1976), I argued strongly for popular democratic forms of administration and for the generalization of competencies among the populace. I am no less committed to these objectives now. What that earlier work chooses to ignore – as so many leftist texts do – is the problems of administering a complex state and economy solely by these means. It is these problems I have tried to examine here.

9. Communitarian and populist practices of control and adaptation, such as have been introduced in China during the Cultural Revolution, are not the same as 'social defence'. The latter notion involves the intervention of specialist knowledges and state agencies. But the popularization of normatization and control is not an unproblematic alternative to 'social defence'. Mass practice unlimited by general rules of conduct relating to specific classes of act can be no less oppressive than norms of conduct enforced by medical or psychiatric functionaries.

10. Jock Young in his introduction to *Capitalism and the Rule of Law* (Fine *et al.*, 1979), refers to the idea of law as pure class oppression as 'soppy',

but this judgement inspires little confidence in view of the fact that this idea was just a few years previous close to his heart.

11. Dworkin accepts fully that rights and claims are not coherent; that rights conflict and must be reconciled or arbitrated by the law itself. His position is subtle and complex, no mere restatement of natural law doctrines. At the same time he conceives certain 'rights' as having priority, even against statute. In the end this conception can be secured only by a doctrine of primacy, by privileging certain entities and attributes.

12. In the present situation positive proposals on abortion law reform must necessarily be rather speculative. The key issue confronting pro-abortion campaigners is to defend the 1967 Act and minimize the damage done by Tory 'reform'. However, in the long run the only possible means of increasing abortion facilities is to push for positive legislation on the one hand and NHS reorganization on the other. The objective of positive legislation should be to circumscribe doctors' discretion in the matter (although it would be difficult to abolish it without eliminating doctors' medical and psychological judgement) and to extend competence in determining the legality of abortion to other agents (day centre nurses and so on). The objective of legislation on NHS reorganization would be to compel the Secretary of State to provide certain facilities in each area. Even so, given professional resistance, doctors' and nurses' claims for freedom of conscience provisions, and administrative tardiness, the results of such action might be far from satisfactory. One effective short-term remedy to such deficiencies would be to strengthen the legal position of the charities (BPAS, PAS, etc.). Licensed charities could then be recognized as agencies competent to determine the legality of abortion and the DHSS required to reimburse their charges for residents of the UK who qualify for NHS treatment. Although this means strengthening formally 'private' medicine, it is probably the most effective way round the resistance of Catholic doctors and the DHSS bureaucracy.

Chapter 8

1. For a discussion of some of these trends, see Hall *et al.* (1978), and Hall (1979a).
2. See Labour Party (1965) and, for a fuller discussion of these themes, Clarke (1979a).
3. For a more detailed discussion of social work education see Jones (1979).
4. See, for example, the literature of *Case Con*.
5. For a fuller discussion of some of the issues here, see Clarke (1979b).

Notes on Contributors

Frank Burton is Lecturer in Sociology at City University, London. Previous publications include *The Politics of Legitimacy* (London: Routledge & Kegan Paul, 1978) and (with P. Carlen) *Official Discourse* (London: Routledge & Kegan Paul, 1979).

Pat Carlen is Lecturer in Criminology at the University of Keele. Previous publications include *Magistrates' Justice* (Oxford: Martin Robertson, 1976), *The Sociology of Law* (Sociological Review, University of Keele, 1976) and (with F. Burton) *Official Discourse* (London: Routledge & Kegan Paul, 1979).

John Clarke is Lecturer in Sociology, North East London Polytechnic. He is co-editor (with Richard Johnson and Chas Critcher) of *Working Class Culture* (London: Hutchinson, 1979). He is also joint author (with S. Hall *et al.*) of *Policing the Crisis* (London: Macmillan, 1978).

Mike Collison is Lecturer in Criminology at the University of Keele and has written *Law in Transition* (London: Academic Press, 1981).

Mark Cousins is Lecturer in Sociology at Thames Polytechnic, London. Previous publications include 'The Logic of Deconstruction', *Oxford Literary Review* (1978) and 'Feminism and Material Arguments' *M/F* No. 2 (1978).

Paul Hirst is Reader in Sociology, Birkbeck College, University of London. Previous publications include *Durkheim, Bernard and Epistemology* (London: Routledge & Kegan Paul, 1975), *Social Evolution and Sociological Categories* (London: Allen & Unwin, 1976) and *On Law and Ideology* (London: Macmillan, 1979). With Barry Hindess he has published *Pre-capitalist Modes of Production* and *Mode of Production and Social Formation*. He is joint author with A. Cutler *et al.* of *Marx's Capital and Capitalism Today* (London: Routledge & Kegan Paul, 1977).

Mary Langan has lectured in social policy at Havering College and is currently a research student at the Birmingham Centre for Contemporary Cultural Studies (CCCS) working on 'State Intervention into Unemployment'. With other members of CCCS she is preparing a book on 'The Emergence of the Interventionist State 1880–1920'.

Phil Lee is Senior Lecturer in Sociology, Sheffield City Polytechnic. He is co-author with David Pithers of 'Radical Residential Child-Care: Trojan Horse or Non-Runner?' in R. Bailey and M. Brake (eds.), *Radical Social Work and Practice* (London: Edward Arnold, 1980). He is joint editor with Roy Bailey of *Theory and Practice in Social Work* (Oxford: Blackwell, forthcoming). With Colin Raban he is preparing two textbooks on the 'Sociology of Welfare'.

Laurie Taylor is Professor of Sociology at the University of York. Previous publications include *Deviance and Society* (London: Nelson, 1973); (with I. Taylor) *Politics and Deviance* (Harmondsworth: Penguin, 1973); (jointly with S. Cohen) *Psychological Survival* (Harmondsworth: Penguin, 1972); *Escape Attempts* (London: Allen Lane, 1976); *Prison Secrets* (London: RAP and NCCL, 1978); and (jointly with R. Robertson) *Crime, Deviance and Socio-Legal Control* (London: Martin Robertson, 1973).

Donald Thompson is Professor of Law at the University of Keele. He has served on the International Commission of Jurists as head of legal staff. He has written articles on constitutional and criminal law for the *Canadian Bar Review*, the *Criminal Law Review*, the *Modern Law Review*, and *Public Law*. He has also contributed a chapter on judicial precedent for G. Treves (ed.), *Studies in Comparative Public Law* (Avione Tipografico-Editrice Torinese, 1971).

Bibliography

Adams, P. (1979) A note on the distinction between sexual division and sexual differences. *M/F* No. 3.

Adams, P. and Minson, G. (1979) The 'subject' of feminism. *M/F* No. 2.

Allen, F. A. (1959) Legal values and the rehabilitative ideal. *Journal of Criminal Law and Police Science*.

Althusser, L. (1971) *Lenin and Philosophy and Other Essays*. London: New Left Books.

Anderson, R. (1978) *Representation in the Juvenile Court*. London: Routledge & Kegan Paul.

Ardrey, R. (1967) *The Territorial Imperative*. London: Collins.

Arendt, H. (1969) *On Violence*. Harmondsworth: Penguin.

Arnison, J. (1974) *The Shrewsbury Three*. London: Lawrence & Wishart.

Arthur, C. (1978) Introduction in E. Pashukanis *Law and Marxism*. Ink Links (1978).

Balbus, I. (1977) Commodity form and legal form. *Law and Society Review* Vol. 11, No. 3, pp. 571–88.

Bankowski, Z. and Mungham, G. (1976) *Images of Law*. London: Routledge & Kegan Paul.

Becker, H. (1963) *Outsiders*. New York: Free Press.

Bellamy, J. (1973) *Crime and Public Order in England in the Later Middle Ages*. London: Routledge & Kegan Paul.

Bentham, J. (1834) *Works* (J. Bowring, ed.). Edinburgh: William Tait.

Bottomley, K. (1979) *Criminology in Focus*. Oxford: Martin Robertson.

Bottoms, A. E. (1974) On the decriminalisation of the English juvenile court. In R. Hood (ed.), *Crime, Criminology and Social Policy*. London: Heinemann.

Brownlie, I. (1968) *The Law Relating to Public Order*. London: Butterworths, pp. 17–22.

Bucholz, E., Hartmann, R., Lekschas, J. and Stiller, G. (1974) *Socialist Criminology*. Farnborough: Saxon House.

205

Burchill, F. and Ross, R. (1977) *A History of the Potters' Union*. Stoke-on-Trent: Ceramic and Allied Workers' Trade Union.

Burton, F. and Carlen, P. (1979) *Official Discourse*. London: Routledge & Kegan Paul.

Cain, M. and Hunt, A. (1979) *Marx and Engels on Law*. London: Academic Press.

Callaghan, J. (1970) *The Sunday Times*, 22 February 1970.

Carlen, P. (1976a) *Magistrates' Justice*. Oxford: Martin Robertson.

Carlen, P. (1976b) *Sociology of Law*. University of Keele.

Carson, W. G. (1974) The sociology of crime and the emergence of criminal laws. In P. Rock and M. McIntosh (eds), *Deviance and Control*. London: Tavistock.

Chambliss, W. J. (1964) A sociological analysis of the law of vagrancy. *Social Problems* Vol. 12, pp. 67–77.

Clarke, J. (1979a) 'Social Democratic Delinquents and Fabian Families'. In National Deviance Conference, *Permissiveness and Control*. London: Macmillan.

Clarke, J. (1979b) Critical sociologists and radical social workers. In J. Parry, M. J. Rustin and C. Satyamurti (eds), *Social Work and the State*. London: Edward Arnold.

Clarke, R. V. G. (ed.) (1978) *Tackling Vandalism*. Home Office Research Studies 47. London: HMSO.

Cockburn, J. S. (1977) *Crime in England, 1550–1800*. London: Methuen.

Cohen, S. (1975) It's all right for you to talk. In R. Bailey and M. Brake (eds), *Radical Social Work*. London: Edward Arnold.

Cohen, S. (1979) Guilt, justice and tolerance: some old concepts for a new criminology. In Downes and Rock (1979).

Cohen, S. and Taylor, L. (1978) *Prison Secrets*. London: NCCL and RAP.

Cole, G. D. H. (1920) *Guild Socialism Re-Stated*. London: Gollancz.

Cole, G. D. H. (1921) *Social Theory*. London: Methuen.

Collison, M. (1981) *Law in Transition*. London: Academic Press.

Connors, W. D. (1972) *Deviance in Soviet Society*. New York: Columbia University Press.

Conservative Party Committee on Policy and Political Education (1946) *Youth Astray*. London: Conservative Party.

Conservative Political Centre (CPC) (1971) *Crisis in Crime and Punishment*. No. 492 London: CPC.

CPC (1977) *The Proper Use of Prisons*. No. 609. London: CPC.

CPC (1978) *The New Vandals*. Contact Brief (Conservative Contact Programme) No. 86. London: CPC.

Conservative Research Department (CRD) (1978) *Protecting the Citizen*. Politics Today No. 7. London: CRD.

Conservative Women's National Advisory Committee (1978) *Delinquents at . . . Large?* London: Conservative Party.

Corrigan, P. and Leonard, P. (1978) *Social Work Practice Under Capitalism: a Marxist Approach*. London: Macmillan.

Cowie, J. Cowie, V. and Slater, E. (1968) *Delinquency in Girls*. London: Heinemann.

Cowley, J., Kaye, A., Mayo, M. and Thompson, M. (1977) *Community or Class Struggle?* London: Stage 1.

Cutler, T., Hindess, B., Hirst, P. and Hussain, A. (1978) *Marx's Capital and Capitalism Today*, Vol. II. London: Routledge & Kegan Paul.

Daintith, T. C. (1966) Disobeying a policeman – a fresh look at *Duncan* v. *Jones* [1966]. *Public Law*, 248.

Derrida, J. (1970) Structure, sign and play. In Macksey and Donato (1972).

Derrida, J. (1976) *Or Grammatology* (trans. Gayatri Chakravorty Spivak), London: John Hopkins Press.

Ditchfield, J. A. (1976) *Police Cautioning in England and Wales*. Home Office Research Study No. 37. London: HMSO.

Donzelot, J. (1977) *La Police des Familles*. Paris: Minuit.

Donzelot, J. (1979) The poverty of political culture. *Ideology and Consciousness*, No. 5, Spring 1979.

Downes, D. (1979) 'Praxis makes perfect: a critique of critical criminology. In Downes and Rock (1979).

Downes, D. and Rock, P. (1979) *Deviant Interpretations*. Oxford: Martin Robertson.

Durkheim, E. (1964) *Rules of Sociological Method*. New York: Free Press.

Duster, T. (1970) *The Legislation of Morality*. New York: Free Press.

Dworkin, R. (1977) *Taking Rights Seriously*. London: Duckworth.

Edelman, B. (1979) *Ownership of the Image*. London: Routledge & Kegan Paul.

Elliot, F. E. (1978) Neurological factors in aggressive behaviour. In R. L. Sadoff (ed.), *Violence and Responsibility*. New York: Spectrum.

Elton, G. (1972) *Policy and Police: the Enforcement of Reformation in the Age of Thomas Cromwell*. Cambridge: University Press.

Engels, F. (1970) The housing question. In K. Marx and F. Engels, *Selected Works*, Vol. III. Moscow: Progress.

Fanon, F. (1967) *The Wretched of the Earth*. Harmondsworth: Penguin.

Fine, B. *et al.* (1979) *Capitalism and The Rule of Law*. London: Hutchinson.

Foucault, M. (1972) *The Archaeology of Knowledge*. London: Tavistock.

Foucault, M. (1973) *The Birth of the Clinic*. London: Tavistock.

Foucault, M. (1978a) *Discipline and Punish*. London: Allen Lane.

Foucault, M. (1978b) *I, Pierre Riviere*. Harmondsworth: Penguin.

Foucault, M. (1979) *The History of Sexuality*. London: Allen Lane.

Fowler, N. (1973) *The Cost of Crime*. No. 521. London: Conservative Political Centre.

Freud, S. (1955) Beyond the pleasure principle. *The Complete Psychological Works of Sigmund Freud*, No. XVIII. London: Hogarth Press.

George, V. and Wilding, P. (1976) *Ideology and Social Welfare*. London: Routledge & Kegan Paul.

Grant, L. (1971) Towards a legal department. NCCL, mimeo.

Greenberg, D. (1977a) *Corrections and Punishment*. Beverly Hills: Sage.

Greenberg, D. (1977b) Review of *The Politics of Abolition. Theory and Society* Vol. 4, No. 1.

Greenwood, V. and Young, J. (1976) *Abortion in Demand*. London: Pluto.

Gunn, J. (1973) *Violence in Human Society*. Newton Abbot: David & Charles.

Gusfield, J. (1963) *Symbolic Crusade*. Urbana, Ill.: University of Illinois Press.

Hall, S. (1979a) Reformism and the legislation of consent. In National Deviancy Conference, *Permissiveness and Control*. London: Macmillan.

Hall, S. (1979b) The Great Moving Right Show. *Marxism Today*, March 1979.

Hall, S., Critcher, C., Jefferson, T., Clarke, J. and Roberts, B. (1978) *Policing the Crisis*. London: Macmillan.

Hay, D. (1975) Property, authority, and the criminal law. In Hay *et al.* (1975).

Hay, D., Linebaugh, P., and Thompson, E. P. (1975) *Albion's Fatal Tree*. London: Allen Lane.

Hegel, G. (1957) *Philosophy of Right*. Oxford: University Press.

Hindess, B. (1971) *The Decline of Working-Class Politics*. London: MacGibbon & Kee.

Hirst, P. Q. (1975) Marx and Engels on law, crime and morality. In Taylor, Walton and Young (1975).

Hirst, P. Q. (1976) *Social Evolution and Sociological Categories*. London: Allen & Unwin.

Hirst, P. Q. (1979a) Introduction. In Edelman (1979).

Hirst, P. Q. (1979b) *On Law and Ideology*. London: Macmillan.

HMSO (1946) *Report of the Care of Children Committee*, Cmd 6922. London: HMSO.

HMSO (1949) *Memorandum on Juvenile Delinquency* (jointly with Ministry of Education). London: HMSO.

HMSO (1960) *Report of the Committee on Children and Young Persons*, Cmnd 1191. London: HMSO.

HMSO (1965) *The Child, the Family and the Young Offender*, Cmnd 2742. London: HMSO.

HMSO (1968) *Children in Trouble*, Cmnd 3601. London: HMSO.

HMSO (1969) *Children and Young Persons Act 1969*. London: HMSO.

HMSO (1972) *Criminal Law Revision Committee Eleventh Report – Evidence (General)*, Cmnd 4991. London: HMSO.

HMSO (1974) *The Law Commission Working Paper*, No. 74. London: HMSO.

HMSO (1978) *Criminal Statistics for England And Wales 1977*, Cmd 7289. London: HMSO.

Hobsbawn, E. (1964) *Labouring Men*. London: Weidenfeld & Nicolson.

Hodges, J. and Hussain, A. (1979) La police des familles: review. *Ideology & Conciousness*. No. 5.

Ignatieff, M. (1978) *A Just Measure of Pain*. London: Macmillan.

Jaggi, M. *et al.* (1977) *Red Bologna*. London: Writers and Readers.

Johnson, T. (1972) *Professions and Power*. London: Macmillan.

Jones, C. (1979) The development of social work education. In J. Parry, M. J. Rustin and C. Satyamurti (eds), *Social Work and the State*. London: Edward Arnold.

Joseph, K. (1975) *Freedom Under the Law*. London: Conservative Political Centre.

Kamenka, E., Brown, R. and Tay, A. (1978) *Law and Society*, London: Edward Arnold.

Kautsky, R. (1964) *The Dictatorship of the Proletariat*. Ann Arbor, Michigan: Michigan State University Press.

Kinsey, R. (1978) Marxism and the law. *British Journal of Law and Society*, No. 2.

Kirchheimer, O. (1961) *Political Justice*. Princeton. University Press.

Kornreich, B. (1978) A critique of social work education. *Bulletin of Social Policy*, Vol. 1 Spring.

Kuhn, T. (1970) *The Structure of Scientific Revolutions*. Chicago: University Press.

Laborit, H. (1978) The biological and sociological mechanisms of aggression. *International Journal of Social Science*, Vol. XXX, No. 4.

Labour Party (1960) *Crime and the Community*, Talking Points No. 8. London: Labour Party.

Labour Party (1965) *Crime – a Challenge to us all*. London: Longford.

Labour Party (1966) *Labour Women's National Survey into Care of Children*. London: Labour Party.

Labour Party (1973) *The Deprived Child*. London: Labour Party.

Labour Party (1978) *Law, Order and Human Rights*. London: Labour Party.

Lacan, J. (1977) *Ecrits*. London: Tavistock.

Leigh, L. H. (1975) *Police Powers in England and Wales*. London: Butterworths.

Lenin, V. I. (1963) *What is to be Done?* Collected Works, Vol. 5. Moscow: Progress Publishers.

Lenin, V. I. (1964) *The State and Revolution*. Collected Works, Vol. 25. Moscow: Progress Publishers.

Lewis, R. (1977) Artful dodgers of the world unite. In C. B. Cox and A. E. Dyson (eds), *The Black Papers in Education*. London: Methuen.

Lombroso C. and Ferrero, W. (1895) *The Female Offender*. London: Fisher Unwin.

Lorenz, K. (1963) *On Aggression*. London: Methuen.

Macksey, R. and Donato, E. (1972) *The Language of Criticism and The Science of Man*. London: Johns Hopkins Press.

Marx, K. (1967) *Capital*, Vol. I. London: Lawrence & Wishart.

Marx, K. (1968) *The Civil War in France*. In K. Marx and F. Engels, *Selected Works*. London: Lawrence & Wishart.

Marx, K. and Engels, F. (1970) *Selected Works*, Vol. III. Moscow: Progress.

Mathews, R. (1979) 'Decarceration' and the fiscal crisis. In Fine *et al*. (1979).

Mathiesen, T. (1974) *The Politics of Abolition*. Oxford: Martin Robertson.

Mauss, M. (1979) *Sociology and Psychology* (trans. Ben Brewster). London: Routledge & Kegan Paul.

Mayhew, P. *et al*. (1978) *Crime in Public View*. Home Office Research Studies No. 49. London: HMSO.

Merleau-Ponty, M. (1969) *Humanism and Terror*. Boston: Beacon Press.

More, H. (1971), *Village Politics* 2nd ed. London:

Morris, A. and Giller, H. (1979) Juvenile justice and social work in Britain. In H. Parker (ed.), *Social Work and the Courts*. London: Edward Arnold.

Morris, D. (1967) *The Naked Ape*. London: Jonathan Cape.

Morris, D. (1969) *The Human Zoo*. London: Jonathan Cape.

Morris, N., and Hawkins, G. (1970), *The Honest Politician's Guide to Crime Control*. Chicago: University Press.

Morris, P. (1978) Foreword to Anderson (1978).

Morris. T. and Blom-Cooper, L. (1979) *Murder in England and Wales Since 1957*. London: Observer Publication.

Newman, O. (1973) *Defensible Space*. London: Architectural Press.

Packer, H. L. (1968) *The Limits of the Criminal Sanction*. Stanford: University Press.

Packham, J. (1975) *The Childs Generation*. Oxford: Blackwell.

Pashukanis, E. (1978) *Law and Marxism*. London: Ink Links.

Paton *v.* Trustees of BPAS and Paton 1978 – Transcript: Lee and Nightingale, Liverpool.

Pearson, G. (1978) Making social workers: bad promises and good omens. In R. Bailey and M. Brake (eds), *Radical Social Work*. London: Edward Arnold.

Perdue, W. C. (1964) *Rorschach responses to 100 murderers. Corrective Psychiatry and the Journal of Social Therapy*, Vol. 10, No. 6.

Picciotto, S. (1979) Theory of the state, class struggle and the rule of law. In Fine *et al.* (1979).

Pinchbeck, I. and Hewitt, M. (1973) *Children in English Society*, Vol. 2. London: Routledge & Kegan Paul.

Piven, F. F. and Cloward, R. (1972) *Regulating the Poor*. London: Tavistock.

Platt, A. (1969) *The Child Savers*. Chicago: University Press.

Playfair, G. (1971) *The Punitive Obsession*. London: Gollancz.

Pollock, F. (1961) *Jurisprudence and Other Legal Essays*.: President's Commission (1967) *On Law Enforcement and Administration of Justice*. Washington D.C.: U.S. Govt. Printing Office.

Pritt, D. N. (1971) *Law, Class and Society*, Vol. III. London: Lawrence & Wishart.

Quinney, R. (1974) *Critique of Legal Order*. Boston: Little, Brown.

Quinney, R. (1977) *Class, State and Crime*. New York: Longman.

Radzinowitz, L. (1966) *Ideology and Crime*. London: Heinemann.

Raeburn, A. (1973) *The Militant Suffragettes*. London: Michael Joseph.

Rawls, J. (1972) *Theory of Justice*. London: Oxford University Press.

Rousseau, J. J. (1913) *The Social Contract* (ed. G. D. H. Cole). Everyman edition. London: Dent.

Rusche, G. and Kirchheimer, O. (1939) *Punishment and Social Structure*. New York: Columbia University Press.

Sachs, A. and Wilson, J. H. (1978) *Sexism and the Law*. Oxford: Martin Robertson.

Samaha, J. (1974) *Law and Order in Historical Perspective*. New York: Harcourt, Brace.

Schur, E. (1973) *Crimes without Victims*. Englewood Cliffs, N.J.: Prentice-Hall.

Scull, A. (1977) *Decarceration*. Englewood Cliffs, N.J.: Prentice-Hall.

Scull, A. (1979) *Museums of Madness*. London: Allen Lane.

Seebohm, F. (1968) *Local Authority Personal Social Services*. Cmnd 3703. London: HMSO.

Sharlet, R. (1974) Pashukanis and the withering away of law in the USSR. In Sheila Fitzpatrick (ed.), *Cultural Revolution in Russia 1928–31*, Bloomington: Indiana University Press.

Smart, C. (1977) *Women, Crime and Criminology*, London: Routledge & Kegan Paul.

de Smith, S. A. (1973) *Judicial Review of Administrative Action*. London: Stevens & Sons, p. 510.

Sorel, G. (1941) *Reflections on Violence*. New York: Peter Smith.

Spicer, R. (1976) Conspiracy law, class and society. In Carlen (1976b).

Stedman-Jones, G. (1971) *Outcast London*. Harmondsworth: Penguin.

Storr, A. (1968) *On Aggression*. Harmondsworth: Penguin.

Sumner, C. (1979) *Reading Ideologies*. London: Academic Press.

Tay, A. (1978) in Kamenka, Brown and Tay (1978).

Taylor, I. and Taylor, L. (1973) *Politics and Deviance*. Harmondsworth: Penguin.

Taylor, I., Walton, P. and Young, J. (1973) *The New Criminology*. London: Routledge & Kegan Paul.

Taylor, I., Walton, P. and Young, J. (1975) *Critical Criminology*. London: Routledge & Kegan Paul.

Taylor, I. and Young, J. (1979) Matthiesen–Greenberg Debate. Unpublished.

Thatcher, M. (1979) *Newsweek*, 7 May 1979.

Thompson, E. P. (1975) *Whigs and Hunters*. London: Allen Lane.

Thompson, E. P. (1978a) The state versus its enemies. *New Society*, 19 October 1978.

Thompson, E. P. (1978b) Introduction to *Review of Security and the State*. London: Julian Friedmann.

Thompson, E. P. (1978c) *The Poverty of Theory*. London: Merlin.

Thompson, E. P. (1979) Introduction to H. Harman and J. Griffith, *Justice Deserted*. London: National Council for Civil Liberties.

Tilly, C. (1969) Collective violence in European perspective. In. H. Graham and T. Gurr (eds), *The History of Violence in America*. New York: Praeger.

Tobias, J. (1967) *Crime in Industrial Society in the Nineteenth Century*. London: Batsford.

Tutt, W. (ed.) (1976) *Violence*. London: HMSO.

Von Hirsch, A. (1976) *Doing Justice*. New York: Hill and Wang.

Whitelaw, W. (1977) see CPC (1977).

Whitelaw, W. (1978) see Labour Party (1978).

Williams, D. G. T. *Keeping the Peace*. 1 KB218. London: Hutchinson.

Wolfgang, M. and Ferracuti, F. (1967) *The Subculture of Violence*. London: Tavistock.

Young, J. (1979) Left idealism, reformism and beyond: from new criminology to marxism. In Fine *et al*. (1979).

Younger, K. (1971) *Report on Young Adult Offenders.* London: HMSO.
Zellick, G. (1974) Prisoners' rights in England. *University of Toronto Law Review*, Vol. 24, pp. 334–9.